The genius of Thomas Hardy

The genius of Thomas Hardy

Edited by Margaret Drabble

WEIDENFELD AND NICOLSON
LONDON

Contents

Illustrations

🌿 Editor's Introduction

Thomas Hardy is one of the greatest and also one of the best loved figures in the history of English literature. He occupies a unique position, as one of the very few writers who achieved great distinction both as a novelist and as a poet: he came from a rural background which had produced few writers, and while he writes very much of a region, he is in no sense merely a regional writer: and he was something of a recluse, although he became one of the most famous and fêted writers in the country. His reputation, and his own work, are full of such paradoxes. He is not a simple man, nor are his works easy to understand or expound. The problems raised by his life and writing have interested and occupied both scholars and the reading public for many years. Yet, complex though he is, he has been read and loved by the widest variety of readers, and his work has probably reached a public wider than that of any author since Dickens.

The writers who have contributed to this volume have little in common apart from their shared enthusiasm for the subject. They include scholars and critics, novelists and poets, experts in Hardy history and topography, British and Americans. We hope that the diversity of approach will help to illuminate the many facets of a man who was architect, poet, novelist, verse-dramatist, would-be actor, lover and recluse. The volume has essays on his life, on various aspects of his work and thought (including one on Hardy as architect by Sir John Betjeman, who is as a poet doubly qualified to write on the subject). It also deals with his relations with critics, and with his posthumous fame, which has reached the furthest corners of the world, as G. Stevens Cox has illustrated. The Hardy industry (of which this book is an example) continues to flourish as healthily as ever, and will doubtless continue to do so, for Hardy's reputation shows not the slightest sign of eclipse. On the contrary, it has grown brighter even since his death in 1928, and his poetry, which was not given full credit during his lifetime, has never been as much admired as it is today. Philip Larkin has included almost twice as many poems by Hardy in his *Oxford Book of Twentieth Century English Verse* as he has poems by other poets, which reflects the esteem in which he is held by living poets as well as by readers of poetry. His novels, which have always been popular (for he intended them to be popular) have reached even larger audiences through films and television adaptations – a fact which, in view of his interest in the theatre, so well described here by Harold Orel, would surely have delighted him. Most writers, after their death, go through a temporary, if not a permanent eclipse of reputation, as did Galsworthy, Bennett and Wells, his immediate successors. With Hardy, this has not been so.

Distinct, in a sense, from the admiration felt for his work, is the curiosity which

Hardy as a man arouses. How could the quiet, shy, and (if the truth be told, rather mean) Grand Old Man of Max Gate have produced the extravagant and passionate novels and poems by which he communicated with the outside world? His biography, by his second wife Florence, was, as is well known, more an exercise in concealment than in revelation, closely supervised by Hardy himself, and it acted as an incentive to inevitable speculation about the private affairs that he tried so hard to keep hidden. There is much biographical material in everything a writer writes, and readers have interpreted Hardy's apparently highly personal work in many different ways. It has always been known that his first marriage was for many years unhappy, and some have seen this unhappiness as the source of the bitterness and tragedy in his work. But, recently, a fellow countrywoman of Hardy's, Lois Deacon, has shed a new and dramatic light on Hardy's emotional life. Her discoveries, understandably, have aroused a great deal of controversy, and not all the contributors to this volume would agree with all the suggestions she makes and all the conclusions she has elaborated; but nobody could fail to find them highly interesting. At the very least, she has provided the reader with a fascinating jigsaw puzzle (as she herself describes it). Some (including, incidentally, myself) believe that she has done a good deal more than that. But Hardy readers will have to decide for themselves. One thing is certain: the Hardy story is by no means a closed book.

Hardy was born in 1840: he died, an old man, in 1928. His life and work span some of the most significant changes in English history, and he saw himself as their chronicler. As several of these essays point out, his attitude to the past was ambivalent, but he was well aware that he was watching the death of many traditional occupations, and change was one of his major themes. Sheila Sullivan, who edited the pictures for this volume, has illustrated not only his own life, but also the lost age that he lived in, an age which inspires nostalgia even in those who never knew it. We hope that they will add to the picture of Wessex which his novels depict. At the same time, one can remember that although Tess and the milkmaids have vanished from the Vale, and the fiddlers from the church gallery, there is much of Hardy's country that is unspoiled, that remains much as it was in his own day. His birthplace is still a place of pilgrimage for Hardy enthusiasts, and many of the sites identified in these pages are immediately recognizable, full of echoes of a fictional and a real past, and as beautiful as they ever were. Perhaps the greatest Hardy paradox of all is the way in which his work achieves the universal through his intense attachment to the particular and timelessness through dwelling on change. He writes of tiny, insignificant hamlets and villages, and gives them the ring of eternity. No wonder that Siegfried Sassoon read Hardy for comfort (Hardy, a tragic and depressing writer) as he sat in the trenches on the Western Front. Hardy's world is a world that can never disappear.

MARGARET DRABBLE

PART 1

The life

The early years

TERRY COLEMAN

There is no point in restating what is already so abundantly known and so easily available in many biographies and in Florence Hardy's posthumous biography of her husband which, since it was mostly written by him in his last years, is better called his autobiography. All I shall try to do is to suggest a few themes, to say (and this is important) what we do not know, and to remark how easy it was, for me at any rate, to be misled by preconceptions which seemed most reasonable but turned out to be wrong.

Wanting to know Hardy, one visits the Hardy country, sees the cottage at Stinsford where in 1840 he was born and the house at Max Gate which he built for himself in 1884 and where in 1928 he died, and by then one knows something of his very early youth, and something of his old age, but is thoroughly misinformed about the years between. This misinformation is much helped by the delightful accident that the cottage and the nearby heath are still as they were when Hardy was a boy and a young man. The lane leading to the cottage is undoubtedly in the same wretched condition. Except that the clumps of pine trees on the heath are probably modern plantations, the heath is much as it was when he walked on it and wrote *The Return of the Native*.

Hardy was a man who could tell in the dark, from the sounds of the wind and rain in the trees along a lane, what kind of trees they were. He wrote novels which were predominantly novels of the country. But it is an error to assume from this, as the assumption naturally follows, that he was only a man of the country. To see and imagine Hardy where he worked and lived, it would be as valuable to go and see the Savile Club in London, of which he was for so many years a member, and reams of whose writing paper he seemed to purloin, to write out on it excerpts from various philosophers who attracted him. He achieved popular success with *Far from the Madding Crowd* in 1874, when he was thirty-four, and on the proceeds of that novel he married: one consequence of the reputation he made from this novel and his ensuing works was that he became a most fashionable man to have to dinner. He was at dinner in half the great houses of London. 'To go to dinners and clubs and crushes as a business,' he said, writing of himself in the third person, 'was not much to his mind. Yet that was necessary meat and drink to the popular author.' It was necessary meat and drink to the man who saw himself as at least in the line of such popular authors as Dickens, the announcement of whose death he had some years before seen not at Stinsford but while he was crossing Hyde Park, or Trollope, whom he heard speak, or Browning, whom he often met. And when he mentioned his doubts about the necessity of clubs and crushes, it was not to his wife but to a Miss Thackeray, who happened to be the sister-in-law of Leslie Stephen, and was to become Lady Ritchie. She of course reassured him that it was a necessity. He dined with Henry James and George Meredith and Lady Galway and the Chancellor of the Exchequer, and spent Christmas at the house-party of Lord Wimborne, who at the time owned a fair bit of London.

Hardy was not obscure. As early as 1875 he was one of a deputation to Disraeli urging the negotiation of American copyright for British authors, something which was later achieved and helped make him a rich man. He visited Henry Irving in his dressing-room, finding him naked to the waist and 'champagne in tumblers'. He was 'well received' (the phrase is his) by Lady Carnarvon. He was for many years an intimate friend of Lady Jeune, wife of a man who became Judge-Advocate General. Sometimes he took his wife Emma Lavinia to London; at other times he did not, and then he wrote to her from the Savile Club or from various great houses where he was a guest, describing the black lace gown of Lady Margaret, daughter of Lord Portsmouth ('dress low'), or the private view at the Royal Academy, or other high moments of the London season. He met de Lesseps, who engineered the Suez canal, saw the funeral of Louis Napoleon, and met the actors of the Comédie Française. He was said not to be able to write about the fashionable and the rich. In his novels, after *The Poor Man and the Lady* and *The Hand of Ethelberta*, he hardly tried; but in his journal he certainly could.

Note [he said] the weight of landau and pair, the coachman in his grey great coat, footmen ditto. All this mass of matter is moved along with brute force and clatter through a street congested and obstructed, to bear the petite figure of the owner's young wife in violet velvet and silver trimming, slim, small; who could be easily carried under a man's arm and who, if held up by the hair and slipped out of her clothes, carriage, etc. etc. aforesaid, would not be much larger than a skinned rabbit, and of less use.

He travelled, not as greatly as Trollope, but throughout Europe. Soon after the publication of *The Woodlanders* he left for Rome and Venice. After he arranged for the publication of *The Trumpet-Major*, he set off to the Hotel Bellevue at Trouville. After *The Hand of Ethelberta* he went to Bonn, Coblenz, and Heidelberg.

All this is not to suggest that he was not the Wessex man of his novels. He was. But he was both that and a worldly man. He was a man who noticed and remembered the exact tone of the church bell of Puddletown, but he was a man who also knew that the bell of the campanile of St Mark's, Venice, had the same tin-tray timbre. He wrote himself of the contrasting planes of his existence, 'vibrating at a swing between the artificial gaieties of a London season and the quaintnesses of a primitive rustic life'. For myself, I do not think he found the London season so artificial, or not unpleasingly

so. He had been born the son of a small builder and had become a celebrated man.
Men of letters could be celebrated in his time.

Of his later and most celebrated novels, two small things are also worth remarking.
The first is that *Jude* was not alone in its theme of the tyranny of marriage. Hardy's
novel has survived. There were many others which have not. He was counted as only
one of the members of what critics called 'The Anti-Marriage League'. At the time,
probably the most famous of those novels was not *Jude* at all, but a book called *The
Woman Who Did*, a hack bestseller, in which what the woman does is to decline on
principle to marry the man she loves, and then lives with him unmarried. She was
greatly daring, and had been a Girton girl. The second thing, now forgotten, is that
Hardy was one of those authors whose success indirectly assured the poverty of all
but the most successful novelists for the next many years, indeed until the present day.
This would have grieved him. When he began to write, a novel was commonly
published in three volumes at half a guinea a volume, making 31s 6d for the work,
which therefore needed to sell only a few hundred copies to feed and clothe its
author for a year. By the time of his last novels (and all his novels except two were
written in the period which the editor of this collection of essays has designated his
early years*), publishers had found it more profitable for themselves to publish novels
in the now familiar format of one volume, not as a subsequent, cheap one-volume
edition, which had been done for years, but as the original edition, at say, six shillings.
This of course sold many more copies. For an author selling as well as Hardy that was
an advantage. Better many small royalties than few large ones; but for the author who
could still only rely on selling his few hundred it was ruinous, and so has continued.
Hardy was not the only or the principal novelist whose success brought this about,
but he was one. *Tess* was published in three volumes, at 31s 6d the set, and sold
1500 copies in the first three months. *Jude* was first published in one volume at six
shillings, and sold twenty thousand in the first three months.

This is all to jump ahead. We must return to the beginning, and to Hardy's young
youth at Dorchester. Not that he even lived in Dorchester, but at Stinsford, which is
a tiny village, nor, properly, even at Stinsford, but rather at Higher Bockhampton,
which is a dirt track and a few cottages. Stinsford was a short walk away. There stood
the church, where Hardy's father and then Hardy played the violin on Sundays
before they pulled the musicians' gallery down; and there also lived the lady of the
manor, who inhabited a Palladian mansion and befriended Hardy. He set his first
published novel, *Desperate Remedies*, in the grounds of this grand house. I suspect
(and here is speculation) that there were, at some time in his youth, daughters of the
manor, one of whom his imagination set in his previous, and unpublished, novel *The
Poor Man and the Lady*. Dorchester was three miles away, and a town of much greater
consequence than it is now. It was the county town of assizes and aldermen and
London papers a day late, the metropolis of its region, not yet overshadowed by

* This has an impeccable precedent. Hardy said himself that he was a child till he was sixteen, a youth
till he was twenty-five, and a young man until he was almost fifty.

Bournemouth or made insignificant by the railway which was to put it only three or four hours from London. As Hardy later spoke about the twin planes of his existence in London and Dorset, in earlier days he talked about the three strands of his life – the rustic at Stinsford, where he lived and played the fiddle; the professional at Dorchester, where he walked each day when he was apprenticed to an architect; and the scholarly, when early every morning from six to eight he read the *Iliad* and the *Aeneid*. Dorchester is now a small country town. Then it was a town not only of aldermen but of so good a scholar as William Barnes. With his fellow architectural apprentices, Hardy disputed points of Greek and Latin, and ran for decisions on some knotty point to Barnes next door. Hardy said the verdict was nearly always in his favour, and the truth is that, although he had very little formal education and often, even after he received the Order of Merit, regretted that he had not been at the university, Hardy was a learned young man, having a lot of Greek and Latin and at least passable French. Today he would become a don, to the loss of all. There is a tale, unsubstantiated by the diocesan records at Salisbury, that he once unsuccessfully offered himself as a candidate for holy orders. If he did, this must have been early, because by twenty-five he could not in conscience have taken them, and said so.

At the age of twenty-one he went to London, and then follow five years about which we know substantially nothing. He practised architecture, and won a small prize for it. He saw the Prince of Wales's wedding, tried the new London Underground, and heard Patti sing. He thought of the theatre as a career and once did appear on stage at Covent Garden as an extra. He wrote verse which was rejected by editors. He heard Palmerston speak in the House of Commons and a little later attended his funeral in Westminster Abbey. All the Cabinet Ministers were there as pall-bearers. Sixty-two years later, Hardy's own pall-bearers in the same place included Shaw, Kipling, and the Prime Minister.

In 1867 Hardy returned to Dorchester, which brings us inevitably to Tryphena Sparks. Miss Lois Deacon, in the following contribution, argues the case for Tryphena. As part author of *Providence and Mr Hardy**, though very much the junior partner, I asserted, and still do, that an engagement between Tryphena and Hardy was pretty well proved. I believe they were lovers. I believe she was *one* of the principal influences on his work. I think it possible they had a child. I think it not impossible that Hardy *believed* she was his niece and that their relationship was therefore, though tenuously, incestuous. But all this is a matter of controversy. Having stated it once in *Providence and Mr Hardy*, with reservations which are not always noticed, I shall urge it no further. The arguments against the thesis are strong, and all the stronger when moderately put, but it *is* a thesis to be considered, and I have been amazed at the intemperance of some Hardy scholars both for and against. For what it is worth, I will say that when I started to sift the evidence for the book I was sceptical,

* For further discussion of the hypotheses of this book see the Editor's introduction to Lois Deacon's contribution (p. 19) and the contribution itself.

that as I progressed I became less so, and that I would not in the end have written as I
did if I had not believed there was a case to set forth. I saw and interviewed Tryphena's daughter. I have seen the deletions in the manuscript of *The Life* in the
Dorset County Museum. What was the 'sorrow of the past' to which Hardy's mind
reverted in his last moments and which Florence Hardy's or some other hand first
recorded and then deleted? This, and many other instances in *Providence and Mr
Hardy*, though conclusive of nothing, probably have some meaning, and I should be
interested to see them differently and consonantly interpreted. Where I know I differ
from Miss Deacon is that I do not believe Tryphena was the sole and dominant love
of Hardy's life, and this brings us back to the five unknown years in London.

In the Dorset County Museum there are two personal notebooks of Hardy's, one
dated 1867–1920, and the other 1921–8. In the first there is not a single detail of the
years 1867 or 1868. On the left-hand side of the first page the date 1867 has been
written, and then ten sheets are missing. They seem to have been cut out. Only the
sheared stumps of the pages remain. Perhaps Hardy did it, or perhaps it was his second
wife after his death. Why? In 1867 he returned from London, and his affair with
Tryphena, if we can assume for the moment that it existed, took place during those
two cut-out years. The question does also arise, why is there nothing at all, and why
does no notebook survive, for the five years in London? It could be harmless chance.
But there once was a diary for those years, because in the few pages Hardy gives these
years in his autobiography he occasionally quotes from it, as:

June 2 1865 Walked about by moonlight in the evening. Wondered what women, if any,
I should be thinking about in five years' time.
   End of July. The dull period in the life of an event is when it ceases to be news and has not
begun to be history.

And so on. The gap of these five formative years in London is important for two
reasons, both to do with the life of the spirit. At the beginning of these years Hardy
was probably still a Christian, and at the end he was certainly not, and of the pro-
cesses by which this change came over such a mind we know nothing. He had read
Huxley and Darwin, and makes later allusions to them both. He had met Huxley,
though he does not say when, only that he had a liking for him which grew with
knowledge. Hardy attended Darwin's funeral in 1882, and recorded this event with
the note that as a young man he had been among the earliest acclaimers of *The Origin
of Species*. And then again in London, and this is more speculation because what
Victorian could write openly of such things, he probably had his first mistress or, if
not that, met the first woman he knew well; and if to wonder about this is only
curiosity, then it is curiosity about the fundamental, because women meant a great
deal to him.

To suppose a man's actions from what he writes is full of perils, and Hardy disliked those who 'grew personal under the name of practising the great historical
method'. But to suppose a man's state of mind from his writings is more reasonable:

a man has only his own mind with which to perceive what he does perceive, and only his own sensibilities with which to feel what he does feel, and what can he write that does not come from his own mind or perception, or that is not at the least moulded by them? And Hardy does go out of his way to hint. He says that his poems are 'in a large degree dramatic or personative in conception; and this even where they are not obviously so'. He says that in 1869 he found the young ladies of Weymouth with whom he danced, 'heavier on the arm than their London sisters', and then gratuitously adds: 'The poem entitled "The Dawn after the Dance" ... is supposed, though without proof, to have some bearing on these dances.' Hardy is persistently indiscreet, usually by allusion though not always so. In May 1874 he met Miss Helen Paterson, who was going to illustrate *Far from the Madding Crowd*. In September he married Emma Lavinia Gifford, largely on his earnings from the serial rights of that novel. In November it was published in volume form by which time, he says, Miss Paterson, 'by an odd coincidence had also thought fit to marry'. Later he told Edmund Gosse, 'Those two almost simultaneous marriages would have been one but for a stupid blunder of God Almighty.' Emma Lavinia lived until 1912, and he loved her for a while.

By the end of his early life, which we have taken to be 1890, Hardy was one of the great men of English letters. That year, at the end of his long youth, he said that he had been looking for God for fifty years, and thought that if God existed he should have found him. In the train on the way to London he wrote the first few lines of 'No line of her writing have I', which was about Tryphena. She was dying at the time. Hardy said he did not know this and that his writing of the poem at that moment was a remarkable example of telepathy. Later he was back at the Jeunes' again, meeting 'Mrs T and her great eyes in a corner of the room'. The most beautiful woman present, he said: but those women, if put into rough wrappers in a turnip field, where would their beauty be? That was the year in which he finished *Tess of the D'Urbervilles*, whose heroine he put in rough wrappers in a turnip field.

At Easter he visited the grave of William Barnes. That summer he went the rounds of the music halls and visited the ballet, noticing the docile obedience of the faces of the dancing women, their passive resignation and their marks of fatigue, and pronouncing that the morality of actresses and dancers should not be judged by the same standard as that of women who led slower lives, because 'living in a throbbing atmosphere they are perforce throbbed by it in spite of themselves'. He met Stanley the explorer. In August he was in France and saw the can-can danced at the Moulin Rouge, but could not keep from his mind the reflection that if he turned from the gaiety and looked out of the back windows he could see the cemetery of Montmartre in which lay the grave of so many gay Parisians and of Heinrich Heine. Travelling back from Paris to Le Havre he saw a woman he called 'a Cleopatra in the railway carriage'. From 8 December onwards he was again with Lady Jeune. 'Lord Rowton, who is great on lodging houses [for down and outs] says I am her "dosser".' That

New Year's Eve, back at Max Gate, he looked out of doors just before twelve and was confronted with the toneless white of the snow spread in front, against which stood the rows of pines breathing out, ''Tis no better with us than with the rest of creation, you see!' The last note in his journal for the last day of the year of his fiftieth birthday, he wrote that he could not hear the church bells.

In the coming year he was to become not merely famous but notorious with the publication of *Tess* in its uncut volume form. He had mercilessly cut it about for its serial publication in *The Graphic*, so much that it hardly made sense, both Tess's seduction and the birth of her baby being excised. He had always been strangely willing to do this with his work, though it was a long time since his ambition had been to be thought a good hand with a serial. He was soon to meet Mrs Florence Henniker, sister of the Lord Lieutenant of Ireland, whom he loved but who did not love him. He was soon to give up writing novels, but at fifty he was known entirely as a novelist. Though he had written poetry, particularly in his first years in London and in the early days of his marriage, he had not published a line. His reputation as a poet was in the future. He had another thirty-seven years to live.

Hardy's secret love

LOIS DEACON

One of the most important contributions to Hardy studies in recent years was made by Lois Deacon, who writes here of her accidental discovery of Hardy's first love, for his cousin Tryphena Sparks. Her revelations caused a storm of controversy, and not all her hypotheses are accepted, but nevertheless Tryphena has been established as a highly influential, though long-concealed factor in Hardy's life and work. There is no doubt about the fact that Hardy loved her, courted her, and broke off his relationship to her. In this essay, Lois Deacon describes her belief that Hardy broke off the relationship because he discovered that Trypyena was in reality not his cousin, as he had supposed, but his niece, being the illegitimate daughter of Hardy's own sister. His love for Tryphena may also have been further complicated by her emotional involvement with Hardy's older friend and mentor, Horace Moule: such an involvement is strongly supported by literary evidence, though there is no factual evidence for it as yet. But, as Lois Deacon points out, there is much still to be discovered about Tryphena's role in Hardy's life.

Moule, Hardy and Tryphena all went their separate ways, breaking up the complex triangle which seems to appear in A Pair of Blue Eyes, *one of Hardy's earliest novels, and* Jude the Obscure, *his last. Moule committed suicide in 1873, Hardy married his first wife Emma in 1874, and Tryphena married Charlie Gale in 1877, after working for some years as a schoolmistress. After his marriage, Hardy never saw Tryphena again. But Lois Deacon believes, and produces much literary evidence to support her view, that his early and tragic love inspired and coloured most of his poetry and prose, though he felt obliged to conceal his sources. Certainly, as we know from his own words, he did not forget her. And it remains a striking fact that a woman who played so large a part in Hardy's emotional life should have remained unrecognized and undiscussed for so long. Here, Lois Deacon tells the story of her discoveries, and suggests reasons for Hardy's long concealment of Tryphena.*

MARGARET DRABBLE

In the summer of 1959 I was living alone in a Dartmoor border village, writing my Dartmoor novels. An isolated Quaker, I was shut off from meeting other Quaker Friends because I had no car. About eight miles away there lived in a remote twelfth-century Dartmoor mill-farm one Eleanor, who was also a Quaker, but she was unknown to me.

Earlier, I had lived for two years at Dartmeet, the heart of the Moor, and a friend who stayed in a nearby caravan, discovering my interest in Hardy as we walked together, began to lend me, one by one, her pocket edition of Hardy's novels. On her death a few years later she unexpectedly bequeathed all her books to me, including the complete Wessex edition of Hardy's works. So I began to read the lesser-known books in my thatched cottage at North Bovey, and it happened that soon after reading the puzzling – but later, quite explicable – *The Well-Beloved*, I decided to join a party of twelve Devon Quakers who were planning to visit the Quakers of the Rhineland.

We twelve Friends were present at a Quarterly Meeting of German Quakers in Darmstadt, and after the Meeting for Worship a Frau from Weisbaden whom I had never met or heard of before seated herself beside me at a tea-table, turned to me without any preliminary, and not even knowing my identity, asked 'Are you an admirer of Thomas Hardy?'

I said I was a student of Hardy, and had *The Trumpet-Major* in my hotel bedroom at that moment. She said, 'There is never a time when I am not reading Hardy,' and added that she did so because he wrote about the Moors; that she herself loved the Moors, having been brought up on the Moors near Bremen.

'I love the Moors also!' I said, 'I love them so much that I live alone on Dartmoor!' She said, 'Then perhaps you know some of these places?' and she produced the *Country Life Book of English West Country Pictures*. I opened the book at random and beheld my village green. I tapped the page excitedly, and said 'This is where I live! My cottage is just above this Green.' I then turned the page, saw Dartmeet and the roof of my former residence, and exclaimed 'This is where I lived before I came to the village of North Bovey!'

That night I related these coincidences to my room-mate, Eleanor, and she said to me:

'My mother is a cousin of Thomas Hardy, and her mother was engaged to be married to him.'

The effect of this was to silence me for that night. In the morning I said, 'You told me that your grandmother was engaged to be married to Thomas Hardy. What was her name?'

'Tryphena.'

'Well, if they were engaged to be married, and they loved each other, why were they not married?'

'She sent back the ring because they were cousins,' said Eleanor.

I came home and started fifteen years of the hard labour of research. But it was not merely a fifteen-year stretch, but a happy life sentence. Incredible coincidences piled up around me, wherever I went, resulting among other things in an avalanche of Tryphena's personal possessions being deposited from a lorry into Eleanor's farmyard – the family Bible of Tryphena's mother Rebecca Sparks, Tryphena's photograph albums, her sampler, worked as a schoolgirl at Athelhampton, near Puddletown, her autograph album, with a handwritten poem – only doggerel, but breathtaking in what it revealed – by her bridegroom, Charlie Gale; a certificate that she won at the training college for drawings of an architectural nature, and many other mementoes. Her album contained the photograph of himself, aged twenty-two which Hardy had given Tryphena five years later. It also contained several photographs of herself, and one of a small boy.*

Tryphena's daughter, Nellie Bromell (the mother of my friend Eleanor), identified the photographs for me, and gave them into my safe keeping, at my bank, until such time as my book about Hardy and Tryphena could be written and published. She eagerly poured out to me, over and over again, everything she could remember about her mother, who had died when Nellie was still a child. She told me how Tryphena was clever at old English lettering – a skill also possessed by Sue Bridehead in *Jude the Obscure*. Nellie showed me pieces of the dresses her mother had worn, and told me how Tryphena had talked constantly to her about 'Tom, Tom, it was always Tom,' and how Tom came to Topsham with his brother Henry after Tryphena's death, and was entertained to lunch by herself, because her father, Charles Gale, did not wish to meet Tom Hardy.

I never questioned Nellie Bromell in my many talks with her, but simply listened to all she told me so eagerly. She insisted on writing out her 'Recollections' and giving them to me, and members of her family told me of their gratitude for my interest. 'Mother is always talking about these things, and we are busy farm folk and haven't time to listen to her!'

In the past fifteen years I think I have studied and restudied every work of poetry and prose that Hardy published, some things that he did not publish, but wrote in his own hand, and a great mountain of books that have been written about him, his literature and his countryside. I have walked in the places where he walked, and where he and Tryphena had their being.

One of the first puzzles to clear up before writing an account of Hardy's secret love was *why* a pair of cousins who had been engaged to each other for five years should then decide that they could not marry because it was 'against the laws of the Church'. At the outset I consulted my own Rector and the Rural Dean on that point, and of course found that it was never against the laws of the Church for cousins to marry, although the Church had sometimes 'frowned upon it'. So there must have been another reason, or reasons, why Tryphena 'sent back the ring', which she undoubtedly did, and we have supporting evidence of this from more than one quarter. There is still new evidence to be found: there is much about this story that is not yet known, as is implied by a letter of Tryphena's that came to light recently, and has been published.

On the original letter Tryphena's nephew, Nat Sparks, Junior (a Royal Academician),

---

* Lois Deacon and Terry Coleman have suggested in *Providence and Mr Hardy* that this photograph was of a supposed illegitimate son of Hardy and Tryphena, a boy called Randy. A monograph by F. R. Southerington, published by J. Stevens Cox, argues the case in favour of this hypothesis more fully. *Hardy's Child. Fact or Fiction?* Monographs No. 42, 1968.

had made a covering note dated 7 November 1955, which included the words
'Thomas Hardy first wanted to marry Martha [Tryphena's sister], but Grandmother
[Maria Hand Sparks of Puddletown] put a spoke in his wheel on the grounds of
its being against the laws of the church. This information was given to me by
my Father, Nathaniel Sparks, Snr' (violin maker of Puddletown, and later of
Bristol).

Photographs of the lovely Martha, closely resembling Tryphena, were long ago
found by me in both Tryphena's album and that of the young Tom Hardy, which
was for a while in my keeping – I having been asked by the owner to identify the old
photographs in the album. I also have a facsimile of a letter written by Tom Hardy,
at the age of twenty-two, from Kilburn, London, to his sister Mary at Salisbury. This
letter was published in his autobiography, *Early Life*, omitting one telling passage
from the original letter – 'I have found Martha Sparks, and went one evening to the
exhibition with her. She is now gone home for a short time.'

Home was the thatched cottage, only a mile from where Hardy's parents lived, at
Sparks' Corner, beside the Mill at Puddletown, where Tryphena lived. When Hardy

PROBABLE TRUTH OF TRYPHENA'S PARENTAGE

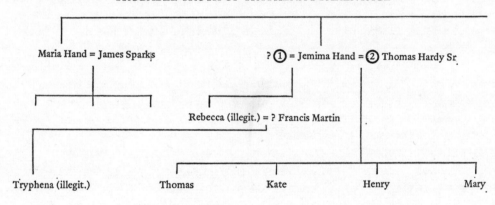

ACCEPTED VERSION OF TRYPHENA'S PARENTAGE

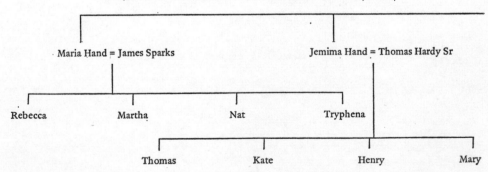

wrote this letter Martha was aged twenty-seven (five years older than Hardy) and Tryphena was eleven (eleven years younger than Hardy).

Gradually, the full explanations of the mysterious relationships between the Sparks family and Thomas Hardy came to me. After many wanderings, hundreds of interviews and exchanges of letters, and endless study, fraught with coincidences, the revelations began to fit together like a gigantic, intricate jigsaw. Many of the pieces so fitted came straight from the pen of Hardy.

The reason why Hardy did not marry Tryphena was as follows. Although Tryphena was ostensibly Hardy's first cousin, living near him on the other side of Puddletown ('Egdon') Heath, she was actually – though we shall never be able to prove it in a court of law – the niece of Thomas Hardy, being the illegitimate child of the illegitimate daughter of Hardy's mother, Jemima Hand. There is evidence that Jemima bore children before her marriage to Hardy's father, Thomas Hardy the second, of Higher Bockhampton, Stinsford, near Dorchester, Dorset. The writer Hardy was Thomas Hardy the third of that place.

It was not too uncommon for countryfolk of that region in those days to bear children before marriage. On the Isle of Portland, for instance, it was known and honoured as 'the island custom'. We need to read Hardy's novel, *The Well-Beloved*, to realize the truth of this.

A close study of Hardy reveals that he necessarily veiled the truth by many a clever but simple device, so that no outsider during his lifetime or that of his family was likely to penetrate his secrets. But at the same time he signposted the truth for the enlightenment of future generations. It is a long time ago that Jemima Hand gave birth to a child who was entered in family Bibles as being that of her respectably married sister.

'Too late! – Too late!' cried the anguished Tess to her remorseful Angel Clare. Hardy, at the age of twenty-seven, found too late that he had unwittingly planned to marry his sister's daughter, which is forbidden in the Church prayerbook.

If, in the mid-nineteenth century, an obscure young Dorset countryman fell deeply in love with a sixteen-year-old cousin, eleven years his junior, and met her secretly in defiance of his and her parents' estrangement and prohibitions, and if, in accordance with the known custom in West Country villages, the girl became pregnant, what would the young man do? He immediately planned to marry her, but if the alarmed parents of the pair tell them that the banns are forbidden 'because of the laws of the Church', what is left to do but to plight their troth privately, and go through their own form of marriage alone in a church? This is what Hardy and Tryphena evidently did, and he tells us about it in more than one poem, novel and short tale; notably and directly in his poem 'A Poor Man and a Lady':

> We knew it was not a valid thing,
> And only sanct in the sight of God.

The plight of the lovers on making the first tragic discovery of their true blood relationship is heartbreakingly presented in Hardy's poem, 'Neutral Tones':

We stood by a pond that winter day,
And the sun was white, as though chidden of God,
And a few leaves lay on the starving sod;
  – They had fallen from an ash, and were gray.

Your eyes on me were as eyes that rove
Over tedious riddles of years ago;
And some words played between us to and fro
  On which lost the more by our love.

The smile on your mouth was the deadest thing
Alive enough to have strength to die;
And a grin of bitterness swept thereby
  Like an ominous bird a-wing . . .

Since then, keen lessons that love deceives,
And wrings with wrong, have shaped to me
Your face, and the God-curst sun, and a tree,
  And a pond edged with grayish leaves.

There is strong literary evidence that Tryphena was the illegitimate daughter of Francis, the Lord of the Manor, who lived at Kingston Maurward, close beside Hardy's home; the squire's wife, Julia Augusta, who passionately loved the little Tommy Hardy, was herself childless. Kingston Maurward was made the setting for at least three of Hardy's earliest novels: he wrote his first novel, *The Poor Man and the Lady*, during the four months in 1867 when he was ardently and secretly wooing Tryphena on Egdon Heath, and the book's heroine is, of course, a 'lady', the daughter of the squire.

The history of that book is now well-known. It was suppressed, resurrected and suppressed again; torn to pieces and privately burned. But careful and – let us confess it – very crafty genius preserved a great deal of its beautiful and valuable contents in *Desperate Remedies, Under the Greenwood Tree* and in the extremely telling and rarely read remnant of the original novel, *An Indiscretion in the Life of an Heiress*, the history of which could fill a whole book. To read this *Indiscretion* is to become completely enlightened about the young author and his love: it is a glorious and rhapsodic piece of writing, though a point that emerges strongly from this idyll is the inevitable opprobrium the illicit lovers encountered in their own locality during their youthful romance. There are echoes of these events in startling personal poems, as well as in other tales and novels. Students of Hardy have noticed other echoes in his fondness for using the same phrases to describe the heroines of different novels: often these cherished phrases can be traced back to *The Poor Man and the Lady*. Of his abundant primary materials Hardy wasted nothing – ever.

By the time that *Desperate Remedies* was written and published, anonymously –

March 1871 – the love relationship between Hardy and Tryphena had developed on
Egdon Heath and had been drastically thwarted by denizens of the Heath – Hardy's
close relations. The desperate remedies of the book were for an impossible situation.

Also, by 1869, Tryphena had met Horace Moule. This unlikely bachelor scholar
and leader-writer, son of the vicar of Fordington St George, Dorchester, brother of
several men who were destined to become eminent clerics and scholars, met Tryphena,
who was twenty years his junior, in London, where she was training to be a teacher.
He fell hopelessly in love with her.* Hardy tells the story very clearly in *A Pair of Blue
Eyes*, and other novels, but most particularly in his personal confession, *Jude the
Obscure*, blaming himself endlessly because he had been personally responsible for
placing his young cousin under the tutelary care and guidance of his trusted mentor
and friend – Moule knowing nothing of the true relationships and ties between Tom
and his supposed young cousin from Puddletown, who could now enter college
because she was eighteen.

Tom Hardy, meanwhile, was trying to earn a little money by part-time architectural work in Weymouth, and was also writing self-revelatory poems and his first
published novel, *Desperate Remedies*. Poems and novel alike demonstrate his desperation, but he was to be far more deeply desperate in a few years' time.

Moving between Weymouth and Stockwell, London, where Tryffie was at training
college, Hardy became aware of the position between Moule and Tryphena – and
himself went what I can only describe as stark, staring mad. (Read all the novels.) I
have shown elsewhere† that there was a natural two-year estrangement between
Hardy, Tryphena and Moule, for which we have abundant literary evidence. But
Moule had not yet committed suicide in his chambers in Cambridge when *Desperate
Remedies* and *A Pair of Blue Eyes* were written, though he appears prominently in
both books, and is immediately recognizable in *A Pair of Blue Eyes*. This novel,
written by Hardy when he was very angry with both Tryphena and Moule, was in
accordance with the ruthless Irony of Circumstance throughout Hardy's life, published under his own name shortly before Moule's suicide. Hardy's original title for the
book was *A Winning Tongue Had He*, and the winning tongue was Horace Moule's.

There is abundant indication that the chastened but flattered Tryffie, with a second
brilliant Abelard at her feet, had seen no harm in promising to marry him, there being
insuperable impediments to her marrying her dearest Tom. *That* is one key to a better
understanding of Hardy's novels.

Tryphena had already been described as she really appeared and behaved, as Fancy
Day in *Under the Greenwood Tree*, and as Cytherea in *Desperate Remedies*, also as the
heroine, Geraldine, of the hidden first novel, but by the time that *A Pair of Blue Eyes*
appeared she had wisely been disguised with the eyes, hair, riding-habit and Cornish
setting of Hardy's future wife Emma, whom he met when they were both thirty, and

* It must be pointed out that although literary evidence for a relationship between Moule and Tryphena
is strong, there is no factual evidence of their having known each other (Editor's Note).
† In *Providence and Mr Hardy*.

married a few years later. Emma's marriage with Hardy was a matter of expedience to them both.

From the moment of the tragic culmination of Moule's inadvertent intervention in Hardy and Tryphena's joint story, it became vitally important to conceal real identities in everything that Hardy wrote in the future. So, in *Far from the Madding Crowd*, *The Return of the Native* and most of the other novels, Hardy adopted the ingenious expedient of telling variations of the true story of his life by means of cutting real life characters into two parts and depicting them and their circumstances in two fictional characters in every book. Sometimes the heroine had three heroes, reminiscent of Thomas Hardy, Horace Moule and Charlie Gale, whom Tryphena married in 1877.

It can be seen that sometimes Hardy moulded together his own characteristics and those of Moule in one fictional character, and occasionally he moulded Emma with Tryffie. Thus we find Tryphena in both Eustacia and Thomasin in *The Return of the Native*, while the two warring sides of young Tom Hardy – passionate reckless fellow and scholarly, austere worthy – are presented in the guise of Damon Wildeve and Clym Yeobright. In the early days of my research I found myself writing the names of these two fictional men side by side and seeing that the real names 'Tom Hardy, Horace Moule and Charlie Gale' were all to be found in the available letters. This would be the sort of way Hardy spoke to Tryphena of matters very weighty to them – without transgressing his self-imposed rule never to see or write to her again, once she was the wife of Charlie Gale.

In *Tess* the 'angelic' side of the writer (the aspect which injures the beloved woman even more than the rascality of the wanton fellow) is portrayed in Angel Clare, and the wild aspect in Alec d'Urberville. Moule is also always to be found in one of the main male characters.

Once we hold the key of Tryphena and the concatenation of affections between herself, Hardy, the spouses they eventually thought fit to marry, and Moule, who by his death turned drama into tragedy, we can faithfully unravel and interpret every tangled tale Hardy ever wrote. None of these stories would have been written but for the part Tryphena played in the author's life, and many of the thousand poems are even more obviously and confessedly personal than the prose. In published monographs, lectures and articles, as well as in unpublished books, I have demonstrated these truths, but only Time can firmly establish them.

Hardy was a stricken, contrite man, deeply immersed in spiritual values and time-lessness; a Seer always, possessed of insight, hindsight and foresight. He endeavoured to work out his expiation – that of the 'obscure Judas Iscariot', as he saw himself while writing his last book. There are close factual links between the names 'Thomas' and 'Judas', as readers will find on studying 'Thomas' in the *Oxford Dictionary of Christian Names*. Our Thomas ('Jude') saw himself as the triple betrayer of his Lost Love, the woman he married without love, and his closest man friend, who is largely 'Phillotson' in the novel *Jude the Obscure*. The strange, un-named children in the book, who were killed by an 'actual' child, 'Little Father Time', are, of course allegorical; that is, children of what might-have-been, but for what-was. Little Father Time himself, the 'Ancient of Ancients', has a compelling resemblance to the boy in Hardy's poem 'Midnight on the Great Western (the Journeying Boy)' and to a small boy with an ancient face in Tryphena's photograph album.*

Working out his 'sad science of renunciation', Hardy bore himself tenderly and with long-suffering during forty years of increasing incompatibility with his wife Emma, and after her death he expressed his regret in beautiful poems of remorse which cannot possibly be mistaken for the passionate poems of a young lover.

I am convinced that Hardy never would have married Emma, nor would Tryphena have married Charlie Gale of Devon after he had persistently wooed her for six years, if Horace Moule had not committed suicide, throwing up the necessity for suppression of facts during the lifetime of all participants in the tragedy. They had become involuntarily involved, like puppets on a stage.

There is much literary evidence in Hardy that before the lovers were forced to go their separate ways with other partners, there was a strong plea from the man to the woman to flee to a far corner of the earth. We are told this in the poem 'The Recalcitrants', which was also a title chosen originally by Hardy for *Jude the Obscure*:

> Let us off and search, and find a place,
> Where yours and mine can be natural lives ...
> We have found us already shunned, disdained ...

Holding the key in our hands we open secret door after secret door, so that even when Hardy writes allegorically it is easy to perceive the inner significance. The truth is signposted for our generation, now that the immediate victims of 'Heredity', and 'the blood's tendence' of the 'Family Portraits' in the poems have been laid to rest – these 'dear people' as Hardy described them when he was eighty-three. That is when the arresting, ingenious *Tragedy of the Queen of Cornwall* was shaped. In this work Tryphena was the dark-haired Queen Iseult; Emma was the unloved fair-haired Iseult (wife of Tristram), and Hardy was Tristram himself. The fact that he wrote this version of the old Cornish love story, after long postponements, shows two things – first, that he still adored his dead Tryphena when he was approaching the end of his life, and secondly that he still thought it necessary to present his romance so that contemporary readers would at once assume that it enshrined memories of his courtship of his wife in Cornwall. Having adopted the same ruse more than fifty years earlier, in the novel, *A Pair of Blue Eyes*, Hardy had specially requested his publisher to take pains to keep this novel, with its Cornish associations, well before the public eye.

The method adopted by Hardy in his old age was to write his autobiography in the third person and to arrange for it to be published posthumously as a biography written by his second wife, Florence, who acted as his secretary, both before and after she married him. She was not born until well after the drama of her husband's early life

* See footnote, page 21.

had been played out to a bitter conclusion. The effects of autobiography masquerading as well-informed but secretive biography are profoundly interesting. Confusion, puzzledom and exasperation are just a few of the inevitable results. In his *Life* Hardy omitted to mention his Sparks relations, only once referring to Tryphena and then as 'a cousin', and, in his published *Pedigree*, Hardy significantly ignored the Sparks family altogether, although Maria Hand Sparks was his aunt, an elder sister of his mother, Jemima, and lived only two or three miles away from Hardy's birthplace.

It has been shown, in print, that the young Jemima Hand's illegitimate daughter Rebecca was almost certainly baptized as being the daughter of James and Maria (Hand) Sparks of Puddletown, and that Rebecca later became the mother of Tryphena – illegitimately.

What Hardy does not tell us in his autobiography he reveals clearly in such poems as 'The Christening', 'A Wife and Another', 'On a Heath', 'At Rushy Pond', 'The Place on the Map', 'The End of the Episode', 'Beyond the Last Lamp', 'Her Love Bird', 'Midnight on the Great Western', 'The Revisitation', 'To a Motherless Child', 'Thoughts of Phena', 'In a Eweleaze near Weatherbury', 'Her Immortality' and dozens of other poems.

Occasionally Hardy omitted from published collections important stanzas which he left in the manuscripts, and sometimes poems were ante-dated or post-dated in collections, for obvious reasons of secrecy. None of the collected poems appeared until eight years after Tryphena's death, which was in 1890.

Some of the most revealing poetry was not published until after Hardy's death, in *Winter Words* (1928). This volume includes the supremely important 'Standing By The Mantelpiece', with Horace M. Moule's initials, indicating the facts behind Moule's suicide.* 'Family Portaits' in the same collection, is also exceptionally important, with its references to veiled secrets in the Hardy family.

What was Tryphena like? We have plenty of indications. A winsome introduction to her can be found, we may assume, in *Under the Greenwood Tree*, a sweet, fresh and happy novel, published anonymously in 1872, before Horace Moule died. The heroine, Fancy Day, shows the 'colossal inconsistency' that characterizes all Hardy's heroines, who almost always had two, sometimes three strings to their bow. Here is Fancy:

Flexibility was her first characteristic, by which she appeared to enjoy the most easeful rest when she was in gliding motion. Her dark eyes – arched by brows of so keen, slender and soft a curve that they resembled nothing so much as two slurs in music – showed primarily a bright sparkle each. This was softened by a frequent thoughtfulness, yet not so frequent as to do away, for more than a few minutes, at a time, with a certain coquettishness, which in its turn was never so decided as to banish honesty. Her lips imitated her brows in

* Lois Deacon and Coleman believe that Moule, who died in 1873, having severed his own wind pipe with a razor, had been involved with Tryphena. The report of the inquest spoke of depression caused by difficulties in his academic career, not unlike Jude the Obscure's, and Moule's brother Charles spoke of 'circumstances to lead to such depression', which may hint at troubles with Tryphena, and his friend Hardy (Editor's Note).

their clearly-cut outline and softness of bend; and her nose was well-shaped – which is saying a great deal, when it is remembered that there are a hundred pretty mouths and eyes for one pretty nose. Add to this, plentiful knots of dark-brown hair . . . and the slightest idea may be gained of the young maiden who showed, amidst the rest of the dancing-ladies, like a flower among vegetables.

This is the Hardyan girl we meet again and again. The phrase about arched brows 'like two slurs in music' is used by Hardy to describe the heroine of more than one of his novels, and her identity with Tryphena, 'the lost prize', is supported by the photograph of Tryphena, aged eighteen, which her daughter, old Nellie Bromell, brought to me from Tryphena's own album.

Of Geraldine in *An Indiscretion in the Life of an Heiress*, Hardy wrote:

The clear, deep eyes, full of all tender expressions; the fresh, subtly-curved cheek, changing its tones of red with the fluctuation of each thought; the ripe tint of her delicate mouth, and the indefinable line where lip met lip, the noble bend of her neck, the waving lengths of her dark brown hair, the soft motions of her bosom when she breathed, the light fall of her little feet, the elegant contrivances of her attire, all struck him as something he had dreamed of and was not actually seeing.

Another notable thing about Hardy's fictional young women is their rich contralto speaking voices, deepening in moments of great emotion, 'in the stopt-diapason note which her voice acquired when her heart was in her speech.' The quotation is from *Tess of the D'Urbervilles* and Hardy so far forgot that he was writing of a *fictional* character that he added to the sentence – 'and which will never be forgotten by those who knew her.' He was quite carried away when he wrote these words, and perceptive readers see what he saw, and heard what he heard. Indeed – ah, indeed – he who runs may read!

Of Eustacia, in *The Return of the Native*, Hardy recorded, 'She had Pagan eyes, full of nocturnal mysteries', and 'In heaven she will probably sit between the Heloises and the Cleopatras.' Hardy's Heloises always sat at the feet of *two* Abelards, and so, I think, did Tryphena.

'Tess' was 'a fine and handsome girl . . . her mobile peony mouth and large innocent eyes adding eloquence to colour and shape . . . Her lower lip had a way of thrusting the middle of her top one upward, when they closed together after a word.' She spoke 'two languages, the dialect at home, more or less; ordinary English abroad and to persons of quality'.

In making Tess say, of a youthful aspect of her appearance, that 'it was a fault which time would cure,' Hardy was actually quoting Tryphena. When she was interviewed for the post of head mistress at a girls' school in Plymouth, she was told that she was very young, at twenty, for the appointment, and she replied, 'That is a fault which time will cure.' She secured the post, and kept it, satisfactorily, until she yielded to Charlie Gale's reiterated proposals at the end of 1877.

Between *Greenwood Tree* and *Tess* we can meet the wayward, loveable girl many times in Hardy's other tales, and very notably as Eustacia in *The Return of the Native*, and as Bathsheba in *Far from the Madding Crowd*.

Hardy had finally parted from his Lost Love before he married Emma, and well before Tryphena married Charlie, and there are many indications that these two marriages may have been largely matters of expediency, to provide an alibi and a refuge to the pair, who were animated by a spirit of atonement and of personal sacrifice.

Hardy indicated that his last novel, *Jude*, was an amplification of the theme already presented in *A Pair of Blue Eyes*, which can clearly be seen from a comparison of the two books. He also explained in the preface to *Jude* that the circumstances of the novel were 'suggested by the death of a woman in 1890' (the year Tryphena died). In a postscript which he added in 1912 to this preface Hardy expressed his earlier hope, which had been disappointed, that 'certain cathartic qualities' might have been found in the book when it was published in 1895. Actually *Jude* had met with a storm of misunderstanding and downright abuse.

In *A Pair of Blue Eyes* and *Jude* the author stressed the 'curious epicene tenderness' and 'unconsciousness of gender' of the young woman at the centre of the complicated plots. She would give her photograph or warm sympathy and attention to any man as naturally as to a friend of her own sex.

After Hardy had written *Jude* he said, 'All my stories are written', and refused to write another novel. But when *The Return of the Native* was being written Hardy was in the early years of his marriage to Emma (the calmest years), and Tryphena was about to be married to Charles. The ill-starred lovers were irrevocably parted, and Hardy was in honour bound never to approach Tryphena again in person, or by letter. So what did he do? He sat in the bay window of his sitting-room, turned his back on Emma (and told us so in a reminiscent poem), and reconstructed the true love story in *The Return of the Native*, with the two real young lovers presented in four different fictional characters. The book is full of tender, loyal, secret yet obvious messages to Tryffie.

The Return of the Native was first printed serially in *Belgravia* from January to December, 1878 – the first instalment appearing in January, the month after Tryphena had married Charles Gale in Plymouth and gone with him to live at Topsham, near Exeter, where she died.

Tryphena read that book. She read all Hardy's books as they appeared, and even gave them to her very young daughter, Nellie Tryphena, to read, telling her 'All the people in Tom's stories are *real* people.' In her old age Nellie Tryphena repeated that information to myself.

Tryphena herself recognized the truth that Hardy was telling, though secrecy, which held that articulate man in her firm grip until his death, demanded often that he should disguise places as well as people; hence, for instance, the setting of *Jude the Obscure* in remoter parts of Wessex – places where Tryphena had never been, and Sue Bridehead is without doubt a portrait of the very Tryphena. Yet, as always, from time to time he whisked off the coverlets by writing such frank poems as 'In a Cathedral City' (Salisbury), telling us that his beloved had never been there, so that he who bore her 'imprint through and through' might sojourn there to gain forget-fulness.

Scores of poems owe their origin in this way to Hardy's secret love for Tryphena: they cover the entire period, from 1867 when he was twenty-seven, to when he was in his eighties, just before his death in 1928.

More than a hundred years have now passed since Hardy and his beloved met 'in a secret year' beside Rushy-Pond on Egdon Heath. The truth about their relationship, so long concealed and so accidentally discovered, can now be told, without harm or distress to any living person, provided we refrain from probing the privacy of living descendants of the protagonists. Hardy himself certainly yearned for the revelation, and employed the power of his pen to bring it about: and Tryphena's grand-daughter Eleanor wrote to me at the outset of my researches; 'All things that are hidden shall be made known,' and 'Truth cannot be hidden at the bottom of a well.' The letter is treasured by me now that Eleanor too has departed.

Hardy's love for Tryphena has rendered her immortal. To those who mistakenly imagine that the truth will damage the reputation of Hardy or Tryphena, one can only point out, with complete sincerity, that she was the lifelong inspiration of his incomparable works.

Friends and critics 1840–1928

SHEILA SULLIVAN

All his life Hardy was a very private person. He retained from early youth to his death at the age of eighty-seven an air of slight withdrawal from the world he lived in and the people he lived with. Hermann Lea, a close friend of Hardy's later years, observes in his notes that Hardy's schoolboy friends found their companion 'somehow different from the rest of us boys, kind of dreaming, seeming to prefer to be by himself'. In *The Life of Thomas Hardy* (largely written by Hardy) the author comments that although young Tom was popular with his schoolmates, he was always irritated if any of them wished to accompany him on the long walk home to Bockhampton. Towards the end of his life, when he was a very old man, his parlour-maid, Miss Titterington, and his secretary, Miss O'Rourke, both remarked on this quality of withdrawal from the world; and T. E. Lawrence found him 'refined into an essence', as if the world could no longer touch him. This habit of retreat from facts and faces and objects arose, not from disdain for the outward trappings of things, but because the intensity of his inner life was such that often the world became an irritation. The retreat was physical as well as emotional. As a child Hardy hated to be touched, as a man he would walk down the centre of the street to avoid contact on the busy pavement; his handshake was always 'slight and nervous'.

His annoyance with casual company lasted a lifetime. As his fame and notoriety burgeoned, with a new burst of growth after every novel, so his need for protection increased. His feelings are reflected both in the design of the house and in the pattern of life at Max Gate. When he built this house, between 1883 and 1885, he set it well back from the Wareham Road and surrounded the large garden with a substantial wall. There was a modest main entrance, but also, round the corner, set in the wall, was a small green door, through which Hardy would emerge secretly for his daily walk. Inside the wall was a solid row of trees; the gardener, Bertie Stephens, told James Stevens Cox (who interviewed him for one of his invaluable series of *Monographs*) that he was allowed to prune and thin those trees only with the greatest caution. The casual visitor would find that the task of breaching this fortress was almost impossible. An appointment must be made first by letter, otherwise the visitor would be politely but firmly repelled by one of the servants, or in later years by the formidable terrier Wessex.

After Hardy's death in 1928, his widow Florence (no doubt acting on Hardy's instructions) arranged for two enormous bonfires in the garden, on to which were piled armfuls of letters, documents, notes, diaries, photographs – all the fabric of Hardy's private life which he wished never to be revealed. Stephens describes how his task was to tend one of the fires, while Florence personally stoked and raked over the other, until no scrap was left unburned. 'It was a devil of a clearout,' said Stephens.

And yet, for all his wariness, Hardy never undervalued love, or friendship. Once he had made a friend he kept him or her until death intervened for one of them. Nor did he despise the pleasures of the world. For thirty years, from about 1877 to 1907, he spent three or four months of every year in London, dining, dancing, party-going, visiting concerts and operas, and clearly (in spite of grumbles in his letters) enjoying the whole performance of lionization in the drawing-rooms of Lady Londonderry, Lady Carnarvon, Lady St Helier, Lady Portsmouth, the Duchess of Marlborough, and so on. (Indeed, George Gissing and many others noted his marked weakness for the aristocracy.)

W. R. Rutland, Hardy's friend and biographer, emphasizes that 'Hardy was not a man who in his maturity gave himself to others.' And Christine Wood Homer, a young friend in Dorset, observed that 'Mr Hardy had to like a person before he would enter into any conversation.' In spite of the sociability of his annual London season, he was in fact a man who had to be won. Always acutely sensitive to the company around him, he was chary of committing himself until he was sure he approved and was approved in return. Once the barriers were breached he gave his friendship and loyally maintained it; but few ever found their way through. In his long life there seem to have been no more than about half a dozen men and women to whom he could write or speak freely, and even they were kept for the most part on the frontiers of his inner griefs and joys. Paradoxically, the only confidant of these was the anonymous world at large, to whom he published his poems.

Hardy's few particular friends had obvious qualities in common. All were people of positive personality and high intelligence, and all with the exception of Hermann Lea were deeply involved in literature. Two of them, Horace Moule and Leslie Stephen, were both eight years older than Hardy. Indeed it seems that in his early life, while he was making the difficult transition from village lad to rising London author, Hardy needed the assurance he found in friendship with an older man. He had grown up with the Moule boys, whose father was vicar of nearby Fordington, and he kept in touch with Charles and Handley all their lives. But it was Horace whom he loved, Horace who guided his reading, encouraged his writing, advised him in his struggle between architecture and literature. It was Horace who helped him with his Greek, taught him part-singing, walked with him in the Frome meadows discussing Bagehot, *Faust*, philosophy, poetry. Hardy did his best to be convinced by Newman's *Apologia* because Moule admired it; he gave up reading Greek with painful reluctance in 1862 because Moule considered he would never make a living as an architect if he was to be up every morning at five, reading Greek drama. Nine years later, after the publication of *Desperate Remedies* in 1871, he followed Moule in a reversal of his advice and decided to press on with writing, in spite of the continual rejection of his poems and the doubtful reception of his first novel. Hardy last saw Moule in Cambridge in 1873, when they climbed on to the roof of King's Chapel (an uncharacteristic jaunt for Hardy) and saw the sun shining on the lantern of Ely Cathedral. There is little doubt that before this time they had survived some darkening of their friendship; it is possible that Horace had fallen in love with Hardy's own love, Tryphena, and had thereby become involved in that painful situation. Nevertheless, by the time of the last visit to Cambridge, it is clear from Hardy's diary, and from certain poems, that his affection for Moule was strong as ever, and Moule's suicide three months later was an appalling shock. The relationship had been one of the most crucial of Hardy's life, and even in death Moule's influence was not ended. In later years Hardy admitted to Sir Sydney Cockerell that Angel Clare was partly based on Moule; but there are many critics who would go much further than this, finding Moule in many of Hardy's heroes, and tracing the triangle of Moule-Tryphena-Hardy in less obvious sources than *A Pair of Blue Eyes*.

Leslie Stephen was a more shadowy figure in Hardy's life, but it is clear that in some measure he took over the role of Moule. Stephen first wrote to Hardy in December 1872, asking for a serial for *The Cornhill*, of which he was editor. He had admired *Under the Greenwood Tree*, which had been published in that year, and although he did not always feel he could publish Hardy's subsequent novels in his family magazine he supported Hardy with encouragement throughout his literary career. He felt he had to refuse *The Return of the Native*, and to his regret he was not offered *The Trumpet-Major*, but he published *Far from the Madding Crowd* and *The Hand of Ethelberta*. His influence was more than that of editor and critic. In the *Life* Hardy describes Stephen as 'the man whose philosophy was to influence his own for many years . . . more than that of any other contemporary.' Stephen's rationalism clarified and confirmed the direction of Hardy's own thought. Both men found themselves renegades from an orthodox Protestant faith, in which Stephen had actually taken Orders and Hardy had once seriously considered the same course. Hardy may well have been surprised to receive a summons from Stephen late one evening in March 1875. He found his friend 'pacing up and down his room and requiring a witness to his signature renouncing Holy Orders.' Hardy complied and they settled down to a discussion of 'theologies decayed and defunct, the origin of things, the constitution of matter, the unreality of time.' Both men held many attitudes in common, not only towards philosophy and religion, but towards morals, marriage, and sexual behaviour. Both were repelled by hypocrisy, both were attracted by plain speaking and sincerity. When Virginia Woolf came to tea at Max Gate in the summer of 1926 Hardy made her particularly welcome, no doubt remembering his affection for her father. 'Your father took my novel, *Far from the Madding Crowd*,' he told her; adding with pardonable pride, 'We stood shoulder to shoulder against the British public about certain matters dealt with in that novel.'

There was another older man for whom Hardy felt deep devotion, and that was the poet William Barnes. He knew Barnes from his own early childhood; and as a young architect of sixteen, training in Hicks's office in Dorchester, he would often drop into Barnes's school next door with some perplexing problem in Latin or Greek. He loved Barnes's poems, which were little read, and he sent to the *New Quarterly* one of the very few reviews he ever wrote, praising the collected edition of Barnes's poems in 1879. After Barnes's death in 1886 he told Edmund Blunden that Barnes's poetry had been doomed by the critics. He acknowledged an immense debt to Barnes in his own poetry and prose, yet it is probable that the vast gap in years between them (Barnes was ten years older than Hardy's father) precluded the kind of friendship Hardy enjoyed with Moule or Stephen.

The other closest friends of Hardy's life were all younger than he. Edmund Gosse first met Hardy in the winter of 1874, when he was twenty-four and Hardy ten years older. They were friends for fifty-three years; their affection and pleasure in each other's company seems never to have wavered, even through periods when Gosse's reviews (notably of *Jude*) were far from adulatory. Gosse was a constant visitor in the winter of 1880 when Hardy nearly died of an internal haemorrhage; whenever Hardy was in London in subsequent years Gosse would take him to dine at the Savile, and invite him to his literary tea-parties. At Gosse's house Hardy met Kipling and the sculptor Thorneycroft. Year after year Gosse was a regular visitor to Max Gate, and in 1901, when Hardy had sent him a copy of *Poems of the Past and the Present* he replied, 'When all speaks to me in the accents of a voice I love so much – in the accents of a man whom of all my living contemporaries I admire and delight in the most – how can I specify?' And in 1919 he wrote to Hardy thanking him for forty-five years' unbroken friendship. For his part, Hardy seems to have written and spoken to Gosse with a freedom which broke far into his customary reticence. Perhaps because of the holocaust of private papers, there is tantalizingly little to go on, but we do know that Hardy discussed with Gosse the painful problems which faced Jude, and the sexual nature of Sue; we know that he revealed to Gosse his own attraction for such women; we know he wrote to Gosse (albeit cryptically) of the feeling he had developed for his illustrator Helen Paterson, in the summer of 1874, before he married Emma.

Hardy was born questioning the lot of man on earth, convinced – as Binyon put it – of the implanted crookedness of things. And there is now little doubt that his basic resentment was cruelly reinforced by the long destruction of love and hope between the sunny autumn of 1867, spent with Tryphena, and his marriage with Emma Gifford in 1874. Clearly Gosse suspected that there were revealing secrets in Hardy's life, and sometimes he probed gently. In his review of *Jude the Obscure* he asks, 'What has Providence done to Mr Hardy that he should rise up in the arable land of Wessex and shake his fist at his Creator?' And in writing of Hardy some years later he observes that 'the wells of human hope had been poisoned for him by some condition of which we know nothing.' Did Hardy ever tell Gosse about those painful years before his marriage to Emma? It seems most likely that he said nothing, even to Gosse.

We know of only one person to whom Hardy definitely revealed something of Tryphena, and that is Hermann Lea. Although Lea was many years younger, he was a man in whose company Hardy seems to have felt cheerfully at ease. Indeed Lea is perhaps the only person ever to describe Hardy as 'jovial'. Many found him some-times genial, but Lea's description of a day's outing in 1916, during which 'Mr Hardy was in one of his jolliest, most jovial moods, when quip and jest marked his interesting remarks . . .' appears to stand unique among the observations of Hardy's friends. Plainly Hardy enormously enjoyed the use of Lea's motor, but equally plainly he enjoyed Lea's company. He and Hermann were friends, and for the most part neighbours, for nearly twenty-five years, and during that time they visited and re-visited, by car, on bicycle, and on foot, all the scenes in the novels and poems which Hardy felt he could identify. The topographical help that Hardy gave enabled Lea to publish two books, *A Handbook to the Wessex Country of Thomas Hardy* and *Thomas Hardy's Wessex*. Lea was devoted to Hardy, and on his side Hardy seems to have responded with uncharacteristic frankness to the warmth of his eccentric and engag-ing friend. 'Mr Hardy responded at once,' writes Lea, 'to many questions of mine, and launched out on many details regarding his work, his methods, his aspirations and his achievements.' (Far from responding 'at once' to such questions, Hardy in most company would refuse to respond at all.) And when at one time in his life Lea found himself confronted by an experience in some ways similar to that which Hardy had encountered with Tryphena, it is clear that Hardy in his endeavour to help told his friend something of the painful secrets of his own past.

James Barrie and Florence Henniker were both people to whom Hardy could write and speak as he felt inclined. Mrs Henniker was one of the many women with whom Hardy fell in love, but he surmounted his feelings (which were not returned) and contrived to retain her as a friend for thirty years, until her death. It is clear from Hardy's letters to her that she influenced the writing of *Jude*, and she should probably be allowed to join the company of Tryphena as a source for Sue Bridehead. No doubt because of the bonfires, only some forty of her letters to Hardy survive, but his to her reveal not only unwavering affection but a determination to do all he could to further her literary career. He even went so far as to write a review for one of her books – one of the only two reviews he ever appears to have written.

This is not the place to describe Hardy's loves, but it is important when discussing his friendships to understand that from youth to extreme old age Hardy was very susceptible to women. He describes in the *Life* how as a little boy his feeling for Julia Augusta Martin, the lady of Kingston Maurward, 'almost was that of a lover'. And at the other end of his life, when he was eighty-four and had weathered many passions, he was still capable of falling in love with Mrs Bugler, who played Tess in Dorchester in the dramatization of the novel. Even when his feelings were not deeply stirred, Hardy blossomed in female company and his manner immediately mellowed in the presence of girls and young women. There are many men whose memories of Hardy in middle and old age are of a silent, depressed, and even morose figure; there seem to be no young women who record anything comparable. In their presence he became open and charming. Christine Wood Homer, who knew him in the nineties, found him 'always very kind and genial to young people'. Mrs Bugler describes him as animated in conversation and his secretary, May O'Rourke, who knew him in the last years of his life, records her impression of his accessibility and charm. Possibly the daughter of Eden Philpotts was a little surprised to find Thomas Hardy O.M., then in his eighties, crawling about with her under the table trying to fix the wires of her radio.

The loving care with which Hardy analyses the heroines of his novels reflects the pleasure he found in the company of women. He told Gosse that the only interesting thing about his first (unpublished and dismembered) novel, *The Poor Man and the Lady*, was 'a wonderful insight into female character' – adding modestly, 'I don't know how that came about.' There are hints that he had something of a reputation among the village girls, but at the same time there is no doubt that his domestic life was, as May O'Rourke puts it, one of iron-clad Victorian decorum.

After his early youth was past, Hardy seems to have moved more easily through the literary and fashionable circles of London than among his own people of Dorset. Despite the fact that he chose to settle permanently only two miles from his childhood home, and despite the affectionate characterization of country people in his novels, he does not seem to have been popular with the local men and women of Dorchester and its countryside. He never in his adult life made any kind of friend of a servant or a social inferior. He never in fact solved the problem of growing from the precocious son of a country builder into a prosperous literary figure of the middle class. From the time he returned to live permanently near Dorchester in 1885 he was shunned by the county set and disliked by the local people. The county disdained him because of his public hatred of blood-sports and the suffering they inflicted on animals. The local people (and indeed most of his family except his brothers and sisters) disliked him for many reasons. His family resented the immorality of his books, and the fact that 'real people' were described in them; they disliked the notoriety Tom had brought upon Dorset. The local people resented his shyness, which they interpreted as superiority, and above all they disliked him for his meanness. 'Miser Hardy, miser Hardy', the children would chant in the streets of Dorchester. And there is no doubt that Hardy was very close-fisted indeed. The food at Max Gate was absolutely minimal; Annie Mitchell, who cooked there early in the century, reported that half a pound of liver had to do for four people. The scarcity of food is described by more than one hungry visitor – only Edmund Blunden appears to have had enough to eat, and he is known to have had scarcely any appetite at all. Nor was Hardy any more generous in the giving of tips and presents. The annual Christmas present for the servants was 2s 6d each, the tip received by Annie Mitchell for collecting a load of sloes for wine, and cycling twenty miles to fetch and deliver them, was 2s.

This streak of parsimony made itself felt not only in money matters, but in Hardy's unwillingness to offer compliments or thanks to servants or providers of services. The gardener, Bertie Stephens, records that 'at no time did Hardy express any appreciation or give any praise for anything that was done in the garden'. Annie Mitchell remembers, because the occasion was unique, that he once praised one of her puddings. It seems fair to say that except in the small circle of his intimate friends Hardy found giving a difficult exercise. To quote W. R. Rutland again, 'Hardy was not a man who in his maturity gave himself to others.' Nor was he a man who easily gave money, or compliments, or thanks.

There were a host of lesser male friendships, mainly literary, enduring over many years. Barrie, Blunden, Cockerell, Kegan Paul, Edward Clodd, Quiller-Couch, Masefield, and at the end of Hardy's life, T. E. Lawrence, were all among those with whom Hardy corresponded and for whom he felt some degree of friendship. Indeed it is remarkable that throughout a long and controversial literary career he made so few personal enemies. Those few who, like George Moore, insisted on flaunting their antagonism, found themselves ignored, or, in Moore's case, dismissed as 'that ludicrous old blackguard'. Henry James and R. L. Stevenson, both of whom expressed strong reservations about Hardy's work, were neatly emasculated as 'Polonius and Osric'.

The fact that Hardy would not make enemies does not mean that he was impervious to criticism. Indeed he was over-sensitive to the point of despair. He describes in the *Life* how in 1871 the *Spectator* review of his first published novel, *Desperate Remedies*, made him wish he were dead. And as that particular review is by no means venomous – parts of it are positively encouraging – it is as well that Hardy had no foreknowledge of the thunder that was to break later with the publication of *Tess of the D'Urbervilles* and *Jude the Obscure*. Although Moule, Stephen, Gosse, and many other of his friends were regular reviewers of books, Hardy from the beginning to the end of his literary life heartily disliked all critics and reviewers. When he was young and indigent, working for Sir Arthur Blomfield in London, he was encouraged by Moule to make money by reviewing; but he would not, then or later. He appears to have written only the two reviews described earlier, one for Barnes and one for Mrs Henniker. An 'old dissatisfaction with the tribe of book reviewers', described by Blunden, remained with him to the end of his career. The Prefaces to his novels and his volumes of verse contain many references to the misconceptions and stupidities of critics. In the Apology to *Late Lyrics and Earlier*, published as far on in his life as 1922, he is still smarting from the injustices inflicted on his own writing and that of others by 'impotent and mischevious criticism; the satirizing of individuality, the lack of whole seeing in contemporary estimates of poetry and kindred work, the knowingness affected by junior reviewers'. The bantering tone of a letter to C. K. Shorter in 1907 does not conceal Hardy's underlying bitterness. 'I endeavour to profit,' he writes, 'from the opinions of those wonderful youths and maidens, my reviewers, and am laying to heart a few infallible truths taught by them, e.g.

    That Thomas Hardy's verse is his only claim to notice
    That Thomas Hardy's prose is his only real work
    That Thomas Hardy's early novels are best
    That Thomas Hardy's late novels are best etc.'

The themes which were to be the main preoccupations of these detested critics begin to emerge very early, with the publication of *Under the Greenwood Tree* in 1872. At once the rustics are under attack for the manner and content of their speech. '. . . they occasionally express themselves in the language of the author's manner of thought rather than in their own,' writes Moule mildly. Again and again in succeeding years the same charge is reiterated, and the mildness of Moule's tone is not always copied. Hardy defended himself in a letter to the *Athenaeum* in November 1878, asserting there that he retains the idiom, the compass and characteristic expression of country people, but does not attempt phonetic transcription. The letter does not squarely answer the main charge, but Hardy must have thought it adequate, for the rustics of future novels do not alter their conversation in order to please the critics.

The charges of sensationalism, inelegance of style, pessimism and immorality succeed each other regularly with the publication of each new work. Indirectly Hardy conceded the charge of sensationalism. Although once hoping to be considered merely 'a good hand at a serial', he came to believe that the magazine serial form was a tyranny that could do only harm. He feared that *The Mayor of Casterbridge* had been spoiled by the need to provide a striking incident for each chapter, and he described to Virginia Woolf how 'one begins to think what is good for the magazine, not what is good for the novel'.

The accusation of pessimism seems first to have arisen with the appearance of *The Mayor of Casterbridge* in 1886, and was immediately repeated with the publication of *The Woodlanders* in 1887. This charge, which was to recur throughout his lifetime (and after), irritated Hardy deeply. He always asserted with the utmost firmness that he was not a pessimist. He defends himself in conversation, in his letters, and in his Prefaces. To Noyes he wrote in 1920, 'it was a mere nickname with no sense in it'. To Vere Collins he said, 'It's only a passing fashion.' He liked to describe himself as a 'meliorist', a man who was prepared to face the worst an indifferent universe might offer, but who believed nevertheless that the will to live persists, and that no life is entirely without its consolations. In an article on Hardy's poems, Gosse shows how Hardy arrives, through his view of the nature of accident, chance, and time, at an involuntary pessimism; but Gosse prefers (as no doubt Hardy preferred) to regard the attitude as one of resignation.

'Pessimist' was an irritating misnomer; the recurring accusation which angered Hardy most deeply was that of coarseness and immorality. Between the publication of *Two on a Tower* in 1882, at which the charge was first levelled, and the final explosion after *Jude the Obscure* in 1896, Mrs Grundy was Hardy's first enemy. In one of his few literary essays, 'Candour in English Fiction', published in the *New Review* in 1890, he writes, 'Life being a physiological fact, its honest portrayal must be largely concerned with, for one thing, the relations of the sexes . . .' If there existed truly adult magazines, he continued, 'the position of man and woman in nature, the position of belief in the minds of man and woman – things which everybody is thinking but nobody is saying – might be taken up and treated frankly.' He describes bitterly the price an artist has to pay for the privilege of writing in English – 'no less a price than the complete extinction, in the mind of every mature and penetrating reader, of sympathetic belief in his personages.'

When Hardy wrote these words in 1890 the friends of Mrs Grundy had not yet closed ranks to face *Tess* and *Jude*. But *Two on a Tower* had been described by the *Spectator* in 1882 'as unpleasant as it is practically impossible . . . objectionable without truth'; and in the *St James's Gazette* as 'little short of revolting'. Doubts had been expressed about the propriety of *The Mayor of Casterbridge* in 1886; *The Woodlanders* had been dismissed by *The World* in 1887 as 'a story of vulgar intrigue' and by the *Spectator* as 'a picture of shameless falsehood, levity, and infidelity'. By the time he was working on *Tess* Hardy was running out of patience with this kind of reception, but no doubt he realized that he still had much to suffer. *Tess* was rejected on moral grounds by both *Murray's Magazine* and *Macmillan's Magazine*, then eventually published in a much bowdlerized form in *The Graphic*. The publication in its full version redoubled the familiar accusations. The book was said to ignore 'the plain, unwritten instincts of morality'. Mowbray Morris, an old enemy, castigated it as 'an extremely disagreeable story in an extremely disagreeable manner'; Henry James described it as 'chockful of faults and falsity'. 'Well,' said Hardy, 'if this sort of thing continues, no more novel-writing for me.' But much worse was to come. Warily on the defensive, Hardy wrote in his Preface to *Jude* that this was a novel 'addressed by a man to men and women of full age' which told 'without a mincing of words, of a deadly war waged with an old Apostolic desperation between flesh and spirit . . .' Published in its full form in 1896, *Jude* was described by the *Pall Mall Gazette* as a work of 'dirt, drivel, and damnation'. The New York *Bookman* found that many scenes recalled the spectacle of 'some foul animal that snatches greedily at great lumps of putrid offal'; the reviewer of *The World* had to open a window to let in the fresh air. Fortunately Hardy did not lose his sense of the absurd. He describes in his Preface to the 1912 edition how the book was burned by a bishop 'probably in his despair at not being able to burn me'; and he remarks in a letter to Henry Harper, his American publisher (whose memory of the uproar is said to have been still green forty years later), that while he would like the novel withdrawn in the United States, as it caused such offence, yet 'I myself thought it was somewhat overburdened with the interests of morality'.

No wonder Hardy was deeply hurt at the reception he was given, and perhaps it is no wonder that he wrote no more novels. Yet, just as when he was a young man wishing he were dead after the publication of *Desperate Remedies*, he over-reacted to the vituperative reviews and failed to find a balancing compensation in the good ones.

For good reviews there certainly were, even for *Jude*. Richard le Gallienne defended it vigorously, as did William Dean Howells in the US. The *Illustrated London News* considered it a work of genius, the *Saturday Review* the 'most splendid' of the novels. Havelock Ellis, writing in the *Savoy Magazine*, found it the greatest novel written in English for many years. Likewise while Henry James dismissed *Far from the Madding Crowd* as 'diffuse . . . verbose and redundant in style' the *Graphic* declared that Mr Hardy excelled everyone but George Eliot and *The Pall Mall Gazette* found the author a man of genius. Although the *Athenaeum* considered *The Return of the Native* 'distinctly inferior to the previous novels', the *Spectator* found it 'a story of singular power and interest', and Lionel Johnson in his book *The Art of Thomas Hardy*, published in 1894, thought it Hardy's best novel. Although *The World* dismissed *The Woodlanders* as a story of vulgar intrigue, Arnold Bennett chose it as the finest of English novels and the *Athenaeum* considered it a masterly work in fiction. *Tess of the D'Urbervilles* was said to lack 'the plain unwritten instincts of morality', yet it was considered by the *Westminster Review* to be the greatest novel since George Eliot died, and by the *National Review* to be a great creation. Time and again, throughout the reviews of the novels, the words 'power' and 'powerful' repeat themselves. Hardy can have been left in no doubt that at least half a dozen of his works impressed their creative strength on all but the pettiest critics. Likewise his skill in description, both of people and of the natural world, is consistently singled out for praise. All in all, few major authors can have had to weather a reception so bewilderingly contrary.

It was with the publication of *Tess* that Hardy became established as a national figure. As we have seen, many of the reviews were terrible; yet Hardy noted with satisfaction that a particularly abusive and sarcastic notice in the *Saturday Review* 'had quickened the sales'. The book became fashionable, everybody had to read and pronounce upon it, the Duchess of Abercorn arranged her dinner guests according to their approval or disapproval of *Tess*.

The reception given to Hardy's poetry was in general colder, but more polite (he was after all a major literary figure before he published his first book of poems in 1898). Appreciation was slow to grow. For twenty years the poetry was derided as wearisome, uncouth, prosaic, stilted; and, as ever, pessimistic. Hardy's plain, overt impressions of love, sensation, incident – what Lytton Strachey, reviewing *Satires of Circumstance*, called 'the undecorated presentments of things' – these were for many years quite unacceptable to readers expecting melody and 'the jewelled line'. Strachey, shouldering against the general current, feels that 'the flat, undistinguished poetry of Mr Hardy has found out the secret of touching our marrow bones', but only other poets, such as the young Blunden, or critics of the perception of Gosse, understood what Hardy was writing. To his great sorrow the public ignored his verse, and sales figures (always of great interest to him) were depressingly low.

His most particular quarrel with the critics of his poetry was over the question of 'music'. When Laurence Binyon wrote in 1915 that Hardy 'is never seduced by sound' he is describing Hardy's endeavour exactly. When the *Spectator*, reviewing

Poems of the Past and the Present in 1901, complains that Hardy is not a master of music, it is accusing him of failing in a direction he never wished to take. He always preferred to pursue 'the quiet unobtrusive melody' which was at last recognized as particularly his own. In an important essay on Hardy's poetry in 1918 Gosse observes how Hardy clogs his line with consonants, in order to avoid the 'melodious falsetto' in fashion for so long. And Hardy, writing to his friend on the same subject in 1919, describes how he has always avoided 'the jewelled line in poetry, as being effeminate'. The avoidance cost him dear with his public, and the reception of his seven volumes of poetry between 1898 and 1928 only confirmed his general contempt for critics.

The Dynasts, in its completed form, was accorded a warm if slightly bewildered reception. Parts I and II, originally published on their own, had not impressed the critics, but with the publication of Part III in 1908 appreciation grew rapidly. It was a work very dear to Hardy, and he must have been gratified to read that *The Times Literary Supplement* found it a great work of art, and Max Beerbohm in the *Saturday Review* 'a noble achievement, impressive, memorable'. Although Hardy insisted that the work was for mental performance only, scenes were produced on the London stage which moved Rebecca West to declare that it emerged as one of the greatest plays that have been on the English stage. Rutland records in his biography the occasion of Hardy's eighty-first birthday, on which over a hundred young poets thanked Hardy 'for all he had written . . . but most of all perhaps for *The Dynasts*'.

On balance, the tribe of book reviewers and their hundreds of reviews, spanning nearly sixty years, did not serve Hardy quite so ill as he supposed. They paid him considerable attention, and it was on the whole because of them, and not in spite of them, that he became the greatest literary institution of his time. They failed him chiefly because they were sidetracked by their conventional outrage at his unconventional morality, and because they could not appreciate his knotted, unvarnished verse; but they failed him also in a matter of which he seems never to have complained. With few exceptions, they – and the public with them – failed to distinguish the novels that to us appear great. *The Mayor of Casterbridge* received scant attention for many years; *The Trumpet-Major, A Pair of Blue Eyes,* and *Under the Greenwood Tree* remained favourites long after the publication of *Tess* and *Jude*. Possibly Hardy did not complain of this lack of discrimination because he was himself only sketchily aware of the relative merits of his novels. Although he took pains with revisions for successive editions, he seems in his old age to have slowly lost interest in the novels (though never in his poetry), and to have had little notion of the scale of his achievement as a novelist. One must believe that when he told T. P. O'Connor that he would not care if all his books were burned, he was in a mood of particularly deep depression; nevertheless Virginia Woolf also found, many years later, that 'He was not interested much in his novels, or in anybody's novels; took it all easily and naturally. "I never took long with them", he said.'

It is arguable that Hardy might have fared better with his critics had he been prepared to write more fully of his own aims and the craft of writing. He wrote only three essays on the subject: 'The Profitable Reading of Fiction' in 1888, 'Candour in English Fiction' in 1890, and 'The Science of Fiction' in 1891. Thereafter he confined his public writing to the Prefaces provided for each novel and volume of verse. These Prefaces are often vigorous, even combative, in his defence, but they are short. The fact is that Hardy did not like being asked to theorize about his work. As a man whose formal education had been brief, and had not included a university degree, he felt himself an outsider among philosophers and literary theorists. Lionel Johnson, in his book on *Mr Hardy's Novels*, complained of the 'plodding and commonplace intellect' revealed in the philosophizing commentary of *Tess*. He wants definitions, he writes, of nature, law, society, and justice. But Hardy did not respond, nor did he set about providing definitions, then or ever. Ten years later he concedes that his arguments in *The Dynasts* 'are but tentative, and are advanced with little eye to systematic philosophy'. Edith Wharton, who met Hardy in the drawing-room circles of his London days, noticed that 'he seemed to take little interest in the literary movements of the day, or in fact in any critical discussion of his craft', and Edward Marsh found him a very silent guest at Gosse's literary teas. When she visited him at the end of his life, Virginia Woolf found the same unwillingness to talk about art. Longing to hear him discourse on his poetry, she began to ask Hardy questions – 'but the dog kept cropping up. How he bit; how the inspector came out; how he was ill . . .'

Perhaps because he had not the equipment to confront it, Hardy felt that the critical intellect was an evil which bedevilled art. This sense of inadequacy, coupled with a temperament of great sensitivity, accounts at least in part for the antagonism he felt all his life towards critic and reviewer. Wary of people, wary of criticism, Hardy was to this extent all of a piece. He did not welcome exposure to the world, he did not readily open himself to friendship, and the satisfaction he found in praise rarely seems to have compensated for the blasts of criticism he had so often to endure. Yet, with the grave simplicity so often observed in him, he took whatever came his way, for better or for worse, and much of it sooner or later became the raw material of his art.

❧ *The later years*

GILLIAN AVERY

'He took no interest in himself as a personage,' Hardy wrote in one of the last chapters he was to supervise in *The Later Years of Thomas Hardy*. In that post-war epoch of his life he was not only sheltering behind the high brick walls of Max Gate, the fir trees and dark shrubberies of the garden, and the protective care that his second wife had built round him. For decades past he had created his own carapace, 'the unassertive air, unconsciously worn [that] served him as an invisible coat almost to uncanniness'. Like the mask in Max Beerbohm's *The Happy Hypocrite* it had grown into him; he was now incapable of discarding it.

The biography which he and Florence concocted, destroying as they went the letters, diaries and memoranda from which it was drawn, can irritate us, so wilfully does the subject of it seem to take a perverse pleasure in presenting himself as a mixture of Augustus Hare and Mr Woodhouse, and record fashionable hostesses, dinner companions and minor ailments. Who could be interested in a dry listing of social occasions that seem to have been copied unelaborated from an engagement diary? Or a holiday that was apparently only noteworthy because Hardy was tempted to stay too long in the water? There is little in the catalogue of names to tell us which were friends and which fleeting acquaintances. We could not guess that he felt a warm bond of sympathy, for example, with T. E. Lawrence, one of the few visitors whom the maids were allowed to admit without query. He is silent about those he disliked, merely remarking that he saw through the pretentious 'as though they were glass'. He set down at the time some cutting and satirical notes on their qualities and compass, but later destroyed all of them, not wishing, he said, to leave behind him anything which could be deemed a gratuitous belittling of others. The death of Emma in 1912 occupies a scant two pages, and then a new chapter is begun with lists of the distinguished with whom he lunched at Cambridge. His marriage to Florence receives only two lines before a record of a second visit to Cambridge when his hosts were, if anything, even more distinguished.

Even the beloved Mrs Arthur Henniker could not, as Barrie commented, 'visibly draw blood'. In the *Life* she is merely a name among scores of other well-born ladies, and if we look at the volume of letters that he wrote to her between 1893 and 1922 we never find a beginning warmer than 'my dear friend', nor does he touch on more intimate topics than the day-to-day health of both of them and their pets, or the progress of their literary activities. Once, it is true, he came closer to a confidence than he ever had before, when he wrote of Emma:

In spite of the differences between us, which it would be affectation to deny, and certain painful delusions she suffered from at times, my life is intensely sad to me now without her. The saddest moments of all are when I go into the garden and to that long straight walk at the top that you know, where she used to walk every evening just before dusk, the cat trotting faithfully behind her, and at times when I almost expect to see her as usual coming in from the flower-beds with a little trowel in her hands.

At last he has let a glimpse of a man of flesh and blood appear through the armour of reserve, the reserve that he usually only managed to discard in his poems.

> Woman much missed, how you call to me, call to me,
> Saying that now you are not as you were
> When you had changed from the one who was all to me,
> But as at first, when our day was fair.

We can detect the donning of the armour at the time of the tumult caused by the publication of *Jude*. Up till then he had been willing to discuss his work, certainly with contemporaries such as Gosse, but also with young admirers like John Cowper Powys, who remembered sitting with him on the Max Gate lawn in the 1890s telling him ardently 'how I detected in his work that same portentous and solemn power of dealing with those abstract-concrete phenomena, such as dawn, and noon, and twilight, and midnight, that Wordsworth displayed in his poetry. He accepted the comparison, I remember, as a just one.' Hardy was even willing to receive strangers who wished to write articles about him, such as Raymond Blathwayt, who made the journey to Dorset in 1892 to interview him for *Black and White*. They sat by the drawing-room fire 'discussing the frail but charming *Tess*', Hardy's reasons for bringing her to a tragic end, the models that he used for his characters.

Hardy told his interviewer how, having decided that Tess must die, he had gone purposely to Stonehenge to study the spot. 'It was a very gloomy lowering day, and skies almost seemed to touch the pillars of the great heathen temple.' And, pacing up and down the grass of the amphitheatre outside Dorchester, 'uninfluenced by modern conventionalism, unrestrained by Mrs Grundy, Mr Hardy and I . . . very seriously discussed the moral aspects afforded to the thoughtful reader by his extraordinary and really magnificent presentment of *Tess of the D'Urbervilles*'.

It was a remarkable interview, when one considers Hardy's later reticence and refusal to discuss his novels. It is also interesting for its reference to Mrs Hardy.

His wife, some few years younger than himself, is so particularly bright, so thoroughly *au courant du jour*, so evidently a citizen of the wide world, that the, at first, unmistakable reminiscence that there is in her of Anglican ecclesiasticism is curiously puzzling and inexplicable to the stranger, until the information is vouchsafed that she is intimately and closely connected with what the late Lord Shaftesbury would term 'the higher order of the clergy'.

From which it would seem that poor Emma had been boasting, as apparently she so often and so embarrassingly did, about her social advantages.

Tess had been attacked for both immodesty and immorality, but this was as nothing compared to the bedlam that broke out in 1895 over the publication of *Jude*. *Jude the Obscene* the *Pall Mall Gazette* called it, a book of dirt, drivel and damnation. 'It is the studied satyriasis of approaching senility, suggesting the morbidly curious imaginings of a masochist or some other form of sexual pervert,' wrote *The Bookman* in New York. 'The eagerness with which every unclean situation is seized upon and carefully exploited recalls the spectacle of some foul animal that snatches greedily at great lumps of putrid offal which it mumbles with hideous delight in the stenches that drive away all cleanlier creatures.' The Bishop of Wakefield was so disgusted with the 'insolence and indecency' that he threw the book on the fire. Emma Hardy herself had reacted as violently as anybody. She had gone to the length of a special journey to London to interview Richard Garnett at the British Museum and implore him to help her persuade her husband to burn the book.

There were favourable reviews and intelligent comments, but Hardy had learned his lesson. After this he retreated within himself, increasingly reluctant to expose his feelings to the outside world. This armour clung to him right to the end. Only once or twice do we see it slip. There was the occasion in 1920 when he spoke to Charles Morgan, then an Oxford undergraduate, and the manager of the OUDS, who were anxious to perform *Tess*. Charles Morgan, who was conducting this immensely distinguished visitor round the University, was startled by the bitterness with which Hardy – who usually affected not to care what the world thought – spoke about his critics, his readers' prejudices and the unjust neglect that he thought he had suffered. Particularly did he resent being classified as a pessimist, 'which they allowed to stand in the way of fair reading and fair judgement'. 'This,' commented Morgan, 'was a distortion of facts as I knew them. It was hard to believe that Hardy honestly thought that his genius was not recognized; harder to believe that he thought his work was not read.'

Charles Morgan was not deceived by the reserve, which he said was a method of self-protection common enough in his grandfather's generation; he realized that it concealed extraordinary fires. But he was amazed by the bitter assertions of neglect, for by the time of that visit to Oxford the Hardy cult was well under way. 'I shall never know a greater man,' Morgan himself had written after the meeting, and this was the attitude of all the hordes who sought admittance to Max Gate. Hardy was eighty then, and was to live for seven more years, a legend and an enigma. Trembling with expectation, the privileged made the journey to Max Gate.

'I found awaiting me a note from Mrs Hardy,' wrote W. M. Parker (who was later to edit Scott's letters). 'I had but to write an acceptance and within two days I should be in the presence of the greatest imaginative genius of modern times. It seemed incredible. But there indeed lay the definite passport to the literary shrine at which I most longed to pay reverent homage.'

The Prince of Wales was dispatched to encounter this genius, between opening a drill hall and inspecting farms. Others came of their own accord: Ramsay MacDonald,

E. M. Forster, Bernard Shaw, Augustus John. A deputation from Bristol University brought him an honorary degree. (He already held honorary degrees from Aberdeen, Cambridge and Oxford.) The Society of Authors sent their most eminent members to Dorset to pay homage on the occasion of his eightieth birthday. Actors from the Garrick Theatre performed *Tess* in the drawing-room to an audience of the author, his wife and two maids who sat on the floor. The Balliol Players brought the *Oresteia*. Anthony Asquith, Walter Oakeshott, Theodore Wade-Gery were in that cast, names undistinguished then, though Hardy recorded them as if prophetically. On their tour of the south-west they had performed in such splendid and appropriate settings as Maiden Castle and among the massive fallen masonry of Corfe. Here they leapt and declaimed on a small lawn outside a mean suburban villa, carrying spikes of spiraea instead of torches.

He was one of the showpieces of the world. Americans stood patiently in the Wareham road; they would wait even if it meant three days' vigil, they said roundly. An Indian travelled ten thousand miles hoping to have words with the great man, and being denied access, was content to meditate in the porch. A little girl of five, on holiday in Devon, was taken by her uncle to hide by the gate and wait to see the gnome-like figure of the greatest man of the century set out for his walk. It would be something she would remember all her life, she was told.

The lustre of the great is always enhanced by old age, especially a quiescent old age, and few of the English novelists had hitherto survived to advanced years. Hardy had behaved with perfect tact so far as the British public was concerned. With *Jude* he had shot his bolt; he withdrew from any kind of writing that could be deemed controversial, and the flutter that it had caused receded from his admirers' memory. *The Dynasts*, whether one had actually read it or not, suggested a man who was setting the seal on his career by celebrating the greatness of the country which had borne him, and the volumes of verse which were to appear at regular intervals from 1898, while they created comparatively little stir, caused no embarrassment either. Thomas Hardy was growing old with grace and dignity, and the world came down to pay homage, marvelling at their good fortune if they were admitted by this recluse. The fact that he had withdrawn to the scene of the novels added to the attraction. He had observed to Powys that it was salutary to a writer to live in his home town; the malice of neighbourhood mitigated the hubris that the admiration of the great world tended to engender. This might have been so, as far as the inward Hardy went, but the presence of the novelist Hardy among the scenes that he had depicted turned Max Gate into a place of awe.

As far back as the 1890s he had had something of a reputation of a hermit – 'a fond delusion,' said Raymond Blathwayt, 'which is disproved by the fact that he is almost more frequently to be seen in a London drawing-room, or a Continental hotel, than in the quiet old-world lanes of rural Dorsetshire.' And it is clear that up to the time of Emma's death he was spending regular periods in London; he was to be found at literary gatherings, at municipal occasions; he mingled with the *haut monde* at society crushes, he and his wife gave garden parties at Max Gate. It was the war that put an end to all this. It broke upon him like a thunderclap.

He recorded in the *Life*:

To Hardy as to ordinary civilians the murder at Sarajevo was a lurid and striking tragedy, but carried no indication that it would much affect English life. On 28 July [he and his second wife] were at a quiet little garden-party near Dorchester, and still there was no sign of the coming storm: the next day they lunched about five miles off with friends at Ilsington, and paid a call or two – this being the day on which war was declared by Austria on Serbia . . . [On August 4] they were lunching at Athelhampton Hall, where a telegram came announcing the rumour to be fact . . . Their host disappeared to inquire into his stock of flour. The whole news and what it involved burst upon Hardy's mind next morning, for though most people were saying the war would be over by Christmas he felt it might be a matter of years and untold disaster. . . It was seldom he had felt so heavy at heart as in seeing his old view of the gradual bettering of human nature, completely shattered by the events of 1914 and onwards.

He repeated this again a few pages further on:

The war destroyed all Hardy's belief in the gradual ennoblement of man, a belief he had held for many years, as is shown by poems like the 'Sick Battle-God' and others. He said he would probably not have ended *The Dynasts* as he did end it if he could have foreseen what was going to happen within a few years.

His reaction in his writing was far slower. He himself had spoken of his 'faculty for burying an emotion in my heart or brain for 40 years', and the poem of 1915, 'In Time of "The Breaking of Nations"', came into being, he said, from memories of the Franco-Prussian war.

I

Only a man harrowing clods
   In a slow silent walk
With an old horse that stumbles and nods
   Half asleep as they stalk.

II

Only thin smoke without flame
   From the heaps of couch-grass;
Yet this will go onward the same
   Though Dynasties pass.

III

Yonder a maid and her wight
   Come whispering by:
War's annals will cloud into night
   Ere their story die.

The life

The earliest known portrait of Thomas Hardy (aged one
year), with his mother Jemima.

RIGHT Thomas Hardy Senior in 1877,
a builder and mason who loved the
countryside. He was also an
accomplished musician.

BELOW Hardy in 1856, aged sixteen
when he first worked in Hicks's
architectural offices in Dorchester.

BELOW RIGHT One of the few portraits
of Hardy in middle age, a period
which according to Hardy himself
began when he was fifty.

Hardy *c.* 1903 photographed by his friend, Hermann Lea. This was one of Hardy's favourite portraits of himself, as indicated in his own hand on the back of the original.

LEFT Another portrait by Hermann Lea, the back of which Hardy signed and presented to him.

BELOW Hardy with his wife and the Prince of Wales in the garden of Max Gate, 20 July 1923. On this occasion the intense summer heat irritated the Prince and to the distress of his *aide de camp* he flung his waistcoat down the staircase.

A portrait of Hardy in his study in 1923 by R. Grenville Eves which now hangs in the National Portrait Gallery, London.

RIGHT Hardy's second wife, Florence, photographed at Max Gate in 1915 by Hermann Lea.

LEFT Horace Moule, Hardy's friend and mentor, who was probably in love with Tryphena Sparks before his suicide in 1873. (See Lois Deacon's contribution.)

Tryphena Sparks, aged eighteen, at one time probably betrothed to Hardy.

Hardy's first wife, Emma Gifford, whose death in 1912 inspired him to write some of his finest verses.

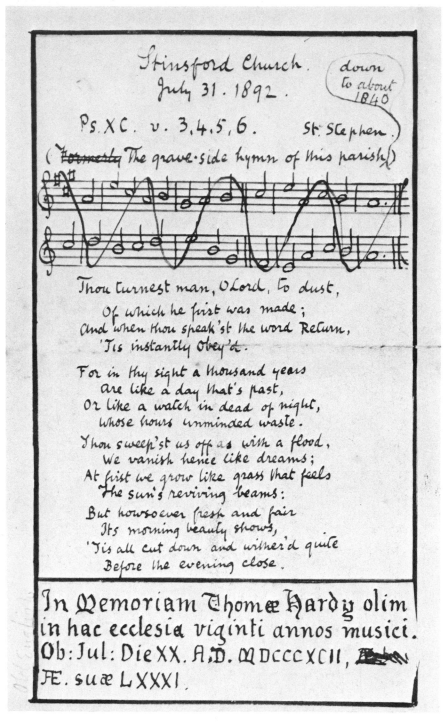

A memorial card in Thomas Hardy's autograph for the service of his father, who died on 20 July 1892.

When the war ended he was seventy-eight. His record of those four years in the *Life* is brief and outwardly undramatic. His sister Mary died, but he lost no close relations in the fighting. His second cousin's son had been killed at Gallipoli: 'Frank George, though so remotely related, is the first one of my family to be killed in battle for the last hundred years, so far as I know. He might say *Militavi non sine gloria* – short as his career has been.' In 1927, two months before his death, he listened to an Armistice Day broadcast of a service from Canterbury Cathedral, and stood for the two minutes' silence, thinking – he told his wife – of this boy whom he had hardly known, who had died in the great holocaust.

By 1918 he felt an old man – in spirit, at least, though his physical vigour remained; at eighty-two he was still cycling round the Dorset roads, and two years before in Oxford he had insisted on a sightseeing programme that had exhausted his hosts but had left him, apparently, still fresh and sprightly. But the last section of *The Later Years* – 'Life's Decline' – is dated from 1918. It was, as it should be, the most tranquil period of his life. He was free from the fret of his uneasy first marriage and Emma's unpredictable, increasingly odd humours and behaviour. Florence, whom he had married in 1914, was concerned only to make the life of the Master as easy as she could; to act as amanuensis, housekeeper and public relations officer – a capacity in which she was much needed, for Hardy's shrinking from the world had coincided with the world's great desire to see him, better still to hear him, before it was too late.

There were plenty who were admitted to the presence, nor did they necessarily have to be distinguished or produce introductions. It was the newspapers or people who might make capital out of printing distorted versions of Hardy's opinions that his wife took care to exclude, and visitors had to undertake that they would not ask him for his autograph, nor write up the interview for publication – in his lifetime at any rate. Even so, there are many records of visits to the shrine, for so great was the sense of occasion in those who were privileged to meet the Master that many were impelled to set down their recollections, and a remarkable set of some seventy monographs edited by J. Stevens Cox from the Toucan Press in Guernsey between 1962 and 1972 sought to record the impressions of those who had had dealings with Hardy.

So we hear how his barber found him:

> I remember him best as a very shy man of kindly disposition, who took good care of his money.
> Q. Did you ever shave him?
> A. Never. He was a self-shaver, and he trimmed his own moustache. I think he would have trimmed his own hair if he could have managed it.

There are accounts of his country motor trips from the point of view of the man who drove him; how his domestic servants found him as an employer. There is even, in the fashion of an earlier age – Edward VII's dog Caesar had written his reminiscences – a dog's-eye view of Hardy by the terrier Wessex. From these leaflets, some trite and ludicrous, some pathetic, one or two throwing a flash of light on the inward Hardy, we can assemble a portrait of the novelist in old age. If they tell us little about what he thought and felt, at least they show vividly how he appeared to those about him.

The admirers who, like W. M. Parker, had asked for the supreme privilege of a few minutes with the Master, found a Lob-like being, small, wrinkled, bright eyed, carefully protected by Mrs Hardy, who offered cups of tea and polite chit-chat and firmly kept the conversation in safe channels – the times of the trains back to London, the views from the Ridgeway, the activities of the moment. Even Vere H. Collins, who felt convinced that Hardy had an instinctive liking for him and who set down every detail of the six visits he paid to Max Gate between 1920 and 1922 in dramatic form, had to supply a great deal of background material of his own to make the interviews sound any different from the small talk a man might have with his dentist.

C. There have been some interesting people in this room, Mr Hardy.

H. Yes (moving forward to open the door of the dining-room, and with the obvious intention of conducting C. into the hall to say good-bye at the front door).

C. Please do not trouble to come out into the cold, Mr Hardy. Good-bye. (He shakes hands, and turns to leave the room. As he does so his eyes meet the portrait of the lady in the blue and white gown. Her gaze is directed straight in front of her – the full red lips half parted as if about to speak. The visitor forgets Stevenson, and Thiers, and Napoleon, and the Great War ... His thoughts go to the Poems of 1912–13; *Veteris Vestigia Flammae*; and to a grave in Mellstock Churchyard where that morning he had stood and watched the rain dripping on to a tombstone inscribed 'Emma Lavinia Gifford – This for Remembrance', one with whose influence, direct and indirect, on the life of her husband, there must be connected so much of the anguish and sadness, and the philosophy, and the beauty, of the works of Thomas Hardy.)

Vere Collins got very little more when he boldly ventured upon a leading question, and asked whether it was criticism of *Jude* that turned Hardy from novel-writing.

H. (shortly) Not just what the papers said. I never cared very much about writing novels. And I should not have – (pause). Besides I had written quite enough novels. Some people go on writing so many that they cannot remember their titles. There was a writer called Nat Gould – I forget how many he wrote.

C. I daresay one every six months. They were racing novels.

H. Yes, I have never read one of them.

Once or twice he was off his guard, though never in interviews such as these. There was, for instance, a revealing exchange with Lady Hester Pinney, whom he had gone to see at Racedown, a few miles off, in 1925. The visit passed with the usual decorum, and then as he was about to leave and was being hustled into the waiting car he asked suddenly, 'Can you find out about Martha Brown? ... I saw her hanged when I was sixteen.' When the sad details of this sixty-year-old local scandal were disinterred from the memories of the oldest inhabitants of the workhouse infirmary and sent to Hardy – Martha Brown had killed her husband with a hatchet when she found him with another girl on his knee, a girl who subsequently tramped for twenty-five miles to see her rival's execution but had finally been turned back by outraged villagers – his reply must have startled his informant, though readers of Hardy's *Life* are more used to the juxtaposition of the macabre and the banal.

I remember what a fine figure she showed against the sky as she hung in the misty rain, and how the tight black silk gown set off her shape as she wheeled half-round and back.

I hope you have not felt the cold much: we have somewhat. Young people love frost, but I for one don't. We shall be glad to see you later on.

And of course there was the affair of Gertrude Bugler. She was a local girl who acted with the Hardy Players in their annual staging of one of the novels. He himself proposed that she should take on the part of Tess in 1924, and, it seems, fell in love, partly perhaps with the girl herself, partly with the Tess he saw realized on the stage for the first time. He had always been susceptible; even the parlour maid remarked that 'Mr Hardy seemed to come out of his shell when talking to younger women as if a light was suddenly breaking through and he could see them in one of his books'. But she added, 'Myself, I do not think he thought of them as women, but just shadowy figures fitting into space like a jig-saw.' Florence Hardy, however, did not see Gertrude Bugler as a shadowy figure. The infatuation stirred her out of her usual outward calm. In her distress she went to the girl herself to beg her not to take the part of Tess in the London production that was planned. 'She said,' Mrs Bugler remembered, 'Mr Hardy was very excited about the play going to London; he was in a nervous state. She feared he would want to go up to town to see it, and, at his age, it would not be good for him . . . She asked me not to go to London.' Whether it was Florence Hardy's appeal or the difficulty of leaving her husband and baby behind in Dorset is not clear, but Gertrude did not go to London to act; at any rate, not during Hardy's lifetime.

It can never have been an easy life for Florence, even without having to cope with the excited romantic fluttering of an octogenarian. She was as reticent as Hardy himself, and has left no comments on their marriage, no reminiscences. Others have described her, though chiefly as a figure hovering in the background. She was the figure who dispensed the tea to the admirers; who had written the notes that allowed them to call. The more deferential noticed her as an attentive hostess, the outspoken remarked on her gloom and melancholy.

'Mrs Hardy was much younger than I expected to see,' a correspondent wrote to Sydney Cockerell,

and the most melancholy person I have ever seen. I think she smiled once but the smile only expressed sadness. She said she longed to go to America – 'but I never shall,' she said with a deep sigh, and with a still deeper sigh she said 'this place is too depressing for words in winter, when the dead leaves stick on the windowpane and the wind moans and the sky is grey and you can't even see as far as the high road'.

She was a distant relative of Hardy's own, who had helped him with research for *The Dynasts* and had come to his rescue in the rudderless days after Emma's death when there was no one to keep the household in order and no one to shield him from the merciless invasion of celebrity hunters. He was seventy-three when he married her, she thirty-five when she found herself immured in the gloom of Max Gate. Nobody, even the most adulatory of the literary pilgrims, could find it a cheerful place. Cynthia Asquith said it was 'of a startling commonplaceness ... closely surrounded by the dreariest shrubberies'; 'a grim cold house,' the parlour maid called it, 'it had only open fireplaces. Mr Hardy would not permit good fires.' 'A dull dispirited house – the solidification in brick of Hardy's intermittent mood of hopelessness at the ugliness in life' – even the adoring secretary could rate it no higher than that.

To this house Florence Hardy brought her pianola and her terrier dog Wessex to brighten up the life there. She at first decided they were a mistake; Hardy detested noise and disturbance of the tranquillity of his elderly routine. What became of the pianola is not recorded, but 'Wessie' became so much a part of the household that visitors always took him to be Hardy's dog. He was an animal of uncertain temper who barked vociferously, tolerated some visitors and attacked others.* 'At times one could pet him,' the parlour-maid recalled, 'and then out of the blue he would have a horrible brainstorm and scare everybody.' The postman, whom he bit three times, carried a lump of wood to defend himself, but Wessex's death in 1926 brought great grief. 'Do you think of me at all, wistful ones?' Hardy made the dog say in 'Dead "Wessex" the Dog to the Household'.

> Do you think of me at all,
>   Wistful ones?
> Do you think of me at all
>   As if nigh?
> Do you think of me at all
> At the creep of evenfall,
> Or when the sky-birds call
>   As they fly?

After Wessex's death the house must have seemed dreary indeed. May O'Rourke,

---

* T. E. Lawrence was the only one he permitted to pick him up. In the doggy memoirs, *Wessex Recidivus*, he is made to say:

There would be a real he-scent that whiffled under the door before Ellen, the maid, could open it, what with bothering about where I had got to. Wow! What a lovely smell it was, a mixed sort of scent with sniffs of sweat and earth, dogs and men, sand and leather and gunpowder. And that would be – as you may have guessed – Lawrence of Arabia ... I can tell you, I never pinned him.

who has left the most sympathetic account of the Max Gate household – young, ardent, a hopeful writer herself, she came to give help typing the literary work, and her affection for Thomas and Florence withstood the daily contact – wrote of the sadder hours which, according to her, overtook the ménage in 1924. Florence's health began to fail, her spirits became very low and her temper uncertain. She went to London for a growth to be removed from her throat, and from that time onwards, Miss O'Rourke guessed, her life was shadowed by the knowledge of the disease from which she suffered. The maids remembered how she stormed at them when she came back from the nursing home and found that Hardy had ordered a special dinner for her of boiled leg of lamb and suet jam roll.

The domestic staff had little use for Hardy.

To us maids Mr Hardy was not the great literary figure he appeared to the world, but just another man having, outside of his writings, no obviously impressive qualities. I was often asked by my friends if I didn't feel highly honoured to be working for such an important person. To which I invariably answered in so many words, 'No, from my point of view Mr Hardy is not very different from other men I have worked for . . .'

I always called it an uneventful household. The only occasions when we had any excitement were when charabancs with trippers stopped near the house and some of the passengers crept up the drive to try and get a glimpse of Mr Hardy. We would go down and turn them out.

To the kitchen he was a little old man, stingy with his tips, who hobbled round the house with his brown crochet shawl over his shoulders, whistling monotonously to himself on one note; ever on the watch for a fire too generously stoked, with a taste for marking down cobwebs. They remembered him for his fondness for mutton broth, apple suet puddings, for the way he had brown sugar with his breakfast bacon, for his inspection of the coal store and apple room before the servants were allowed to draw from them.

We piece together an account of the last few days at Max Gate in the biting January cold of 1928 from the banal trivia supplied by the maids: the tottering steps to the lavatory over a carpet of eiderdowns laid on the cold oilcloth, the piping voice protesting at the extravagant warmth the kitchen was permitting itself – 'that's a big fire you've got there, Nellie.' His death to them was not a great grief, not even a great event. The parlour maid's comment was, 'My seven years there were not the happiest of my life. These were to come later, when I worked for Mr Henry Pomeroy Bond of Moignecombe, Dorset.'

It all makes a poignant contrast with the splendour of the funeral rites: the service in Westminster Abbey with Barrie, Galsworthy, Gosse, Housman, Kipling and Shaw as pallbearers, the thousands waiting for admission in the cold January rain, the crowds at Stinsford church, where his heart was buried in Emma's grave, the municipal pomp of the service at Dorchester. It was a contrast that Hardy himself would have appreciated. But he had composed his valediction as long ago as 1917, on quite different lines – one of the most poignant of any poet's leavetakings.

When the Present has latched its postern behind my tremulous stay,
    And the May month flaps its glad green leaves like wings,
Delicate-filmed as new-spun silk, will the neighbours say,
    'He was a man who used to notice such things'?

If it be in the dusk when, like an eyelid's soundless blink,
    The dewfall-hawk comes crossing the shades to alight
Upon the wind-warped upland thorn, a gazer may think,
    'To him this must have been a familiar sight.'

If I pass during nocturnal blackness, mothy and warm,
    When the hedgehog travels furtively over the lawn,
One may say, 'He strove that such innocent creatures should come to no harm,
    But he could do little for them; and now he is gone.'

If, when hearing that I have been stilled at last, they stand at the door,
    Watching the full-starred heavens that winter sees,
Will this thought rise on those who will meet my face no more,
    'He was one who had an eye for such mysteries'?

And will any say when my bell of quittance is heard in the gloom,
    And a crossing breeze cuts a pause in its outrollings,
Till they rise again, as they were a new bell's boom,
    'He hears it not now, but used to notice such things'?

PART 2

The work

The major novels

J. I. M. STEWART

In the most widely anthologized of his poems, 'The Oxen', Hardy says that, if invited to visit the lonely barton on Christmas Eve and see the 'meek mild creatures' kneeling in their strawy pen, he would go along, 'hoping it might be so'. But the trip would be made 'in the gloom' – in part a figurative gloom, betokening the poet's knowledge that it *wouldn't* be so. He regrets having this knowledge, but at the same time it is what gives him breadth of view and generates the poem, so that he must regard having acquired it as a good thing.

The possession of contrary strains of feeling such as is here exhibited is regularly a fecundating, even while potentially a confusing, agent in Hardy's art. There is another and greater poem, 'Afterwards', in which he describes himself as a man who notices the hedgehog and the wind-warped upland thorn, and hopes that it is as such a man that he will be remembered. But there is an implication that, although he would be well content to be remembered simply as this rural sensitive, the 'bell of quittance' will in fact be commemorating one on whom there had rested some range of knowledge, some burden of thought, which defined the man and which has brought his poem to birth.

There is thus always an ambivalence about Hardy's thought. He set store by his own reverence for the natural world, for the venerable and immemorial, for the antique works and ways of men. But it is a reverence that cannot have been uncommon in the humble folk among whom he grew up, and it is detectable that he set even more store by what was antithetical in him to this: a speculative rather than a contemplative habit, concerned with 'the views of life prevalent at the end of the nineteenth century, and not those of an earlier and simpler generation'. In his heart he was chiefly proud of having made himself what the age called an advanced thinker. This pride, and a good deal of dogmatism attending it, remained with him throughout his life, side by side with all those more traditional modes of believing and behaving still current in the society into which he had been born. It is thus that, in a variety of ways, conflicting tides of appraisal, thought and feeling are regularly part of the dynamic of his writing.

A percurrent theme in the novels – one viewed as their central theme by many critics – is the passing of an older order of society in England and its supersession by a new. We are commonly told with some confidence on which side we shall find Hardy's sympathies to lie: he is the celebrant and threnodist of sanctities and salubrities

passing away. It is true, obviously, that here lay his sentiment; and to that sentiment he early lent such potent literary charm that he came to be a good deal trapped
in it while establishing himself as an acceptable and successful novelist. But his
intellect – in the operations of which he had all the confidence of an autodidact
conscious of his own achievement against brutal odds – his intellect set over against
this an awareness of the past as a dark theatre of tyranny, penury and superstition.
Looked at squarely and disenchantedly, our forefathers are seen to have been happier
than we are only within those areas of life in which ignorance is bliss – or at least in
which it curtains much cause for melancholy and despair.

This persuasion is expressed again and again in the novels. In *The Return of the
Native* Egdon Heath is made an explicit symbol of modern man's hopelessness as he
progressively uncovers 'the defects of natural laws'. When in *Tess of the D'Urbervilles*
the heroine chants the Magnificat as she walks, we in our latter-day disillusionment
know that 'probably the half-unconscious rhapsody was a Fetichistic utterance in a
Monotheistic setting', and at Talbothays Angel Clare becomes for a time 'wonder-
fully free from the chronic melancholy which is taking hold of the civilized races with
the decline of belief in a beneficent Power'. In *Jude the Obscure* we have it on medical
authority that the preternaturally joyless Little Father Time is just the sort of child
now being brought into the world as a consequence of our new and juster sense of
that world's place in the universe. Thus the advantages of having been born into an
earlier time prove to be of a negative sort, while today 'the plight of being alive' (as
it is called in *Tess*) is something men must simply strive to attenuate 'to its least
possible dimensions'.

In all these places Hardy may seem to be telling us that even if we commanded
Wells's Time Machine we still couldn't win. Yet this is not quite what he presents us
with. When he declares himself to be a meliorist he is saying something essentially
correct. Means can be taken – means discoverable by the free intelligence – to sort
things out a little, to improve the general human lot. He is certainly far from enter-
taining this rational hope with any largeness or facility; his forward-looking people
and his backward-looking exhibit equally heavy casualty lists; human character is not
necessarily elevated through acquiring modern views; Donald Farfrae is no improve-
ment on Michael Henchard, nor Angel Clare on his clerical father, believer in 'an
untenable redemptive theolatry' though he be. On the whole, however, modern
enlightenment is to be approved. It may darken our sense of human destiny. There is
something Promethean about it, all the same.

We know little of the course of Hardy's intellectual development towards this
position, and nothing whatever of any specific struggle or crisis which may have
attended his abandoning the orthodox pieties of his time in favour of the philosophical persuasions which underlie the Wessex Novels. The entire reticence here of
The Early Life of Thomas Hardy may well suggest to us the existence of a phase of
mental and spiritual tension which he judged too private for exhibition in a biography. Few things are clearer about him than his vulnerability to the stresses generated

by conflicting and divisive emotional states. They were acute in him and enduring, shaking his frame at eve with throbbings of noontide. The 'Poems of 1912–13' are the most striking evidence of this. A man who has been for half a lifetime a broodingly disenchanted and resentful husband, obsessed by the folly and wickedness of the marriage laws of his country, proves to have preserved a lover's passion through this long winter of discontent to an effect notable in the history of English poetry. He is seen to be one constrained to register keenly, and retain tenaciously, patterns of feeling so conflicting in themselves as to be ordered and harmonized only through the medium of artistic expression: in ambivalent constructs, we may say, satisfying to the imagination rather than to the logical faculty. He is often in two minds to an extent exposing him to hazard as a creative artist – although bereft of this power-house of warring elements he might well have been a creative artist only of a very minor sort.

When we have distinguished this native mental constitution in Hardy we shall not be surprised to find elements of inconsistency and fluctuating purpose alike in his theory and practice as a novelist.

It is in a preface to the fifth edition of *Tess of the D'Urbervilles* that he expresses the hope that his novel does indeed embody 'the views of life prevalent at the end of the nineteenth century, and not those of an earlier and simpler generation'. But a novel, he says in the next sentence, 'is an impression, not an argument'. Even the 'contemplative' parts of *Tess* were intended 'to be oftener charged with impressions than with convictions'. He himself, he adds, is 'a mere tale-teller, who writes down how the things of the world strike him, without any ulterior intentions whatever'.

Hardy often offers his critics equivocal-seeming statements of this sort, and I believe it is customary to regard them as essentially disingenuous. An 'impression', a 'view of life', an 'argument' constitute a blurry series of terms conducing only to a designed obfuscation; and nothing could be more absurd than for Hardy to represent himself as being, whether in prose or verse, the idle singer of an empty day. His novels are, at their core, 'purpose' novels as definitely as are Charles Reade's. In the majority of them 'ulterior intentions' gain admission freely, and the two greatest reverberate with 'convictions' from cover to cover.

This is true, yet we cannot say that Hardy offers his periodic disclaimers entirely with his tongue in the cheek. He was capable of feeling it unfair that there should be such a to-do about his novels – bishops denouncing them, publishers refusing them, editors insisting they be bowdlerized – when novels *were*, after all, essentially idle performances, produced to earn a writer unassuming bread. For the fact is that Hardy never made up his mind about the status of the Novel; about its weight and significance, actual or potential, as one of the higher literary kinds. He inclined now one way, and now another. Sometimes he did this even as he wrote.

We may guess that the autodidact, once more, weighed significantly on the depreciatory side. It is impossible to imagine the hero of *Jude the Obscure* (that very paragon of autodidacts) forming a high regard for prose fiction. The self-educated man, even if not instinctively conservative in feeling, is always liable to be rather behind the times. Hardy was aware of this. In some fields he was alertly on his guard against it – hence that resolute advanced thinker that he saw in himself. But his literary canons were scarcely modern, and – at least in phases of self-distrust – he viewed the Novelist as very much a poor relation of the Poet or Dramatist. Something even of class-feeling may have influenced his estimation. In *A Pair of Blue Eyes* the socially superior Henry Knight is not a novelist but a 'reviewer and essayist', perhaps because around prose fiction there still lingered an aura of Grub Street and bourgeois origins. It lingered, indeed, after Hardy's active time; when Virginia Woolf, halfway through her career, confides to her diary the hope that a novel is something she will never be accused of again her feeling is, in a shadowy way, as much socially as aesthetically determined, novel-writing being associated in her mind with what she calls 'the thick dull middle class of letters'.

Hardy, of course, had good reason to feel that a thick dull middle class of *readers* imposed upon prose fiction an obtuse moral censorship adverse to the achieving of serious art. Most of the novelists of the day – including even Henry James, whose urge to bring a blush into the cheek of the young person can never have been strong – felt at a disadvantage here as compared with their continental fellows. But Hardy's almost settled disposition to disparage the Novel appears to go deeper than this, and to repose upon a persuasion that there is something inherently inferior in the form. Thus he is on record as having felt distress upon learning that Tennyson (a great admirer of his) had taken to novel-reading in old age; it was, Hardy said, an incomprehensible 'downward step'. It is possible to bring together, from every stage of his career, a large body of evidence seemingly substantiating the view that he really did think slightingly of his craft. When his first effort, *The Poor Man and the Lady*, was declined, he at once accepted Meredith's advice to have a shot at what we should call a thriller, and turned in *Desperate Remedies*. Steadily thereafter he sustained what might not unjustly be termed a coarsened version of Trollope's robustly commercial note. To the first of the major novels, *The Return of the Native*, he gave a conclusion which he confessed contrary to his artistic instinct – and this not because of any constraint in terms of sexual tabu but merely to incorporate a popular 'happy ending' close; years later, moreover, he appended to the passage a cavalier note sketching how his readers might, in their imaginations, improve matters if they chose.

This is the Hardy whom Hardy, looking back upon his career, is for obscure reasons concerned to obtrude on us: the man whose only ambition had been to have a few poems in a good anthology; who hadn't wanted to be a novelist at all – but who, having become one, was simply concerned to be reckoned a good hand at a serial with no nonsense about higher artistic considerations getting in the way; and who, when he bowdlerized *Tess* for the *Graphic*, 'carried out this unceremonious concession to conventionality with cynical amusement'.

There is, no doubt, much to suggest that all this was little more than the defensive-ness of a thin-skinned man. Like Wordsworth and Tennyson, the elderly Hardy didn't much care for talking about his work. Just as Wordsworth would turn the conversation to the state of American railroad shares and Tennyson confide to you that he liked his mutton cut in chunks, so would Hardy announce that he could put you in touch, should you desire it, with a thoroughly reliable monumental mason. When Virginia Woolf made a properly reverent pilgrimage to Max Gate, and thought to prompt Hardy to some discussion of his novels by saying that she had been reading *The Mayor of Casterbridge* on the train, he produced a deflating 'And did it hold your interest?' and went on to regret that none of his books were fitted to be wedding presents.

Yet this depreciation of the Novel and of his own labour as a novelist is only another exemplification of the fact that Hardy, like Kipling, had two sides to his head. With it, indeed, we are in the presence not of an affectation but of an authentic strain of feeling; nevertheless it is not hard to produce answering evidence that he was capable of viewing novel-writing as a very serious business indeed – a medium through which it is possible to challenge the traditionally accepted heights of literary achievement. Egdon Heath, he tells us in *The Return of the Native*, 'it is pleasant to dream . . . may be the heath of that traditionary King of Wessex – Lear'. Only a dull reader could fail to gather from this that the novelist is proposing no middle flight for his own tragic story. And in fact we find that the reliable hand at a serial and cynical bowdlerizer for the *Graphic* regularly regarded Shakespeare and the Greek dramatists as his masters. When addressing himself to the history of a Wessex milkmaid who kills her seducer with a knife snatched up from the breakfast-table he got in training for his task by rereading Sophocles. Again, there are places in which Hardy betrays, almost inadvertently, that sense of the much he has attempted and the little he has achieved which surely characterizes the dedicated artist. Thus there was an occasion upon which Coventry Patmore (who shared, oddly, with Proust an extravagant admiration for *A Pair of Blue Eyes*) paid him some compliment to which he replied, 'It is what I might have deserved if my novels had been exact transcripts of their original irradiated conception, before any attempt at working out that glorious dream had been made – and the impossibility of getting it on paper had been brought home to me.'

Hardy, then, wavered in his view of the right pitch and scope of the Novel, and was without a constant and single sense of its function. Is prose fiction best regarded as a vehicle for entertainment, whether robust or refined, or ought it to enlighten and edify? Hardy has no consistent answer to the question, and in this differs strikingly from the most eminent of his immediate predecessors, George Eliot. She had no doubt whatever that to offer mere diversion to one's readers was as reprehensible as to peddle gin and opium to babies. We must wonder why Hardy, with Sophocles and Shakespeare in his pocket, finds some similar if less extreme assertion difficult.

There is – after all, and as we have seen – no real question about his instinctive stance. That he is very much one who harbours improving designs upon us is a fact so patent as to stand in little need of documentation. The major novels – *Far from the Madding Crowd, The Return of the Native, The Mayor of Casterbridge, The Woodlanders, Tess of the D'Urbervilles, Jude the Obscure* – represent something like an ascending or intensifying series of assaults upon what is implicitly asserted to be the darkened state of our minds on matters of grave moral and social moment. They are this as uncompromisingly as are those plays of Ibsen's which so fascinated Hardy in his middle years.

Yet a Hardy novel is not at all like an Ibsen play. Nor – to come to a more obvious contrast – is Hardy's masterpiece, which is undoubtedly *Tess*, at all like *Middlemarch*, which is George Eliot's. They do share much common ground, most notably in their concern with the play upon individual destinies of the assumptions and prejudices of a specific society. But George Eliot's is here by far the wider view. It is her cardinal tenet (stated explicitly in *Felix Holt*) that 'there is no private life which has not been determined by a wider public life', and pervasively in *Middlemarch* we are drawn to acknowledge that this is true. In *Tess* there is no such extensive analysis, even although the idea is present and receives powerful embodiment at crucial points in the story. Thus we do feel that Angel Clare has had bad luck in being exposed to movements of thought which he lacks the stuffing to cope with. But Alec d'Urberville floats free of any formative influences inherent in a social situation; Hardy has barely thought about him; has accepted a piece of mere social mythology, grabbed a ready-made stage villain and made him the puppet of a plot. It is on Tess alone that all impact of the kind bears, and while much of the tremendous drive of the novel arises from this concentration the method involves Hardy in a good deal of reliance upon material of inferior interest to fill up his tale.

And whether we look back to *The Return of the Native* and *The Mayor of Casterbridge* or forward to *Jude the Obscure* we find that something of the same sort holds. Despite the strong general impression (poetic, significantly, in its actual contrivance) that the folk of Egdon Heath are the children of a specific soil, there remains something socially nebulous about both the Yeobrights and the Vyes – a fact pointed for us by the discovery that Hardy as he worked was in two minds about the class background of these principal personages. Michael Henchard predominates in his story precisely as Tess does in hers; he is the representative of 'old' ways as Farfrae no doubt is of 'new'; but whereas George Eliot would have interwoven with this salient theme other and related themes, steadily developing and interacting throughout the book, Hardy is content with the single march of a protagonist to his doom – the general ineluctable fatality of things announcing itself loudly by means of a series of sensational set-pieces en route. *Jude the Obscure* is a shattering book, and packs punches that George Eliot would have been as much without the brute force as the inclination to contrive. At the same time it has interest as evidencing an endeavour to confine within something at least approximating to the modesty of nature its exhibitions of Crass Casualty at work. There is a very real effort to show the aspirations of Jude and

Sue as steadily and variously abraded by the prejudices and insensibilities of the society within which they are condemned to struggle.

Yet the fundamental impression rendered by *Jude the Obscure* is that of an artist impatient of the medium in which he is working – conscious of the painful paradox that he is at once circumscribed by it and inadequate to certain of its essential demands. We need not attribute to the abuse heaped on the book by bigoted persons the fact that it was to prove Hardy's last novel. He had come to the end of a road, so that it was indeed fortunate for him that he had only to jump over the hedge and continue on another sort of wayfaring. Mr Alvarez has made this point succinctly in remarking of *Jude* that 'the feelings are those which were later given perfect form in Hardy's best poetry'. In the novel these feelings are insufficiently embodied in any fully realized representative fiction: consider the tiny but significant fact that the children hanged in the closet by Little Father Time are never so much as given names; they have been born simply thus to die and thereby afford their father an occasion to reflect sombrely on 'the coming universal wish not to live'. We are made too much aware of a writer with urgent inner pressures to relieve and an inadequate ability or inclination to command that sort of aerial perspective (as Hardy himself might have called it) which is the novelist's means of lending felt life, with a just gradation of emphasis, to all the depths and peripheries of the total spectacle with which he is concerned. Jude's is the bleak story of one who, alike as a promising boy and a striving man, is perpetually at the wrong end of the stick; he is clobbered, and clobbered again, through an unending sequence of educational, social, and sexual deprivations. And Hardy pours so much emotion into this that he has little energy left for anything else. His own final sense of the book as a failure appears to have been overwhelmingly strong. Of nothing else that he wrote is he on record as expressing so convinced a sense of the disparity between what he had proposed and what achieved.

We are now a long way from George Eliot, and should have to return to *The Woodlanders* to consider Hardy coming nearest to her in his major fiction. There everything flows from the wrong-headed social ambitions of Melbury in an orderly way; a harmony of effect is preserved throughout the whole course of the narration; the harsh polemical impulse is subdued. But *The Woodlanders* is, for Hardy, a book of restricted power. For he possesses the great writer's ability to make extravagance, strong accentuations, even the monstrous and bizarre, break in upon common experience and illuminate it. And in fact Hardy will be found to have sketched for himself an aesthetic of fiction which takes account of this predisposition.

At the beginning of the second part of *Adam Bede* George Eliot speaks of her delight in the 'precious quality of truthfulness . . . in many Dutch paintings', and it may have been this remark that prompted Hardy to give to *Under the Greenwood Tree* the subtitle *A Rural Painting of the Dutch School*. But this was not eventually to be his school, despite the faithfulness of so many of his effects in *genre* and in landscape studies. He was by temperament an Expressionist. He admired Grünewald and would have responded to Munch. 'My art,' he wrote, 'is to intensify the expression of things as is done by Crivelli'; what he chiefly prized in an artist was his 'idiosyncratic mode of regard'. This is one reason why he is so unlike George Eliot; why, in novels ambitiously designed to reach the pitch of tragedy, he embodies so much that hazards no more than melodramatic effect. It is why, for example, Tess spends her last night as a free woman at Stonehenge, asleep on what her creator supposed to be a sacrificial altar.

But this rigidly held aesthetic is not the sole explanation of a certain hit-or-miss quality in Hardy's grand effects, nor of his neglect of that unity of tone and facture, that care for the flow and harmony of the completed work, which commonly, if not always, marks achievement in major prose fiction. For here we have to return, quite simply, to what we have distinguished as the intermittent character of Hardy's faith in the medium that first brought him fame. Is not a novelist imagining things, fancying himself, when he judges himself other than as being, or not being, a good hand at a serial? This seems to have been a question which he often asked himself in moments of fatigue or depression – and which he answered, in effect, in the affirmative by thinking up some startling episode good enough for the *Graphic* or *Harper's Bazaar*.

It seems, on the face of it, absurd to charge with a lack of stamina the man who produced *A Laodicean* under the conditions recorded of it, and who was still writing a vigorous poetry in his later eighties. Yet Hardy was certainly prone to discouragement, slack writing, inadequate revision. When *Tess* incurred the moral disapprobation of the periodical press he wrote to Walter Besant, a successful novelist active in organizing the profession of letters, to ask whether he ought to resign from the Savile Club. Again, he was, it must be reiterated, primarily what he believed himself to be, a lyric poet and a balladist, and a factor in his regular depreciation of the Novel may have been simply the exhaustion that the fabricating of long prose fictions is likely to induce in anyone not, as it were, born to that activity. It had been, he said, a hand-to-mouth business, living by writing serials. Yet, in a fashion, the serial form may have held certain advantages for him. *The Mayor of Casterbridge*, for example, appeared not in monthly but in weekly parts, and he believed that he had damaged it in answering the need to incorporate some strongly accented action in each brief section. But working to such a pattern, or within such a rhythm, may have been less taxing than would have been the building up of more sustained narrative units and a lesser recourse to sensational material; it may have been both less taxing and more in consonance with the free working of his imagination.

Yet however all this may be, it is undeniable that when Hardy is in difficulty with the development of his subject at a level of high seriousness he is prone to decline upon the less elevated of his conflicting estimations of his craft, offering us as a substitute for the Pierian spring a succession of quick swigs from the brandy bottle of popular romance.

The latter part of *Tess of the D'Urbervilles*, in particular, exemplifies the vulnerability. As he approaches his heroine's marriage, confession and rejection by her husband, difficulties loom ahead. The grand difficulty must have been nervous rather than technical. He was achieving a novel the sheer painfulness of which is almost unexampled in our literature. *Jude the Obscure* itself was not to be so painful, but only more depressing. We do not know whether Hardy wept over Tess as Dickens is supposed to have done over Little Nell Trent, but it is scarcely rash to suppose that the story he was telling moved him very deeply indeed. There were aspects of it, moreover, with which he was not particularly well equipped to deal. 'Midnight contiguity' (as it is absurdly called somewhere in *Jude*) was not his strong suit, and the subject of Clare and his bride on their wedding night bristled with problems. It is when this climax is only a few hours ahead that Hardy begins noticeably to cast around for a few Gothic stays and props to help him out. Tess has a *déjà vu* experience when confronted with the conveyance provided for the bridal couple, and Clare at once supposes that she has 'heard the legend of the D'Urberville Coach'. She is ignorant of it, and he speaks thus:

Well – I would rather not tell it in detail just now. A certain D'Urberville of the sixteenth or seventeenth century committed a dreadful crime in his family coach; and since that time members of the family see or hear the old coach whenever— But I'll tell you another day – it is rather gloomy. Evidently some dim knowledge of it has been brought back to your mind by the sight of this venerable caravan.

Shortly after this a cock crows thrice: an ill omen for the marriage, this is supposed to be – although we may chiefly think of it as presaging badly for the sobriety of the tale. We next learn that the wedding night is to be spent in one of Tess's 'ancestral mansions', and view a couple of portraits of long-dead D'Urberville women, malign-looking but also rather like Tess as well. Tess is given some jewels sent by Clare's mother, and when she has put them on we are told that Clare 'had never till now estimated the artistic excellence of Tess's limbs and features'. Bizarrely bad writing like this is regularly a sign that Hardy is in trouble – and now he feels that nothing is to be done but pile on the agony. On the next page we are told that one of Tess's companions in the dairy has tried to drown herself for love of Clare, and on the page after that that another has taken with miraculous celerity to drink. Clare then confesses to his 'eight-and-forty hours' dissipation with a stranger', prefacing the avowal with some remarks on plenary inspiration and quotations from St Paul and Horace. This tone and manner and intermittent ghastly writing goes on and on through Tess's own confession and its aftermath; we are offered a thought of M. Sully-Prud-homme, and told that Tess has failed to consider that her love for Clare 'might result in vitalizations that would inflict upon others what she had bewailed as a misfortune to herself'. Clare, who we have earlier been told is liable to 'freaks' in his sleep, now puts on his somnambulistic turn, carrying Tess across a 'speeding current' on a bare plank and depositing her in 'the empty stone coffin of an abbot'. Matters might be worse, we may feel, were an abbot still in residence – but not very much worse, since all this is about as bad as it could be.

The truth is that in Hardy we are never many pages away from eruptions of slap-dash writing by a fatigued hack; from the spectacle of passing kicks being given, without propriety or keeping, to persons or poems or institutions apparently distasteful to the author; from the answering spectacle of similarly extraneous matter commendatory of sages – Huxleys, it may be, or Darwins or Mills – of whom the author approves; from images drawn at random from history, classical mythology and the graphic arts having no organic consonance with what is on hand; above all, from ingeniously concocted demonstrations of the proposition that it is the ordinary experience of mankind constantly to be meeting quite extraordinary bad luck. This last territory Hardy had discovered to be very much his own as far back as *A Pair of Blue Eyes*, and he never ceases recklessly to deploy amid its booby traps tragic characters of a potential stature as impressive as, outside Shakespeare, English literature shows.

Of some aspects of all this artistic confusion Hardy was sufficiently conscious to feel that a defence was required. He saw, he maintained, no malign principle in the universe – only a vast unregardingness or neutrality which it is our natural human frailty to minimize or ignore. It is the task of the artist, he believed, so to concentrate and accent the existence of misfortune and misery as to bring us, through a species of shock treatment, to a realistic and disenchanted sense of our true situation.

Whether this – again Expressionist – aesthetic is more than a rationalizing of fallen man's impulse to let others feel no happier than he happens to be feeling himself is a problem touched on by Hardy's critics often enough. Whether – 'vitalizations' as we are, who live crouching by the mere flame of life – whether we are much heartened and strengthened by the spectacle of Elfride or Henchard or Tess or Jude getting an implausibly rough spin all through would appear to be equally open to debate. There are those who declare Hardy's to be a morbid or Manichaean vision: T. S. Eliot was once very clear about this, although eventually he modified his view. Yet the test, the appeal, is to experience. When we have admitted that in Hardy there is much inferior artistry, and that he was too viewy, quirky, dogmatic, glum, divided and confused to stand with the greatest; when we have admitted this we have to acknowledge that his novels, although so little concerned to cheer us up, are not in their total effect dispiriting – as is today so much of the literature of despair and of the absurd. We see man as a minute 'vitalization' amid the dust of the stars, and individuals as crawling specks on a Roman road, an immemorial heath, a brutal terrain of hacked turnips. But pervading the vision is some principle that makes for life, for human life and its worth and meaning in a universe not very largely cognoscible even by the most approved advanced thinkers of an age. Hardy himself offered as his ultimate apologia the proposition that if a way to the better there be it exacts a full look at the worst. He often provides us with the worst in a distillation so extreme as to strain our sense of the verisimilar, but the proposition itself does speak to our condition. In part it sounds a pragmatic and practical note: honest stock-taking is necessary if we are to mend our affairs, improve our condition. In part it is a psychological statement, affirming the classical theory of catharsis. The confronting of spectacles of pity and terror is purgative, so that we *feel* better – or do so (Aristotle seems to assert) provided the personages we are invited to contemplate are moral beings much like ourselves (or perhaps a little better than that). And here is the nub of the matter when we are assessing the final salubrity of Hardy's art. His people are moral agents, constantly aware of the paradox that, in a neutral universe, significance and dignity are theirs because they see good and evil around them and own a duty to conduct their lives, however senselessly tormented, in terms of that perception. Our sense of this fact is what saves for us *Jude the Obscure*, the bleakest book of them all.

Sue and Arabella

ELIZABETH HARDWICK

Sue and Arabella, in Hardy's *Jude the Obscure*, are like a Pre-Raphaelite painting of Sacred and Profane Love. There they stand – assuming the absent man, the abashed, overwhelmed Jude. Sue is thin, pretty, with a light, abstracted, questioning gaze; Arabella is round, sly-eyed, sleepy, with the dreaming torpor of a destitute girl pondering an exchange of sexual coin. It is scarcely worth noting that they are different, almost opposites. The sources of feeling could not be more reflective than they are in Sue, or more immediate and formless than they are in Arabella. Experience, with them, is not merely the sum of events gone through; it is the response of their differing consciousness to love, want, greed, or renunciation.

In the novel, Sue and Arabella are *connected* as women with Jude Frawley. But he does not initiate or control. Instead, he is identified by them and his situation is dominated by what they offer or withhold. In youth he comes under the sexual domination of Arabella, a surrender rather flimsy that immediately becomes a trap very steely. With Sue, a miserable life is redeemed by the joys of enlightenment and by the special importance that is given to a love or an attachment by one who cares to think about it in a deep way.

There is every kind of suffering and failure in *Jude the Obscure*. This is its great glory as a novel – the passion, the complexity, the completeness, if you will, of petty, mean, bitter failure. Waste, oppression, injustice, indifference have soaked into the very soil of life, washing away all of the yearnings and rights of those with unlucky natures or unfortunate birth. Social and spiritual deprivation bears down on these modest persons who have asked only the lightest measure of possibility. Every single character fails – falls, in great pain, each one. The children, the lovers, the married, the ignorant, the intellectual. The only moments of happiness are the innocence of early hope and perhaps those instances of love and respect that Sue Bridehead, a singular, deep creation, brings to the lives about her. Love and respect – or is it, instead, affection and sympathy, emotions a little more distant.

Sue is an original, mingled being. The outlines of her nature waver and flow. She is as we find it often in our lives: one of those striking, haunting persons who endlessly talk, act and analyse and yet never quite form a whole as a simpler and more rigid character would. Too many parts and each with its quality and interest; the design is there but it fades suddenly. This sort of person, like Sue, *thinks* and that is her mystery. It is not at all the usual mystery. The most fascinating and startling complications of her character have to do with sex and with the power of abstract ideas upon a truly superior female mind.

Sue Bridehead is frail, delicately balanced. She is a radical sceptic and it is her custom to ponder and question the arrangements and tyrannies of society. She is intense, 'all nervous motion', and yet 'artless' and 'natural'. Sue is more or less self-educated and has encountered avant-garde ideas about religion, art, and Biblical interpretation. When we first meet her she is reading the chapter in Gibbon on Julian the Apostate. Somehow her involvement with critical, radical thought, the cluster of aesthetic and social attitudes, form a frame for her disappointments and for the rebukes of society. It is the common thing of an intellectual alienation that gives an assurance to one's character and even a measure of tranquillity and resignation to balance the shatterings and shakings of psychological intensity.

In quite a different way, the pained, stumbling efforts of Jude to gain knowledge have about them a despondent, almost imprisoning aspect. His books, his noble, baffled yearnings create in us a great pity for him, but it is as if a necessary sense had been denied him along with the cruel denials of society. Jude's hopes for education are linked with the natural hopes for a profession, whereas with Sue ideas and learning have a gratuitous, spontaneous, somewhat unprofessional character, that of the deepest inclination. When Jude is brutally turned down in his dream to enter Christ-minster (Oxford) – '. . . and, judging from your description of yourself as a working man, I venture to think that you will have a much better chance of success in life by remaining in your own sphere and sticking to your trade than by adopting any other course . . .' – he adjusts his hopes and plans to study theology, with the idea of making his life in the church. He is astonished by Sue's light-hearted dismissal of much of religion and by, for instance, her contempt for the Church's efforts to deny the erotic meanings of the Song of Solomon. He cries out several times that she is a 'perfect Voltairian'.

In the end what is so poignant is that Sue's brightness and will to freedom cannot save her. She goes down into despair with Jude and, finally, under the strain of life, sinks into a punishing denial of her own principles about marriage and religion. She has not, through ideas and strong personal leanings, been able to break out of poverty and defeat and the undermining force of an accumulation of disasters. Life simply will not open itself to her frail unsupported brightness. In despair she tries to name the mystery of implacable barriers. 'There is something exterior to us which says, "You shan't!" First it said, "You shan't learn!" Then it said, "You shan't labour!" Now it says, "You shan't love!"'

Jude the Obscure is about poverty and the crushing of the spirit that goes along with it like a multiplying tumour. It is also about sex and marriage. Marriage is, as the plot develops, an experience violated by need, by the drastic workings of chance, and by the peculiar limitations of choice. It is also seen as an idea, an institution, open to the 'higher criticism' in the same manner as religion and scriptural problems. At best it is a thunderclap, the sky lights up, and then a storm of entrapment, manipulation, and bad feeling rains down. Wholeness and freedom are violated and, for Sue at least, these qualities are of the first value. In putting this value upon them she creates a violent uneasiness in what would otherwise have been a more usual plotting of forces and resolutions.

The price of sex is a destruction for every fulfilment, and often a destruction without fulfilment. Love exhausts itself as a spur to action in any case and its claim upon the soul is not greater than the claim of pity – even less at times. Part of the peculiar quality of this suffering, tragic novel is that the relationships, worn down as they are by life, have, nevertheless, a kind of loveliness. Perhaps it is the glow spread by Sue's complicated candour and by her patient, analytical effort to understand her feelings and convictions. Only Arabella, limited, greedy, 'normal' at least in her lack of the fastidious scrupulosities of Sue – only she is outside a certain grace and sweetness.

Arabella is as much a convention in the history of the novel as Sue is an original. It is the rule of conventions to ask us to accept as given a certain gathering of traits and motives. Arabella represents the classical entrapment by sex: the entrapment of an 'innocent' sensual man by a hard, needy, shackling woman. Arabella's coarseness is a mirror of Jude's weakness. Her qualities are a force of a negative kind; their bad effects upon others are far more devastating than any advantages she may reap for herself. Advantage is forever in her mind and in many ways the failure of dishonest sex to bring about anything prosperous is always interesting. The person exploited by dishonest sex is weakened, distracted, and a falling off of personal and worldly fortune is likely to be observed. This is true for both the men and the women and especially striking if both are poor since, in that case, the entrapment has not found its proper object. In Arabella, sexual exploitation is combined with other deceits. Indeed the deceits are inevitable, since she has no plan, conviction, or order that could give her relations with men a genuineness. What is absent in Arabella is love. Her compulsions arise from the survival struggle and not from obsessional passion. All of these exigencies are meant to signal that she is 'bad' in some intrinsic way.

Arabella begins with the physical charms of youth, a bosomy air of possibility. But this is presented as a fraud. Her tendency is to face life as a desperate improvisation and she will naturally lack the discipline that might protect her small, early capital of beauty. Arabella's driven poverty, the crude urgings of an unenlightened family, the scheming habit of the other poor girls in the village have severely limited her vision. Hardy's presentation of her ignoble struggle scarcely hints at the numbness inside.

And her sullenness: only this has the shape of a deeply personal and meaningful condition of Arabella's feeling. It is a sullenness shrouded in peasant melancholy. The sullenness is her own comment on her deceitfulness and is some always dawning awareness of its futility. Even deceit needs a more nourishing soil than society has allowed Arabella. Her efforts are the traditional ones the novelist will give her: she works as a barmaid and early unsettles Jude with her knowledge of malts and hops. In the course of the novel she will move on to Australia; she will marry for the second time without unmarrying the first. She always ends up without money or help. She has a pitiful child whom she looks upon as one would look upon a mongrel loosely and accidentally attached to one's life.

For a poor and lonely young man like Jude, pleasure is not to be taken without cost. He is not hard enough for his encounter with Arabella – that is the way it has been designed. In the same way he is not gifted enough for the life of scholarship and learning his heart is set upon. Jude's longings have falsely come to rest in his dream of Christminster. He is a man who would sacrifice everything for the journey and yet takes the wrong road. Arabella's offering of sex is seen as a menace to learning and ambition and that does not prove to be wrong. There is a heavy consequence, a large bill to be paid for the most perfunctory surrender. Latin and Greek are not acommodating. After he has been with Arabella he comes home to the reproachful books: 'There lay his book open, just as he had left it, and the capital letters on the title-page regarded him with fixed reproach in the grey starlight, like the unclosed eyes of a dead man.'

We are given Jude's collision with Arabella as a weakness, but one of those weaknesses most critics believe make men human, real. Arabella is deeply in tune with the consequential. By asserting cause and effect the weak avenge themselves and, of course, not always upon the strong. They avenge themselves as they must and can. They demand, they imprison. When Jude thinks of ending his affair with Arabella, she deceives him about pregnancy and they marry, in hopelessness, without any joy or understanding of each other. Jude must sell his books 'to buy saucepans'.

The misery of this marriage is so great that Hardy has dipped the courtship and early days in the slow, filthy waters of the pigsty. Arabella and Jude undertake to kill a pig they have raised. Jude hears the animal scream and wishes to get it over quickly; but Arabella has a country knowledge of pigs and their killing. She cries out in anger against the idea of a quick passage to death. 'You must not! The meat must be well bled and to do that he must die slow . . . I was brought up to it and I know. Every good butcher keeps un bleeding long. He ought to be up to eight or ten minutes dying, at least.' The connection with Jude hastily comes to mind. His life is to be a long-drawn-out suffering and pain. The gentler tones of nature surround the brute factuality of a hard existence only as an accompaniment, an aside. 'A robin peered down at the preparations from the nearest tree, and not liking the sinister look of the scene, flew away, though hungry.'

'Married is married,' Arabella says when the child does not appear in due time. She grows tired of Jude and mercifully moves on, to Australia. It cannot be the end, for there is no end to consequence, connection. 'But she's sure to come back – they always do,' Jude says. It is hard to tell what has real power over Arabella except the depressed, sullen downhill slide based on flirtations, marriages, alliances made and dropped, hopes grabbed and abandoned, listless enterprises, absence of plans. These liabilities and follies are not in the real sense her own. They are part of the *given* and of the absences. She is destitute, anxious, brutalized by the absences in the tradition, the only one she knows, a tradition she has to live out in the lowest, rural, most diminished terms. It is in no way softened as it is in more fortunate women, such as Eustacia Vye, who live also by manipulation and deceit.

Arabella is harshly treated by Hardy because she is so great a part of Jude's paralysis and despondency. In his other novels there is usually a great insistence upon the virtues of the poor folk who are hemmed in by nature and custom. The furze-cutters, the reddlemen, the country mothers are heroic in their simplicity, authenticity, and constancy of feeling. Restlessness – Eustacia Vye, Lucetta, Mrs Charmond – is inclination to spoil, to appropriate, to introduce a worldliness and standard that corrupt. The waste of talents is condemned by Hardy with a strong class feeling in a doctor like Fitzpiers in *The Woodlanders* who neglects his work, in an engineer such as Wildeve in *The Return of the Native*, who out of sloth and distraction ends up running a tavern. There is a repetitiveness in this rural life that Eustacia Vye is overwhelmed by. It is the same repetitiveness Arabella is doomed to, although, in her, it is stripped of its romantic, dark, and arresting aspects.

Arabella is the bad side of the ignorance and pain of the country, just as Tess is the good part of rural courage and beauty and naturalness. The thing that finally seeps through the story is that a 'sensual' risk like Arabella is really as abstract about life as Sue, as much a creature of sceptical reaction if not of thought. In her relentless trudging after the relief of love affairs, Arabella looks for the hopeless ideal. The numbing disappointments, the raging need for the means of survival, make the ignorant Arabella finally show the same lack of reverence for conformity, for the legalities of things, the same vaulting of the stony fences of convention that are found in Sue's fascination with ideas. Of course there is nothing critical or reforming in Arabella's delinquencies. She is blackness in action, and yet she is as miserable with Jude as he with her. Her tricking him into marriage, her lies, her abandonment of him on his deathbed are the deepest betrayals that follow on the first betrayal, their lack of real meaning for each other.

Arabella finds Jude's goodness and yearnings boring; it is her habit to consider them as a rebuke to herself. Jude's exacerbated sensitivity, his bouts of drunken frustration, his passion for the refined and the gentle in life – these can scarcely be offered for Arabella's realistic approval. Her sense of things is different. Pigs have to be killed and the robin's dismay is not to the point. Arabella's flaws are traditional; she is harsh, but comprehensible. A contrast indeed to Sue Bridehead.

Bridehead: it is curious that Hardy should have chosen this name for Sue. It is a curiosity, and something of an embarrassment, because the plot of Sue's life circles around two great reservations – refusal of sex and grave misgivings about marriage. Is 'maidenhead' to be thought of? Is the idea of attaching 'bride' to the name of a young woman genuinely questioning about marriage meant as a telling incongruity? Yet there is a sound to the name that does not impugn the high tone of Sue's discourse or her ambivalences that are like a deep tattoo on the skin of her being.

Sex and marriage – of the two, marriage is the easiest surrender and Sue rather thoughtlessly submits to it with the unsuitable Mr Phillotson, the schoolmaster. He is confused to learn that the other submission is not forthcoming. Sue asserts her right to chastity as one would, without shame, assert any other inclination. Chastity – how embarrassing it is in a love story. And how odd that it is faced so candidly and childishly rather than as a distortion and disguise, a great, devouring secret, veiled in subterfuge and duplicity. Sue is very unsettling in the prodigal openness with which she greets these dark holes of withdrawal. She tells Jude of the most important experience of her youth, her meeting with a young undergraduate at Christminster:

He asked me to live with him, and I agreed to by letter. But when I joined him in London I found he meant a different thing from what I meant. He wanted to be my lover, in fact, but I wasn't in love with him; and on my saying I should go away if he didn't agree to my plan, he did so. We shared a sitting-room for fifteen months; and he became a leader-writer for one of the great London dailies; till he was taken ill, and had to go abroad. He said I was breaking his heart by holding out against him so long at such close quarters. . . I might play that game once too often he said . . . I hope he died of consumption, and not of me entirely. I went down to Sandbourne to his funeral, and was his only mourner. He left me a little money – because I broke his heart, I suppose. That's how men are – so much better than women!

Jude is distressed and cannot understand her 'curious unconsciousness of gender'. And yet Sue is all charm and sympathy. Jude and Mr Phillotson are in no way graceful or inspired enough to be her companions but it would never occur to us that some 'better' man would alter the curious course of Sue's character. We might say that the brute reduction of her prospects, the bleaching rural impoverishment, the rootless, unprotected strangeness of her life with Jude are a terrible burden upon her great intelligence and upon her wandering, artless courage. Those calamities do indeed push her to the edge, but there is the *essential* Sue, mixed and misty as it is, that is not in any way circumstantial.

Sue's marriage to Mr Phillotson is the baldest inconsistency. She has a sort of unworldliness and caprice that allows her to undertake this union. The schoolmaster has none of the stirring pathos of Jude. He has early been overwhelmed by the hypocrisy and deadness of the small educational institutions of his time. He sees the lightness of Sue, her indifference to advantage, and he believes that he might appropriate some of her wayward magic to relieve his own heavy spirits. Sue, as it turns out, feels a profound aversion to Mr Phillotson. She is aware of it – awareness of feeling is, as Irving Howe says in his brilliant portrait of Sue, part of her *modernity*, her fascinations – awareness not as an idea, but as an emotion completely personal and pressing. She hides in a dismal closet rather than enter the bedroom. Once, dreaming that he was approaching her, she jumped out of the window. Is this neurasthenia and hysteria? To look at it in that way is to impose a late abstraction of definition upon a soul, one might almost say a new kind of human being, struggling to take form in history. The personal, the analytical, the passion for self-knowledge that raise *authenticity* above everything, and certainly above duty and submission, come so naturally to Sue that she is almost childlike. Hypocrisy, especially in matters of feeling, is to her a sacrilege. At one point, Jude asks her if she would like to join him in evening prayers and she says, 'Oh, no, no! . . . I should feel such a hypocrite.'

After she has been married to Phillotson for eight weeks, Sue tries to voice her feelings. 'Perhaps you have seen what it is I want to say – that though I like Mr Phillotson as a friend, I don't like him – it is a torture to me to – live with him as a husband!' She goes on to say in despair that she has been told women can 'shake down to it', and yet 'that is much like saying that the amputation of a limb is no affliction, since a person gets comfortably accustomed to the use of a wooden leg or arm in the course of time'. In addition to aversion, she laments 'the sordid contract of marriage . . . the dreadful contract to feel in a particular way, in a matter whose essence is its voluntariness.'

Authenticity, chastity, renunciation. Of course, Sue is not able to live out completely the deep stirrings of her nature. She feels a sympathy for Jude that is a transcendent friendship as profound and rare as love. It is sanctified by their sufferings and by the ever-spreading insecurity of their existence, by the unreality of themselves as a plan of life. In the absence of *surroundings* – they are like itinerants with no articles to offer as they wander in a circle from town to town – in the way their need has no more claim upon society than the perching of birds in the evening, they come to fall more and more under the domination of the mere attempt to describe themselves. They live under the protection of *conversation*, as many love affairs without a fixed meaning, without emotional space to occupy, come to rest in words. Their drama is one of trembling inner feeling and of the work to name the feeling.

Sue does have children – an inauthenticity for her. The children come under the doom of thought, of analysis. They die in the nihilistic suicide *decision* of Little Father Time, the watchful, brooding son of Arabella and Jude. Nothing seems more sadly consequent than that the tragedy should finally come to Sue, after the pain of it, as a challenge to principle, a blinding new condition in her struggle to give shape to her sense of things and of herself. She begins to go to church and gradually moves away from her old self to the decision that her original marriage to Phillotson has a remaining churchly validity and therefore the highest claim on her. She returns to him and also at last submits in every sense. An immolation. In this ending Sue is faithful to her passion for an examined life; for indeed religion is at least an idea for her, not a mere drifting. The necessity for this is pitiful and even if it seems to have a psychological truthfulness as the end of the road for one who has been utterly rejected by destiny, religion and the bed of Phillotson are like those cerebral strokes that destroy the life of a living mind. The defeat of Sue is total.

Accident and coincidence in 'Tess of the D'Urbervilles'

THOMAS HINDE

The plot of *Tess of the D'Urbervilles* turns on a succession of accidents and coincidences. Again and again Tess's tragic fate depends on some disastrous mischance. One or two of these may seem possible – life after all is full of mischance – but heaped on top of each other they produce a final effect of gross improbability. Does this matter? Are we to see them as blemishes on an otherwise fine novel; or are they such a pervasive part of it that they must either condemn it or form part of its success?

At its face value the novel suggests not only that these accidents and misfortunes are included by intention but that it is the author's view that life does give human beings just such a succession of kicks downhill to disaster. The refrain 'where was Tess's guardian angel?' is more than an attack on the conventional Christian idea of a benevolent and protecting Almighty; it implies the exact opposite. Our problem, if we don't share this view, is that we see Tess as not so much the victim of Fate, nor as the victim of her own character and circumstances, but as Hardy's personal victim.

It is he who appears to make her suffer her improbable sequence of accidents. In criticizing this effect I do not imply that probability is a criterion by which we should universally or invariably judge. A novel sets its own standards, and no one, to take an obvious example, expects the same 'realism' from Kafka as from Tolstoy. The problem with Hardy's novels is that in most other ways they set up expectations of a quite conventional realism. It is against this self-established standard that the plot of *Tess*, as much as that of any of his novels which came before it and which it otherwise excels, at first sight appears equally to offend.

I say at first sight because my purpose is to suggest a way of looking at *Tess* which sees its many accidents and coincidences neither as blemishes, nor as valid samples of Hardy's neither credible nor particularly interesting view of the part played in life by a persecuting fate; if encouragement were needed to search for such a view it would be provided by *Tess*'s many admirers who seem undismayed by its improbabilities, though these begin on the very first page and feature regularly throughout the book.

Setting the scene, and necessary if there is to be any novel at all, is the coincidence of names: the rich north country manufacturer Stoke who buys his way into the southern landed gentry has arbitrarily chosen from a British Museum list of defunct families the name d'Urberville to add to his own, and this is the original name of the family from which Tess Durbeyfield is distantly descended. The story opens with Parson Tringham telling Tess's father about his aristocratic ancestors, which till now he has not known about. John Durbeyfield puts two and two together and makes five, concluding not only that he is related to the Stoke-d'Urbervilles but that he probably belongs to the senior branch.

Up to this point all could be said to be reasonable enough. If it is an accident it is one which sooner or later seems possible if not probable. In any case, even a realistic novelist may, without offending against his own criterion of probability, precipitate his story with such a single event, then stand back to demonstrate with no further interference the inevitable consequences. To take one modern example, John O'Hara's *Appointment in Samara* employs just such a scheme. The single angry gesture, the highball thrown by Julian English in the face of Harry Reilly, precipitates the whole tragic sequence which follows. Not only is no other interference needed, given the characters and their circumstances, but the accident itself achieves in retrospect a kind of inevitability, as if sooner or later Julian must have made this or some similar gesture.

There seems no such inevitability about the next kick downhill which Fate gives Tess. Driving her father's cart to market at night because he is too drunk to go, she is run down by the mail coach, and Prince, the horse on which his livelihood as a haggler depends, is pierced to the heart by the mail coach's shaft. Tess's guilt at what she has done persuades her to agree to her mother's plan that she should visit the *nouveaux riches* Stoke d'Urbervilles in the hope of making a prosperous marriage.

Here she meets the young and buckish Alec d'Urberville; once again a flavour of managed accident surrounds her seduction by him. Her quarrel, late at night in open country, with the drunken Trantridge village women provides her with just the motive which makes plausible her acceptance of Alec's offer of a pillion ride when he spurs up at a convenient moment. Criticism is only disarmed by the splendid dramatic quality of this scene, set as it is with sinister omen and diabolic detail.

At Talbothays, where Tess goes a few years later and after the death of her child to become a milkmaid, who should she meet but Angel Clare, the young man who, in a more insidious but surer way, is to lead her to her tragic end. And Angel, it turns out, has met Tess before when, on a walking tour with his two priggish brothers, he discovered the maidens of Marlott celebrating May Day and danced with her.

. . . he seemed to discern in her something that was familiar, something which carried him back into a joyous and unforeseeing past, before the necessity of taking thought had made the heavens gray. He concluded that he had beheld her before; where he could not tell. A casual encounter during some country ramble it certainly had been, and he was not greatly curious about it. But the circumstance was sufficient to lead him to select Tess in preference to the other pretty milkmaids.

From this moment the plot turns on Angel's plan to marry Tess, and on whether or not Tess can bring herself to confess her sinful past with Alec d'Urberville before their wedding day. Though she can't tell Angel to his face she at last makes herself write to him and late at night pushes the letter under his door. Only on her wedding eve does she discover that Fate has struck again: she has accidentally pushed it under the carpet as well as the door and Angel has never received it.

Her confession after her marriage leads to their separation, Angel to go to Brazil, Tess to return to Marlott. He has left her an allowance but a succession of minor misfortunes – in particular the neediness and imprudence of her parents – leaves Tess destitute by the time winter comes. Angel has told her that she should go to his parents if she is ever in need, but Fate, which has already put him personally beyond her reach, closes this escape too. She walks to Emminster and finds Angel's father, the vicar, out. Before she can try his door again Angel's brothers discover her walking boots which she has hidden on the outskirts of the village and Miss Mercy Chant bears them off for charity. Tess's courage fails her and she turns for home. 'It was somewhat unfortunate,' Hardy writes, 'that she had encountered the sons and not the father, who, despite his narrowness, was far less starched and ironed than they, and had to the full the gift of Christian charity.' Though we may read this as a confession of clumsy plotting, that is far from Hardy's intention. His tone is ironic. The world may consider that Tess here suffered an improbable and untypical stroke of ill luck, but Hardy, better informed about the working of Fate, knows that such accidents are in fact typical and probable.

Meanwhile Tess has taken on the humblest and most oppressive sort of agricultural labour: work on arable land. The description of her grubbing up swedes for cattle food, creeping across the icy uplands of Flintcomb Ash in drenching rain, is one of the most memorable in the book. And who should turn out to be her employer but a farmer who knows her past and whom Angel once struck on the jaw when he insultingly hinted at it during the last days before their marriage. Inevitably he takes his revenge on Tess.

Here any chance that Angel might send her help is cut off by an even more gratuitous stroke of ill fortune. On his way to the boat Angel has casually – and not at all convincingly – made a pass at Izz, one of Tess's fellow milkmaids, inviting her to go with him to Brazil. Tess is told of it and concludes that Angel never really loved her. She can no longer bring herself even to write to him.

Alec d'Urberville's conversion to evangelical Christianity – coincidentally performed by Angel Clare's father – now gives Alec the chance to harass Tess again and, more important, weakens her power to resist him. The scene is set for her final disastrous return to Alec. The various letters Angel ultimately receives from her and from others reach him at moments which time his return exactly too late to save her from the murder of Alec and ultimately the gallows.

Though this is only a brief selection of the blows which Fate strikes Tess, I hope it is sufficient to show that the plot of the novel turns on a succession of disastrous accidents which far exceeds realistic probability. But as in all such abstracts, vital elements which seem unrelated to the book's plot have been left out, in particular one to which Hardy persistently returns even though his attention is overtly directed towards Tess and her personal tragedy. This is the equally sure and tragic destruction of the traditional society of the English village.

Twice he shows us mechanized agriculture at work; on the first occasion he describes how the reaping machine, with its red arms in the shape of a Maltese cross, gradually reduces the standing corn.

Rabbits, hares, snakes, rats, mice, retreated into a fastness, unaware of the ephemeral nature of their refuge, and of the doom that awaited them later in the day when, their covert shrinking to a more and more horrible narrowness, they were huddled together, friends and foes, till the last few yards of upright wheat fell also under the teeth of the unerring reaper, and they were every one put to death by the sticks and stones of the harvesters.

It needs little intuition to see that Hardy is here describing by parallel the fate of the human inhabitants of such a village as Marlott.

Humans themselves are the victims on the second occasion: Tess and her fellow workers who feed the monstrous itinerant threshing machine at Flintcombe Ash, with its diabolical master.

By the engine stood a dark motionless being, a sooty and grimy embodiment of tallness, in a sort of trance, with a heap of coals by his side: it was the engineman. The isolation of his manner and colour lent him the appearance of a creature from Tophet, who had strayed into the pellucid smokelessness of this region of yellow grain and pale soil, with which he had nothing in common, to amaze and to discompose its aborigines.

What he looked he felt. He was in the agricultural world, but not of it. He served fire and smoke; these denizens of the fields served vegetation, weather, frost, and sun. He travelled with his engine from farm to farm, county to county ... He spoke in a strange northern accent; his thoughts being turned inwards upon himself, his eye on his iron charge, hardly perceiving the scenes around him, and caring for them not at all.

Still more symptomatic of the destruction of a village society by the new rich and their industrial money is the chicken house where Tess keeps the Stoke-d'Urberville chickens, once a copyholder's cottage.

The descendants of these bygone owners felt it almost as a slight to their family when the house which had so much of their affection, had cost so much of their forefathers' money, and had been in their possession for several generations before the d'Urbervilles came and built here, was indifferently turned into a fowl-house by Mrs Stoke-d'Urberville as soon as the property fell into her hand according to the law.

Apart from the implications of such incidents, Hardy as author continually comments on the changing and deteriorating condition of rural Wessex. The May Day dance, for example, where we first meet Tess, is 'a gay survival from Old Style days when cheerfulness and May were synonyms'. The refreshments which the rural labourers of Trantridge drink on Saturday nights are 'curious compounds sold to them as beer by the monopolizers of the once independent inns'. Still more important, it is the tenant farmers, deprived of their independence, who are 'the natural enemies of bush and brake', and to whom Tess falls victim at the lowest point of her decline at Flintcombe Ash.

And it is because Tess's family are victims of another aspect of this destruction of rural independence that she is finally exposed once more to Alec d'Urberville. As soon as her father dies her mother loses her right to their cottage, and the family must join all those other labourers' families which take to the road on Lady Day, their worldly goods loaded on to hired waggons, to hunt for new jobs and homes. Oppressed by responsibility for her family, she no longer feels she has the moral right to resist his advances when they could bring with them the financial help she so badly needs.

Indeed, a good many of Tess's misfortunes turn out, on closer inspection, to have economic causes which seem almost as important as the random vengefulness of Fate to which Hardy attributes them. It is only a short step from realizing this to wondering whether Hardy is not – consciously or unconsciously – concerned throughout the book not so much with Tess's personal fortune as with her fate as a personification of rural Wessex.

Just why Tess should be an appropriate figure to play this part is clearly explained in Chapter LI, in a passage which holds the clue to the book's social message.

The village had formerly contained, side by side with the agricultural labourers, an interesting and better-informed class, ranking distinctly above the former – the class to which Tess's father and mother had belonged – and including the carpenter, the smith, the shoe-maker, the huckster, together with nondescript workers other than farm labourers: a set of people who owed a certain stability of aim and conduct to the fact of their being life-holders like Tess's father, or copyholders, or, occasionally, small freeholders. But as the long holdings fell in they were seldom again let to similar tenants, and were mostly pulled down, if not absolutely required by the farmer for his hands. Cottagers who were not directly employed on the land were looked upon with disfavour, and the banishment of some starved the trade of others, who were thus obliged to follow. These families, who had formed the backbone of the village life in the past, who were the depositaries of the village traditions, had to seek refuge in the large centres; the process humourously designated by statisticians as 'the tendency of the rural population towards the large towns', being really the tendency of water to flow uphill when forced by machinery.

At once much that appeared arbitrary becomes logical. The destruction of the haggler's daughter no longer seems a cruel mischance, but inevitable. And many more of the accidents she suffers, which on a personal level seem so excessive and gratuitous, become those which her class *must* suffer.

The mail coach which runs down the haggler's cart and kills his horse is the vehicle which will destroy the livelihood of all hagglers, whether they are drunkards like John Durbeyfield, or sober and hard-working. Deprived of their former independence, the children of this village middle class will be driven downwards into just the sort of menial labouring jobs that Tess is forced to take. Her downward progress from milkmaid to arable worker of the lowest sort is the path ahead for all of them.

In their distress they will turn to the new rich, as Tess's parents are driven to send Tess to call on her 'cousins', and these, represented by Alec d'Urberville, will offer only the further exploitation which Tess's job as poultry girl followed by her seduction represents. If they turn to the old upper middle class for relief, as Tess turns to Angel, they are again betrayed, and the mistaken (in Hardy's view) ethics of the Anglican church are employed as an additional moral stick to beat them with. Because, for all his superficial emancipation, Angel does represent this class and is basically not only priggish but as conditioned and conventional as his father and brothers. 'With all his attempted independence of judgement, this advanced and well-meaning young man, a sample product of the last five-and-twenty years, was yet the slave to custom and conventionality when surprised back into his early teachings.' As soon as we see him in this rôle, Tess's failure to confess her past to him ceases to seem an improbable accident and becomes merely the hook on which he happens to hang a betrayal which sooner or later is inevitable. She is not of his class and it can never accept her.

Much else now falls into place. Tess is rejected by the women of Trantridge on the night of her first seduction not just because they are jealous of the way Alec d'Urberville favours her but because she is not really a labourer of their kind. Farmer Groby ill-treats Tess not just because of the coincidental attack made on him by Angel but because tenant farmers *are* the destroyers of such families as Tess's.

Tess is of course many other things as well. She is, for example, the embodiment of 'nature' and in particular of natural womanhood. 'Women whose chief companions are the forms and forces of outdoor Nature retain in their souls far more of the Pagan fantasy of their remote forefathers than of the systematized religion taught their race at later date.' And however much she may stand for a principle or a passing society, she remains a lost and frightened human being in a world which misleads then persecutes her. Scenes such as the splendid but appalling one in which she baptizes her dying child in her bedroom wash basin may indeed seem to establish her tragedy too clearly as a personal one for the interpretation I am suggesting.

But such a view of Tess becomes less and less satisfactory as Hardy inflicts on her a less and less probable sequence of accidental and coincidental misfortune. It is only when she is seen to some extent also to be a daughter of the doomed rural England which Hardy loved, and in particular of that class in the rural community from which Hardy himself came and which was once 'the backbone of the village life' that her fate no longer seems arbitrary and author-imposed but inescapable.

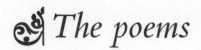 # The poems

GEOFFREY GRIGSON

I

Sift *The Life of Thomas Hardy*, of which Hardy is the real author, and you find much evidence of how he came into his mode of poem-making, how he reached at last the freedom of his creativity; and how his poems and his novels are related. He began as a poet. He jilted poetry to write novels. Then at last, when he was fifty-five, he set novels aside to write poetry. First love and last love. He wanted us to remember him as a poet. About taking again to poetry Hardy excused himself by saying that he had tried to keep his narratives 'as near to poetry in their subject as the conditions would allow'. He said poetry 'had always been more instinctive with him': from his early years he had just been able to keep poetry alive 'half in secrecy, under the pressure of magazine writing' – the pressure of keeping up instalments as the novels were serialized.

It was some time between 1857 and 1860, between seventeen and twenty, that Hardy wrote his first poem 'Domicilium' – his dwelling-place, a poem of the kind many poets begin with, an act of natural piety towards his home, his childhood, his opening consciousness.

Though it was first printed within Hardy's lifetime, in 1916, 'Domicilium' wasn't included in Hardy's *Collected Poems*, perhaps because in the *Life* (where it is reprinted) he had called it 'Wordsworthian', and had spoken of its 'naïve and obvious fidelity'. In fact these 'Wordsworthian lines' were surprisingly and promisingly individual. If Hardy began with description or celebration of the Higher Bockhampton cottage, the 'lonely and silent spot between woodland and heathland' where he was born, he at once set the two elements of the situation against each other, the domestic:

> Red roses, lilacs, variegated box
> Are there in plenty, and such hardy flowers
> As flourish best untrained. Adjoining these
> Are herbs and esculents –

against the independent, the wild, the indifferent, the black threat of the heathlands, which fill the hollows of the Dorset chalk:

> Behind, the scene is wilder. Heath and furze
> Are everything that seems to grow and thrive

The cottage in Upper Bockhampton where Hardy was born in 1840, photographed by Hermann Lea.

The cottage as it is today.

ABOVE Max Gate, built in 1885, showing its inaccessability, the trees the gardener was discouraged from pruning, and the 'dreariest shrubberies' described by Cynthia Asquith.
BELOW High West Street, Dorchester, 1841. 'Casterbridge was the complement of the rural life around; not its urban opposite. Bees and butterflies in the cornfields at the top of the town, who desired to get to the meads at the bottom, took no circuitous course, but flew straight down the High Street . . .' *The Mayor of Casterbridge*.

ABOVE South Street, Dorchester, 1898. 'Over the pavement on the sunny side of the way hung the shopblinds so constructed as to give the passenger's hats a smart buffet off his head . . .' *The Mayor of Casterbridge.*

LEFT The King's Arms, Dorchester. 'The building before whose doors they [the town band] had pitched their music stands was the chief hotel in Casterbridge – namely, the King's Arms. A spacious bow-window projected onto the street over the main portico . . .' *The Mayor of Casterbridge.*

ABOVE A Dorsetshire stone bridge: 'These bridges had speaking countenances. Every projection in each was worn down to obtuseness, partly by weather, more by friction from generations of loungers . . .' *The Mayor of Casterbridge.*

RIGHT ABOVE Puddletown, the birthplace of Tryphena. 'Weatherbury. It was where Bathsheba had gone two months before. This information was like coming from night to noon.' *Far from the Madding Crowd.* '. . . the Weatherbury folk were by no means uninteresting intrinsically. If report spoke truly, they were as hardy, merry, thriving, wicked a set as any in the whole county. Oak resolved to sleep at Weatherbury that night . . .' *Far from the Madding Crowd.*

RIGHT Egdon Heath, the Roman Road. 'In many portions of its course it overlaid the old vicinal way, which branched from the great western road of the Romans . . . though the gloom had increased sufficiently to confuse the minor features of the heath, the white surfaces of the road remained almost as clear as ever.' *The Return of the Native.*

Lanhydrock House, Cornwall. 'A little further, and an opening in the elms stretching up from this fertile valley revealed a mansion. "That's Endelstow House, Lord Luxellian's," said the driver.'
A Pair of Blue Eyes.

St Juliot Church, Cornwall. 'On the brow of one hill, of rather greater altitude than its neighbour, stood the church . . . The lonely edifice was black and bare, cutting up into the sky from the very tip of the hill.' *A Pair of Blue Eyes.*

Country gate painted with a text. 'Frequently when they [Alec and Tess] came to a gate or stile they found painted thereon in red or blue letters some text of Scripture . . .' *Tess of the D' Urbervilles.*

Stonehenge in 1910, photographed by Hermann Lea. 'The next pillar was isolated; others composed a trilithon; others were prostrate . . . and it was soon obvious they made up a forest of monoliths grouped upon the grassy expanse of the plain . . .
"It is Stonehenge," said Clare.
"The heathen temple, you mean?"
"Yes. Older than the centuries; older than the D'Urbervilles." '
Tess of the D'Urbervilles.

Bournemouth, 1871. 'At eleven o'clock that night, having secured a bed at one of the hotels . . . he [Angel Clare] walked out into the streets of Sandbourne.' *Tess of the D'Urbervilles*. 'This fashionable watering-place, with its western stations, its piers, its groves of pines, its promenades, and its covered gardens, was, to Angel Clare, like a fairy place . . .' *Tess of the D'Urbervilles*.

> Upon the uneven ground. A stunted thorn
> Stands here and there, indeed; and from a pit
> An oak uprises, springing from a seed
> Dropped by some bird a hundred years ago.

Enter – the next words are 'In days bygone' – that past, which so often animates the painful present of Hardy's verse, his father's mother telling him in the rest of the poem how much more wild the domicilium had been when she and her husband first settled there, how it swarmed with snakes and efts and how the 'heathcroppers' on the hills – the shaggy heathland ponies – had been their only friends.

This is the Hardy who in his thirties would note '*May*. In an orchard at Closeworth. Cowslips under trees. A light proceeds from them, as from Chinese lanterns or glow-worms'; and then '*September* 28. An object or mark raised or made by man on a scene is worth ten times any such formed by unconscious Nature. Hence clouds, mists, and mountains are unimportant beside the wear on a threshold, or the print of a hand.'

Looking backward from 'Domicilium', Hardy has left us snapshots of the child whose consciousness of his local past and present and of himself had increased – a child who preferred his own company, who then, as through all his life, disliked being touched; who did not wish to grow up – 'he did not want at all to be a man, or to possess things, but to remain as he was, in the same spot, and to know no more people than he already knew (about half a dozen)'; a child who delighted in dancing and music ('this sensitiveness to melody, though he was no skilled musician, remained with him through life'); a child who attached himself dumbly and ideally to a succession of girls; who was fascinated by real or supposititious accounts of his ancestry; a child unusual in having had two experiences of death – death by hanging.

He describes one of these experiences. When he was sixteen he remembered, one summer morning, that a man was due to be hanged at Dorchester at eight o'clock. He took up the family telescope, climbed a heathland hill which gave a view of the town, and focused on the gallows:

> The sun behind his back shone straight on the white stone facade of the gaol, the gallows upon it, and the form of the murderer in white fustian . . . At the moment of his placing the glass to his eye the white figure dropped downwards, and the faint note of the town clock struck eight.

It had all been so sudden that Hardy nearly dropped the telescope:

> He seemed alone on the heath with the hanged man, and crept home wishing he had not been so curious. It was the second and last execution he witnessed, the first having been that of a woman two or three years earlier, when he stood close to the gallows.

It would make no bad epigraph to much of Hardy's feeling and much of his verse: 'He seemed alone on the heath with the hanged man.'

2

Hardy was fairly talkative about his first considerable outflow of poems, in his middle and late twenties. He was then the 'young Gothic draughtsman who could restore and design churches and rectory-houses', working, in offices overlooking the Thames, in the Adelphi, for the architect Arthur Blomfield; 1865 was the first year of this efflorescence. He read nothing but verse, he talked verse to Blomfield's staff and pupils when work was slack. Spenser, Donne, Shelley, Wordsworth, Scott – he read his way backwards and forwards in English verse, he read the living, and the new poets. The 1860s were the years of Browning's *Dramatis Personae* and *The Ring and the Book*, more explosively the years assaulted by Swinburne, and – a little belatedly in England – by Whitman. Hardy recalls in a much later poem, after Swinburne's death, the 'quick, glad surprise' of reading Swinburne's *Poems and Ballads*, when they came out in 1866:

> – It was as though a garland of red roses
> Had fallen about the hood of some smug nun
> When irresponsibly dropped as from the sun,
> In fulth of numbers freaked with musical closes,
> Upon Victoria's formal middle time
>   His leaves of rhythm and rhyme.
>
> O that far morning of a summer day
> When, down a terraced street whose pavements lay
> Glassing the sunshine into my bent eyes,
> I walked and read with a quick glad surprise
>   New words, in classic guise.

He walked from Hyde Park to the office every day with the green *Poems and Ballads* in his pocket. Two years later, in 1868, he was reading Whitman, that other villainous poet of the time, in the first English selection of him introduced by William Michael Rossetti (and published by the same not very respectable John Camden Hotten who had brought out Swinburne's book). He must have been affected by these new words from America, unless he found them too unclassic. In the *Life* he just mentions Whitman – no comment, which is a pity; whereas to Swinburne and to Browning he comes back again and again, a note here, a note there. When Browning died years after, in 1889, he copied out a quotation from Browning, as if to summarize his own mature response: 'Incidents in the development of a soul! little else is worth study.' From Swinburne a favourite line about Man – Hardy thought of it on the day of Swinburne's funeral – was 'Save his own soul he hath no star'.

Meantime in these late sixties of poetic innovation and rebellion, Hardy was writing his own poems, without confidence in himself and without certainty about his own future. Some of these poems were lost, some remain. One of them is among Hardy's best, the wry 'Neutral Tones' (1867), beginning:

> We stood by a pond that winter day,
> And the sun was white, as though chidden of God,
> And a few leaves lay on the starving sod;
> – They had fallen from an ash, and were gray . . .

and ending (after 'The smile on your mouth was the deadest thing/Alive enough to have strength to die'):

> Since then, keen lessons that love deceives,
> And wrings with wrong, have shaped to me
> Your face, and the God-curst sun, and a tree,
> And a pond edged with grayish leaves.

There are other poems about life which proceeds to death, and love which fails to deliver its promised consolation and benison. Twenty-six-year-old Hardy thinks of walking down 'Life's sunless hill' ('She, to Him III'). The girl in the same poem is 'Numb as a vane that cankers on its point'. This pupil of

> A senseless school, where we must give
> Our lives that we may learn to live!
> ('A Young Man's Epigram on Existence', 1866),

this young restorer of Gothic decay stands with a girl among the dead:

> The two were silent in a sunless church,
> Whose mildewed walls, uneven paving-stones,
> And wasted carvings passed antique research;
> And nothing broke the clock's dull monotones.
> ('Her Dilemma', 1866)

Hardy sent his poems to magazines, editors sent them back. He was in confusion. Inclination said writing, prudence said architecture (very much a rising profession at that time). Could Hardy realize himself, achieve individuality and freedom, in a profession which would always mean bending to a client? Should he be a critic of art and architecture (Hardy was a frequenter of art galleries)? Would being a clergy-man (an old dream of Hardy's) combine with literature? Should he go on the stage?

In retrospect, Hardy felt that association with living poets would have helped him. Swinburne, Browning might have encouraged him and stimulated him; meeting them would not have been difficult. But he was aloof, and he never thought of it. This young Hardy might be in London, the country builder's son a rung at least up the social ladder, in his work in the office of a leading architect; but what was con-ceivable for Hardy continued far short of *knowing* poets and writers. In London or back in Dorset, he found these late twenties of his life a time of despair arising from uncertainty and indecision. As 'cures for despair' he prescribed for himself Wordsworth's 'Resolution and Independence' (which isn't so encouraging when it says:

> We poets in our youth begin in gladness
> But thereof come in the end despondency and madness)

and the chapter 'Of Individuality, as one of the Elements of Well-being' in Mill's *Liberty*, which students then knew by heart; but if his own character was 'uncustomary', in Mill's term, how was he to attain independence for his own individuality? 'He who lets the world, or his own portion of it, choose his plan of life for him, has no need of any other faculty than the ape-like one of imitation.' Exactly. Mill as a cure for despair could increase despair.

Writing novels might or might not be the way out. By the time Hardy made his note about reading Wordsworth and Mill – 1 July 1868 – he had finished his first novel, *The Poor Man and the Lady*. When he sent the manuscript off to Macmillan, he was still thinking about poems, 'Perhaps I can do a volume of poems consisting of the *other side* of common emotions.' What he did in fact was to edge the making of poems to one side and drift unsteadily from architecture into fiction.

There is irony about the linkage of events in Hardy's life, in the years 1868 to 1872 or 1873. Though Alexander Macmillan, and then George Meredith, for the publishers Chapman and Hall, dissuaded him from publishing *The Poor Man and the Lady* (Macmillan shook his head and declared that it 'meant mischief'; Meredith thought – though the actual words are Hardy's, not Meredith's – that the tendency of the writing was 'socialistic, not to say revolutionary'), he was at least encouraged enough to his second novel, then to his first success, *Under the Greenwood Tree*. Yet it was architecture, now slowly abandoned by Hardy, which brought him to the great emotional experience of his life, to the threshold of delight, dismay and eventual remorse and exultation, when he travelled down to St Juliot in north Cornwall to report on the restoration of the church, and was received at the distant rectory above the Atlantic, on the night of his arrival on 7 March 1870, by the rector's sister-in-law, the girl he was to marry four years later, by which time novel had succeeded novel – *Desperate Remedies* (1871), *Under the Greenwood Tree* (1872), *A Pair of Blue Eyes* (1873), and then *Far from the Madding Crowd*, in the marriage year of 1874.

Architecture gave him Emma Lavinia Gifford, his success as a novelist enabled him to marry her, and Emma Gifford, Emma Hardy, in the end, when he came back from fiction to poetry, was to be the delayed cause of his greatest poems.

A mix-up. Novels made him independent, well-to-do and famous. (Did Hardy, among the plaudits, the reviews, and the royalty statements, remember John Stuart Mill, 'Genius can only breathe freely in an atmosphere of freedom,' and 'It is the privilege and proper condition of a human being, arrived at the maturity of his faculties, to use and interpret experience in his own way'?) Novels were not what he cared for. He realized, as the novels followed each other, that fiction prevented him from carrying on his life 'as an emotion'; that 'he was committed to novel-writing as a regular trade, as much as he had formerly been to architecture'; whereas to write poems was to be himself. Looking back to 1866 and 1867 the old Hardy attributed to the young Hardy the total view that 'in verse was concentrated the essence of all imaginative and emotional literature'.

On that he had never changed his mind.

3

How absolute was Hardy's abandonment of poetry in his long fictional career? He spoke of those early poems, some refused by editors, most of them never submitted, all of them kept private, as 'consigned to darkness till between thirty and forty years after' – until, that is, he had finished with novels. In 1895 *Jude the Obscure* was published, in 1897 *The Well-Beloved* (which had been serialized in 1892). Hardy was free; and at the close of 1898 *Wessex Poems*, his first book of verse, revealed to a world not much impressed to begin with, that the grand novelist of the day was also a poet. In a sense Hardy was back at the beginning. As if paying back Macmillan and his adviser John Morley and Chapman and Hall and Meredith for their strictures on *The Poor Man and the Lady*, he had now signed off with a swingeing, more than 'socialistic' novel, which 'meant mischief', to recall Alexander Macmillan's apprehension. Hardy, fifty-five when *Jude the Obscure* appeared, was in his fifty-ninth year when *Wessex Poems* signalled his return to poetry. The collection began with some of the few poems of the 1860s which had for so long been consigned to darkness. 'Neutral Tones' was one of them.

That Hardy wrote few poems between 1869 or 1870 and the late nineties is certainly true. The abandonment, the abstinence, was complete save for a few slight occasional pieces, and a single poem, 'He Abjures Love', which was wrung out of his pangs in 1883. Yet to say the abstinence was nearly complete is not to say that poetry at any time ceased to appeal to him, or ever lost its status in his mind. He was thinking about it always, and, it may be supposed, reading it always. Again and again he makes pronouncements to himself about poetry – more, or more felt ones, about poetry than about fiction. And since these notes are applicable to all the poems he was to write, as though disburdening himself of his whole past, between 1895 and his death in 1928, it is well to recollect some of them, and then to set against these the disheartening and disillusioning experiences of his middle years.

His pronouncements, his comments, are negative as well as affirmative. Repeatedly, as the novels succeed each other, he speaks out to himself against fiction, and that exchange of the architect's trade for the novelist's trade. In 1874 during the serialization of *Far from the Madding Crowd* he tells his editor Leslie Stephen that his present circumstances led him 'to wish merely to be considered a good hand at a serial', and fiction being his enforced and prudential second string, he tells himself the next year, in between *Far from the Madding Crowd* and his sixth novel *The Hand of Ethelberta*, that to prose style he can carry the knowledge he has acquired – where? in poetry: the knowledge 'that inexact rhymes and rhythms now and then are far more pleasing than correct ones.' He slighted his livelihood. By 1866, after another eleven years, *The Mayor of Casterbridge* just out and acclaimed, *The Return of the Native, The Trumpet-Major, A Laodicean* and *Two on a Tower* all behind him, Hardy, by his later testimony, 'had quite resigned himself to novel-writing as a trade, which he had never wanted to carry on as such. He now went about the business mechanically.' In old age, in 1918, he wrote of himself, and poetry and his career – and of fiction, by slighting inference – that:

A sense of the truth of poetry, of its supreme place in literature, had awakened itself in me. At the risk of ruining all my worldly prospects I dabbled in it ... was forced out of it ... It came back upon me ... All was of the nature of being led by a mood, without foresight, or regard to whither it led.

Here are more of his remarks on poetry or on writing poems or on resuming poetry:

1 July 1879, quoted from Leslie Stephen – Hardy at the time writing *The Trumpet-Major*:

The ultimate aim of the poet should be to touch our hearts by showing his own, and not to exhibit his learning, or his fine taste, or his skill in mimicking the notes of his predecessors.

November 1880 – Hardy now forty years old, ill and in bed, *The Trumpet-Major* out, and *A Laodicean* relentlessly in hand to meet the serialization dates:

At the end of November, he makes a note of an intention to resume poetry as soon as possible.

19 April 1885 – Hardy having just written the last paragraphs of *The Mayor of Casterbridge*:

The business of the poet and novelist is to show the sorriness underlying the grandest things, and the grandeur underlying the sorriest things.

29 May 1887 – Hardy having that year brought out *The Woodlanders* and his *Wessex Tales*:

Instance of a *wrong* (i.e. selfish) philosophy in poetry:

> Thrice happy he who on the sunless side
> Of a romantic mountain ...
> Sits coolly calm; while all the world without,
> Unsatisfied and sick, tosses at noon.
>   THOMSON

5 August 1888 – Hardy by this time making plans for *Tess of the D'Urbervilles*:

To find beauty in ugliness is the province of the poet.

18 December 1890 – *Tess* in preparation and no other major fiction to come now except *Jude the Obscure*:

The highest imaginative genius – that of the poet.

Christmas Day, 1890:

While thinking of resuming 'the viewless wings of poesy' before dawn this morning, new horizons seemed to open, and worrying pettinesses to disappear.

4

Jude finished and out by the late months of 1895, within two years Hardy had his *Wessex Poems* ready, having resumed life as emotion, and poetry as 'emotion put into measure'; himself reborn. The abusive reception of *Jude* made it easier for him to come to the boil and reject his self-imposed trade at last without regret:

17 October 1896:

Poetry. Perhaps I can express more fully in verse ideas and emotions which run counter to the inert crystallized opinion – hard as a rock – which the vast body of men have vested interests in supporting. To cry out in a passionate poem that (for instance) the Supreme Mover or Movers, the Prime Force or Forces, must be either limited in power, unknowing, or cruel – which is obvious enough, and has been for centuries – will cause them merely a shake of the head; but to put it in argumentative prose will make them sneer, or foam, and set all the literary contortionists jumping upon me, a harmless agnostic, as if I were a clamorous atheist, which in their crass illiteracy they seem to think is the same thing . . . If Galileo had said in verse that the world moved, the Inquisition might have let him alone.

Poems multiplied. Hardy – like other poets – had a preservative memory, from which he could exhume impressions years old but still fresh and unimpaired. After the *Wessex Poems* in 1898, which he called 'in a large degree dramatic or personative in conception', he quickly produced the *Poems of the Past and the Present* in 1901, a much larger collection, and then in three parts, in 1904, 1906 and 1908, that enormous and I think rather burdensome dramatic hybrid of verse and fiction *The Dynasts*. Another six collections of verse were to be assembled and published, the last, *Winter Words*, appearing in 1928, in the autumn after his death.

Some nine hundred poems, in twenty-nine years, many of the ones towards the end written with as much brio as the poems of his second beginning, his second poetic birth. The total, the skill, the variation and the power, are extraordinary, but then this small, strong, nimble poet, who moved on quick feet like a dancer, came of longevity, on either side. And he had developed, if quickly in mind, slowly in body; 'a child,' he said of himself, 'till I was 16, a youth till I was 25; a young man till I was 40 or 50.'

Hardy had soon felt at ease again in poetry, and as if to symbolize his regeneration, his new dawn, he had changed his study in Max Gate, that rather glum house he had built for himself and Emma Hardy between Dorchester and his birthplace. Fiction had been written facing west, poems were now written in a new study facing east.

Experience forearmed him against criticism. He complained a little, but was not hugely upset, when characteristics which resulted from consciousness and conviction were slated (they still are sometimes) as lack of skill. Irregularities, neologisms – it was neither here nor there if they did not always work, if (as with every poet) some poems in his deliberate style worked out less well than others. Hardy now considered poetry vis-à-vis his old practice of architecture. He took into his verse, part consciously, part, he said, unconsciously, 'the Gothic art-principle in which he had been trained – the principle of spontaneity, found in mouldings, tracery and such like – resulting in the "unforeseen" (as it has been called) character of his metres and stanzas'. For him it was stress rather than syllable, 'poetic texture rather than poetic veneer' – a deliberated art enlivened by the broadest investigation of forms and metrics, the most extensive reading of verse, old and modern, Horace and medieval Latin lyrics, John Ford, Donne, Edgar Allen Poe and Wordsworth and Crabbe, Shelley ('our most marvellous lyrist'), Browning, Swinburne, Patmore, and William Barnes. No insincerity either of language or attitude – 'The Poet takes note of nothing that he cannot feel emotively' (1906). No divergence from his own particularity – Poetry is 'a particular man's artistic interpretation of life' (1918).

He had too his ideas about poetry in conjunction with the quick-eyed contemplation of human life and nature and incident, about art as 'a disproportioning (*i.e.* distorting, throwing out of proportion) of realities, to show more clearly the features that matter in those realities, which, if merely copied or reported inventorially, might possibly be observed, but would more probably be overlooked' (1890). So art wasn't realism, and truth in art was truth to the artist's impressions which expressed his idiosyncratic view: 'I hold that the mission of poetry is to record impressions, not convictions.' Wordsworth, and Tennyson, he berated because in their old age they recorded convictions instead of those impressions by which they were moved. 'Absit omen!' he added for himself (1917). He insisted, although of course he speculated and philosophized, that he had no philosophy, 'merely what I have often explained to be only a confused heap of impressions, like those of a bewildered child at a conjuring show'. People would look, Hardy protested, for a single theory in all his 'mood-dictated writing' (1920).

The impression of wind oozing through blackthorns, the impression of the undulating floor of St Mark's, in Venice, the impression of a girl holding 'a long-stemmed narcissus' to his nose, as he passed her in Piccadilly at night, the impression of a garden-seat lacking its paint – such things prompted mood, such things were felt by Hardy; and by likeness or analogy they might produce further impressions:

New Year's Eve. Looked out of doors just before twelve, and was confronted by the toneless white of the snow spread in front, against which stood the row of pines breathing out: ''Tis no better with us than with the rest of creation, you see!' I could not hear the church bells. (1890)

It was the impression of this 'churchy' poet, as he described himself, that all men pursue a shadow, which is the Unattainable; it was his impression that there is no god – 'I have been looking for God for 50 years, and I think that if he had existed I should have discovered him' (1890); it was his impression that if there was a god, he could be no more than 'an indifferent and unconscious force at the back of things', or a vague being who might ask:

> Wherefore, O Man, did there come to you
> The unhappy need of creating me—
> A form like your own—for praying to?

who might admit he was:

> One thin as a phasm on a lantern-slide
> Shown forth in the dark upon some dim sheet,
> And by none but its showman vivified,

who might complain to man, now he was dwindling day by day and was about to disappear altogether, that:

> The truth should be told, and the fact be faced
> That had best been faced in earlier years:
> The fact of life with dependence placed
> On the human heart's resource alone,
> In brotherhood bonded close and graced
> With loving-kindness fully blown,
> And visioned help unsought, unknown.
> ('A Plaint to Man', 1909–10)

It was Hardy's impression, as well, Hardy's emotion, that if there was a god, he had gone too far in adding consciousness to the human part of his creation.

5

Certainly enough disheartening, disillusioning experience helped to form and to colour Hardy's impressions, and in turn his poems. Central in his experience of life – no matter what over-ingenious fancy imagines but has so far failed to establish about the other women who appealed to Hardy – was Emma Lavinia Gifford, Emma Hardy, whom he met by lamplight in the doorway of St Juliot rectory in 1870, and married in 1874, and lived with, or as it became, alongside, for thirty-eight years until her death in 1912. That experience at first contradicted and then greyly confirmed feelings over which Hardy brooded already as he contemplated transience and the irremediability of disappointments and death; and if doing so may not be the most scintillating function of poetry, it is certain that in dealing with his experience in poem after poem, especially in the 'Poems of 1912–13' in his *Satires of Circumstance*, Hardy touches our hearts by displaying his own.

To be a little cruel to Emma Hardy, she was lucky indeed to have found Hardy, and acquired him as a husband. She was not beautiful, though fair and fresh, and full-figured, with hair shining and coloured like ripe hazelnuts. She was not of more than middling intelligence and education, though she had a childlike spontaneity and naïvety. She was penniless. She was already thirty years old when she and Hardy met on that evening in March. Her father was a failed solicitor, an impoverished idler, given to drink, and living at that time in a rented house outside Bodmin in Cornwall, where he nervously hung on to his decayed gentility. Emma and her sister had both been governesses for a while. The sister had then been fortunate enough to marry a middle-aged widower, who was the incumbent of the poor living of St Juliot. She filled a vacated position, and she had taken Emma to live with her.

From Emma's father Hardy received a letter in which he protested against their intended marriage, calling him in the grandiose language of his kind, a 'low-born churl who has presumed to marry into my family'. The low-born churl and the not so very high-born young woman, who must have believed herself on the shelf before Hardy's arrival, married; and continued in love with each other – for a while. They had no children, they grew estranged and indifferent, Emma succumbing to her father's illusions of superior rank and to her own illusion of superior intelligence, looking down on her husband, jealous of his increasing fame, deriding and objecting to his impressions of existence, and clinging to her Christian orthodoxy, even as a climax going from Max Gate to London, to the British Museum, to beg the eminent librarian Richard Garnett to persuade her husband to suppress *Jude the Obscure* and burn the manuscript.

What can be declared with assurance is that this disillusion above all disillusions, this emotional separation from his wife, more than colours poem after poem by Hardy about every other kind of miscarriage of hope, love, happiness, and about all the mishaps of blind chance. What Hardy felt about life was confirmed; and he was the man who already, in the brief happy period after his marriage, had noted that at times he looked on 'all things in inanimate Nature as pensive mutes', as mourners, that is to say, at the perpetual funeral of life.

What must have surprised Hardy is the wave and tide both of remorse and re-animated or re-imagined love which gulfed him after his estranged wife died so suddenly and unexpectedly in 1912. Twenty-nine years before Hardy had written in that poem 'He Abjures Love':

> —I speak as one who plumbs
>   Life's dim profound,
> One who at length can sound
>   Clear views and certain.
> But—after Love what comes?
>   A scene that lours,
> A few sad vacant hours,
>   And then, the Curtain.

After Emma's death it was as if, remorse or no, the curtain had lifted – for a while.

> Summer gave us sweets, but autumn wrought division?
>   Things were not lastly as firstly well
>   With us twain, you tell?
> But all's closed now, despite Time's derision.

Yes, but it was now, in the exceptional poems first published in the autumn of 1914, as if the young woman of the rectory and the cliffs had returned, 'despite Time's derision', as if the primacy and unassailability of love had been re-instated, against all experience. Hardy recalls how Emma had possessed him, and irradiated him after their first meeting.

> When I came back from Lyonnesse
>   With magic in my eyes,
>   All marked with mute surmise
> My radiance rare and fathomless,
> When I came back from Lyonnesse
>   With magic in my eyes!

Odd as it seems, Hardy in his fourth collection was to place that now most familiar of his lyrics next to a poem about another woman he had been in love with, more or less, 'A Thunderstorm in Town'. But the old man had revisited St Juliot, and there had followed – *veteris vestigia flammae* he called them, out of the mouths of Virgil and Dido, 'moments of an ancient blaze' – that sequence of poems including 'After a Journey', 'Where the Picnic was', and 'The Phantom Horsewoman':

> A ghost-girl-rider. And though, toil-tried,
>   He withers daily,
>   Time touches her not,
>   But she still rides gaily
>   In his rapt thought
>   On that shagged and shaly
>   Atlantic spot,
>   And as when first eyed
> Draws rein and sings to the swing of the tide.

Hardy once more loved and longed for his young wife as he had first known her, in a total of 116 poems, about an eighth of all the poems he ever wrote.

   Yet it would be error to see in these late poems, in which Emma Hardy, or Emma Gifford reappears,

> Facing round about me everywhere,
>   With your nut-coloured hair,
> And gray eyes, and rose-flush coming and going,

a reversal of Hardy's pervasive emotions and impressions of the human situation. The backward vision of the girl who had been and now is again, consoled him intermittently, but he still had plenty to say of 'the melancholy marching of the years', he had still to ask *Why?*, expecting no answer, to talk of the rotten rose ript from the wall, to repeat that he was one who never expected much. In the poems which came out after his death in *Winter Words* there are epitaphs; one begins:

> I never cared for Life: Life cared for me,
> And hence I owed it some fidelity.

and more savagely, 'A Necessitarian's Epitaph':

> A world I did not wish to enter
> Took me and poised me on my centre,
> Made me grimace, and foot, and prance,
> As cats on hot bricks have to dance
> Strange jigs to keep them from the floor,
> Till they sink down and feel no more.

Of our whole situation he still has to admit:

> We are getting to the end of visioning
> The impossible within this universe,
> Such as that better whiles may follow worse,
> And that our race may mend by reasoning.
> We know that even as larks in cages sing
> Unthoughtful of deliverance from the curse
> That holds them lifelong in a latticed hearse,
> We ply spasmodically our pleasuring.
> ('We are Getting to the End')

Those who begin as devotees of Hardy's verse, entranced by his impact and the quiddity of his vision, the quiddity of his impressions (read that favourite poem 'Afterwards'), sometimes end by finding all of this too much, as if Hardy represents mortality creeping on the dung of earth (the phrase comes from a play he admired, *The Broken Heart*, by John Ford) with less consolation or less spasmodic pleasuring than the case permits.

John Ford goes on that mortality, creeping on this dung of earth, cannot reach 'The riddles which are purposed by the gods'. In our own later contemplation of the Absurd, that element of Hardy's emotions and impressions may worry us less, and we may admit that an evensong hand does go up in some degree of blessing in Hardy's rhetoric and rhythms; more than elsewhere in those defiant poems of the fresh and fair Emma at St Juliot and in a few others as well – among them, according to my choice, at any rate these ten: 'Neutral Tones', 'A Broken Appointment', 'The Ballad

Singer', 'Friends Beyond', 'Overlooking the River Stour', 'Afterwards', 'A Tramp-woman's Tragedy' (that verse story, in a movement borrowed from his admirer Coventry Patmore, which Hardy thought to be 'on the whole, his most successful poem'), 'Lausanne – In Gibbon's Old Garden' (on truth continuing to come like a bastard into the world), 'Lying Awake', and his poem on the armistice of 1918, 'And there was a Great Calm'.

Hardy and the theatre

HAROLD OREL

Hardy's interest in the theatre – a lifelong love-affair – is worth a chapter in itself, though here we will concern ourselves only with *The Dynasts* (written in dramatic form) and *The Famous Tragedy of the Queen of Cornwall*. A few words rapidly sketching that interest, however, may serve as a prologue.

In a lovely painting of a theatre audience that included Mr D'Oyly Carte and Lily Langtry awaiting the dimming of house-lights in the New English Opera House on the occasion of the first performance of Sir Arthur Sullivan's *Ivanhoe* (1891), Hardy is depicted with his attention apparently focused on a programme in his hand;[1] he seems perfectly at home in the theatre. Indeed he was. As one example, he had seen and thrilled to several mumming plays in Dorchester while he was still a child, and late in 1920 he was to 'concoct' a recension of 'The Play of "Saint George"/As Aforetime Acted/By the Dorsetshire/Christmas Mummers, etc.' for a dramatization of *The Return of the Native*. As a young man in London, studying architecture, he volunteered for a walk-on role in *The Forty Thieves*, a pantomime staged at Covent Garden; he paid frequent visits to the 2s pit seats of Drury Lane; he held in his hand a copy of the Shakespearian play that Samuel Phelps was declaiming on the stage ('a severe enough test for the actors', if in fact they noticed his monitoring of their speech, as Hardy noted in his autobiography). He preferred Phelps to Charles Kean. Letters published in the *Dorset County Chronicle* in 1902 indicate that Hardy (who was writing about Edmund Kean's appearance in Dorchester in 1813) was an eager student of the history of the local theatres. He attended, as often as possible, the dramatic readings by Charles Dickens at the Hanover Square Rooms. He knew a great deal about how Pinero corrected actors at rehearsal, and Barrie's relations with actors. He knew Ibsen's plays well, and joined Meredith and George Moore in support of the Independent Theatre Association's efforts to produce them; close friends like William Archer and Edmund Gosse kept him posted on developments in Scandinavian drama. He was a devoted follower of the acting styles of Ada Rehan, Mrs Patrick Campbell, and Henry Irving. One biographer has written a lengthy review of his debt to Shakespeare.[2]

Hardy dramatized *Far from the Madding Crowd* for the managers of the St James's Theatre (1882), and was keenly disappointed to have it rejected; and in the first years of this century he went 'so far as to shape the scenes, action, &c.' of a tragic play before deciding that the subject matter would prevent its ever getting produced, whereupon he converted the story to a ballad entitled 'A Sunday Morning Tragedy'.

He was particularly pleased by the efforts made by the members of the Dorchester Debating, Literary and Dramatic Society to popularize dramatized versions of his prose fictions. Having suffered still another disappointment in the late 1890s over a version of *Tess* that he had prepared for the theatre (two other versions were produced, in London and New York, before Hardy could complete arrangements for his own), he put his script aside for twenty-seven years; not until 1924 was it brought out again for the amateur players of the Dramatic Society. It proved to be a hit both in Dorchester and London, and was revived more than once in later years. Other productions – though not prepared by Hardy himself – followed: a scene from *The Trumpet-Major*; several scenes from *Under the Greenwood Tree* bound together as *The Mellstock Quire; The Three Wayfarers* and *The Distracted Preacher; Desperate Remedies; The Return of the Native* and *The Woodlanders*. Hardy's concern in these productions was the preservation of the past, country manners, rustic dialect, and musical airs that the seventy-five-year-old fiddler Harry Bailey – almost alone – remembered how to play. Hardy attended rehearsals faithfully, and even changed lines sanctified by decades of reprintings in their original form to make them 'sound right'. Although he urged actors and actresses to interpret the lines as they understood them, he was ever-watchful lest his characterizations be misunderstood, and he once mildly rebuked Norman Atkins, a handsome and energetic Alec, for being 'too nice' to Tess. Atkins, who felt that 'Alec must have had some charm of manner to have attracted Tess', had been acting on the basis of that conviction; he had received Florence Emily's blessing for his interpretation; and he could not help being chagrined that he 'was the only member of the cast to have received a direct criticism from the author himself'.

Yet Hardy's views on the commercial theatre were more than a little mordant, despite his delight in the dozen productions of the Hardy Players given between 1908 and 1924. He contributed to a symposium in the *Pall Mall Gazette* (31 August 1892) a series of responses to set questions that the editor was publishing under the title 'Why I Don't Write Plays'. Hardy cited as his reasons the conviction that a novel was a better way of 'getting nearer to the heart and meaning of things' than a play; the fact that parts had to be moulded to actors rather than the other way around; the unlikelihood that managers would support 'a truly original play'; the need to arrange scenes 'to suit the exigencies of scene-building'; and, more generally, the subordination of 'the presentation of human passions' 'to the presentation of mountains, cities, clothes, furniture, plate, jewels, and other real and sham-real appurtenances . . .' For the *Weekly Comedy* (30 November 1889), he argued that the 'regulation stage-presentation of life' impressed a middle-aged spectator thus: 'First act – it may be so; second act – it surely is not so; third – it cannot be so; fourth – ridiculous to make it so; fifth – it will do for the children.' Moreover, if one could only 'weed away the intolerable masses of scenery and costume', one might popularize the theatre among intelligent adults ('a good many hundred people'), who would be willing to come from considerable distances

to see a play performed in the following manner: – The ordinary pit boarded over to make a stage, so that the theatre would approach in arrangement the form of an old Roman amphitheatre, the scenery being simply a painted canvas hung in place of the present curtain, the actors performing in front of it, and disappearing behind it when they go off the stage; a horizontal canvas for sky or ceiling; a few moveable articles of furniture, or trees in boxes, as the case may be indoors or out; the present stage being the green room. The costumes to be suggestive of the time and situation, and not exclusively suggestive of what they cost.

Hardy always thought that censorship belonged to this list of depressing problems. On a later occasion he responded quickly to the appeal of John Galsworthy, who was accumulating documents that might be submitted to a Joint Committee of Lords and Commons, under the leadership of Lord Plymouth, to strengthen a campaign against irresponsible censorship. He wrote a letter to *The Times*, printed on 13 August 1909, to say that 'something or other – which probably is consciousness of the Censor – appears to deter men of letters, who have other channels for communicating with the public, from writing for the stage'. Even 'an eminently proper and moral subject' could not be brought on to the boards if the author in any way implied that conventions might or should be transgressed for the sake of fuller expression of 'natural feeling'.

Still, his play-going was ardent, and an important element in his crowded social life whenever he visited London. His writing of the longest, most ambitious work of his full half-century of creative endeavours was deeply indebted to his knowledge of classical and English theatre.

The sub-title for *The Dynasts*, however, refers to it as 'An Epic-Drama of the War with Napoleon', and the term suggests that the form in which Hardy cast the events of the critical decade of 1805–15 mingles elements of epic tradition with elements of dramatic composition; and that the process of mingling has required the coinage of a term to describe its genre.

The Dynasts has its literary antecedents in the great epics of the western world. Hardy, during the long period of gestation that preceded its writing, at one time thought of writing several ballads, about various campaigns, Moscow, and the Hundred Days, that he might entitle – once they had been brought together – 'An Iliad of Europe from 1789 to 1815'. This possibility, dated 1875, was recorded by Hardy as his 'earliest note', and although the epic he finally wrote began more appropriately with that moment of Napoleon's greatest arrogance, the hubris of the crowning at Milan in 1805, the fact of his familiarity with Homer, Virgil and Milton is worth stressing because the multiple original features of *The Dynasts* have misled some reviewers and critics into a judgement that Hardy, in this work at least, is a modernist comparable to Joyce, Proust, Kafka, Eliot and Pound. Hardy would not have thought so. Indeed, he found the developing tendencies of twentieth-century literature as depressing as Wordsworth, in an earlier age, had found the excess of those who were writing (and reading) imitative German shockers.

Yet though he fleetingly thought of *The Dynasts* as a work that might illustrate 'the difference between what things are and what they ought to be (stated as by a god to the gods – i.e. as God's story)', he also understood the dangers inherent in the temptation to write 'a Homeric Ballad, in which Napoleon is a sort of Achilles' (a note made on 27 March 1881). Such a 'ballad' would inevitably exalt Napoleon's life, and suggest that dynasts exercised a greater degree of control over the working-out of their own destinies than was compatible with Hardy's well-developed notions of a supreme and universal Will. Hardy adapted epic conventions for his own purposes. One fruitful approach to the task of understanding the dimensions of Hardy's achievement is to compare and contrast *The Dynasts* with *Paradise Lost*. He always considered Milton to be one of 'the illustrious', consulted his works frequently and mentioned *Paradise Lost* specifically in his preface to *The Dynasts*. But he was also interested in depicting the events of 1805–15 as 'a Great Modern Drama'. Working his way towards the appropriate tone ('spectral'), perspective ('A Bird's-Eye View of Europe at the beginning of the Nineteenth Century'), cast of characters ('Title: "A Drama of Kings"' and humanity as 'a collective personality'), structure (three parts, the first dealing largely with the aborted invasion of England, Ulm, Trafalgar, and Austerlitz; the second with the peace treaty signed at Tilsit and the Peninsular Campaigns; and the third with Wellington's final victories in Spain, the French invasion of Russia, Napoleon's retreat and abdication, and the Hundred Days), Hardy deliberately chose a 'play-shape'. As he wrote in the *Times Literary Supplement*, such a shape 'is essentially, if not quite literally, at one with the instinctive, primitive, narrative shape'.[3] Perhaps he exaggerated when he added, somewhat testily, 'The methods of a book and the methods of a play . . . are fundamentally similar.' Nevertheless his last effort to define the genre of *The Dynasts* – 'a spectacular poem . . . more or less resembling a stage-play, though not one'[4] – is at least as satisfactory as the definitions that were proposed by contemporary reviewers. Moreover it allows a reader some freedom of judgement on the question of whether Hardy was more interested in writing an epic than a drama. The coinage 'epic-drama', looked at more closely, seems a carefully chosen compromise.

In some ways, the problems associated with its unconventional form make *The Dynasts* as difficult to approach today as it must have been when Arthur Bingham Walkley, the distinguished literary and dramatic critic of *The Times* during the first quarter of this century, was trying to define its genre. Walkley was so baffled by its originality that he finally decided a semi-dramatic work which emphasized the inability of its major characters to act freely, and to shape their own destiny, might best be produced as a puppet-show. Despite Hardy's sense of outrage that Walkley, in a *TLS* review dated 29 January 1904, seemed to deny him the privilege of using dramatic conventions in a new way, Walkley's problem – perhaps best paraphrased in the following form, 'How are we to relate this work to Hardy's earlier literary achievements?' – is understandable. This epic-drama, consisting of three long parts, in turn made up of nineteen acts with one hundred and thirty-one scenes, span the full decade between 1805 and 1815 and include more than two hundred speaking rôles, not to mention hundreds of thousands of nameless civilians, attendant lords 'to swell a progress' and soldiers and sailors, demanded the kind of sympathetic patience that many reviewers did not have. *The Saturday Review* spoke harshly of 'many, slovenly, slipshod, uncouth verses, stilted in sentiment, poorly conceived and worse wrought', and concluded that Hardy, 'by his own deliberate act', had 'discredited that judgement on which his reputation rested'. George Meredith, an old friend, held serious reservations about Hardy's word-coinages. The *Spectator* (20 February 1904) identified phrases like 'an untactical torpid diplomacy' and 'the free trajection of our entities' as 'impossible in any music, aerial or otherwise', and Hardy hastily changed many such awkward constructions to more felicitous expressions in a revised edition of Part First (1904); the decision to publish Part First as a separate volume before the subsequent two parts had been more than outlined and partially written he subsequently regretted.[5]

Not that friendly reviews had been unknown, and Meredith, to whom Hardy had appealed for advice on whether to continue the vast project, encouraged him ('needlessly', Meredith wrote within parentheses in a letter dated 2 July 1905, a word that suggests Hardy had already made up his mind). Moreover the completion and publication of the second and third parts led to fuller understanding of his intentions, as well as a less carping appreciation of his accomplishments. Hardy's bitter note in his autobiography – 'The appraisement of the work was in truth, while nominally literary, at the core narrowly Philistine, and even theosophic' – reminds us, when it is related to the reviews of the poetry preserved in the Memorial Library at Dorchester, that Hardy was extraordinarily sensitive to adverse criticism, which he remembered to the exclusion of many of the favourable comments that appeared during the first decade of the century.

We need to look closer at the work itself, of course, to judge for ourselves. But some observations may well serve as preparation for that pleasurable task. The epic-drama has 10,553 lines (exclusive of the stage directions and the more than thirty dumb-shows), and is one of the longer poetical works in English literature.[6] Hardy, who had never written anything remotely resembling *The Dynasts* before, never attempted anything like it again. For the rest of his life he regarded it as his most ambitious undertaking and his greatest literary achievement. He gratefully acknowledged the birthday tribute (2 June 1921) sent to him by St John Ervine, and 'signed by a hundred and six younger writers', that concluded with the stirring sentences:

From your first book to your last, you have written in the 'high style, as when that men to kinges write', and you have crowned a great prose with a noble poetry.

We thank you, Sir, for all that you have written . . . but most of all, perhaps, for *The Dynasts*.[7]

It is perhaps no great praise in itself to say that *The Dynasts* is the fullest and most serious treatment in English imaginative literature of all that Napoleon's career meant to Europe. The few passages lamenting Napoleon's downfall in Byron's *Childe Harold's Pilgrimage*, the few chapters about Waterloo in Thackeray's *Vanity Fair*, and the less than a thousand lines of Meredith's *Odes in Contribution to the Songs of French History*, testify by their loneliness on the Victorian landscape to the puzzling fact that the cataclysmic aftermath of the French Revolution – the phenomenon of Napoleon – held very small appeal to major poets and novelists. (Robert Buchanan's *The Drama of Kings*, 1871, which treated many of the same events, has sometimes been identified as a source of *The Dynasts*; but it is a mediocre work, and Buchanan's interests were not focused, as Hardy's were, on England's rôle as Nemesis to Napoleon.) 'As far as English is concerned,' William R. Rutland has written, 'it is likely to remain without successors, as it was without forerunners. No major English poet before Hardy had cared to dedicate himself to that theme; and after Hardy none will either dare or desire to sing again the lay he sang once for all.'[8]

Writing towards the end of the century of *Pax Britannica* that Wellington's victory in Belgium had made possible, Hardy was keenly conscious of his originality. In the Preface to Part First, dated September, 1903, he reminisced about the publication of *The Trumpet-Major* in 1880: 'I found myself in the tantalizing position of having touched the fringe of a vast international tragedy without being able, through limits of plan, knowledge, and opportunity, to enter further into its events; a restriction that prevailed for many years.' Hardy went on to identify at least one major reason for beginning his work: 'But the slight regard paid to English influence and action throughout the struggle by so many Continental writers who had dealt with Napoleon's career, seemed always to leave room for a new handling of the theme which should re-embody the features of this influence in their true proportion.' So much has been written about the melancholy implications of the deterministic philosophical substructure of the work – mankind, the Spirit of the Years informs us in the Fore Scene, is made up of 'frail ones' who 'gyrate like animalcula/In tepid pools' – that it is all too easy to forget one of Hardy's primary intentions: to write a patriotic poem that would for the first time render justice to England's determined resistance against Napoleon's ambitions.

Hardy recognized the historical realities: Englishmen might desert on the battle-field, act from venal impulses at home, share a simple-minded relish over the unedifying scandals associated with the Prince Regent's behaviour. But *The Dynasts* is about heroes as well as puppets, and they are, for the most part, Englishmen, and three Englishmen in particular: Pitt and Nelson, whose lives are most important in Part First, and Wellington, who comes into his own in the final section. Hardy borrowed from his sources what appealed to his own sense of fitness of conduct: Pitt's thorough detestation of the anarchic self-interest that Napoleon's career symbolized, Nelson's knowledge that his destiny prevented him from acquiring permanent happiness ('the philosopher's stone no alchemy/Shall light on in this world I am weary of'),

Wellington's professional judgement at Waterloo that the French strategy 'looks a madman's cruel enterprise'. These men were giants, and one scholar's shrewd comment about Pitt – that at moments he exemplified free will not by reshaping events, but by transcending them[9] – might be equally well applied to his two fellow-Englishmen, and even to Fox, who, in an extraordinary scene (II, I, i), rejects on moral and ethical grounds the offer of a would-be assassin to rid the world of Napoleon. Moreover, Napoleon throughout the epic-drama recognizes that his most formidable opponent is England, architect and financier of a 'tough, enisled, self-centred, kindless craft' that ultimately undoes him. As other dynasts reel before Napoleon's onslaughts, rush to offer him concessions or even the hands of princesses to insure the principle of dynastic succession, or despair of their own future, they think of England as steadfast, unbribable, implacable. In the words of Pitt at the Guildhall and the Lord Mayor's banquet (versified by Hardy with little change from the scene recounted in Earl Stanhope's *Life of the Right Honorable William Pitt*):

> My lords and gentlemen: – You have toasted me
> As one who has saved England and her cause.
> I thank you, gentlemen, unfeignedly.
> But – no man has saved England, let me say:
> England has saved herself, by her exertions:
> She will, I trust, save Europe by her example!
>
> (I, V, v)

Finally, as evidence of the consistency with which Hardy chronicled as affirmative and magnificent the achievements of his ancestors (in the arms of his own relative, after all, the great Nelson had died), we should add that the Spirits, who speak in cutting terms of the pretensions to grandeur of Napoleon and all who follow him, are properly respectful of the heroic qualities of Pitt, Nelson and Wellington.

We have spoken of the Spirits, and it is time to identify them more clearly, for Hardy's resurrection of the celestial machinery of earlier epics was accomplished with full awareness that the religious faith of Milton's age, or for that matter of the Greeks or of the Vikings, had become an anachronism in the twentieth century. Anthropomorphic gods had vanished; men no longer spoke of God as 'He'; God now was thought of as 'the First or Fundamental Energy', and the monistic theory of the Universe made impossible 'the importation of Divine personages from any antique Mythology as ready-made sources or channels of causation, even in verse'. *The Dynasts* has compelling interest not only because Hardy is saying something about the most sanguinary decade of the nineteenth century that English writers had failed to say in imaginative and creative form, but because of his devising a set of 'phantasmal Intelligences', or Spirits, to function as 'the modern expression of a modern outlook'. He freely admitted that what he was doing with these 'impersonated abstractions, or Intelligences', diverged in significant ways 'from classical and other dramatic precedent which ruled the ancient voicings of ancient themes'.[10] He noted, in his Preface, that the Pities came closest to 'the spectator idealized' (he was quoting Schlegel) of the Greek Chorus, and that their views were deeply affected by events. Another group approximated 'the passionless Insight of the Ages', and included the Spirit of the Years, whose 'unpassioned essence' is perhaps best defined as Stoical. The names of the Spirits Sinister, Ironic and Rumour were self-explanatory. The Shade of the Earth functioned in some respects like Earth in *Prometheus Unbound*, and Shelleyan influences may be marked in several speeches by other Spirits.

The Spirits comment on the action. Sometimes they speak directly for Hardy; the game of determining exactly when they do has challenged critics for almost three quarters of a century. Occasionally they interfere with or shape the direction of human actions. (Hardy never committed himself to a complete or consistent 'universal necessity'.) And sometimes, too, they bring to human beings messages or intimations from the Immanent Will. Taken altogether, their invention is one of the notable features of a literary work filled with novel perceptions of an historical decade long taken for granted.

The Spirits are at the service of the Immanent Will and – privileged spectators though they be – inextricably meshed within its absent-minded weaving. Hardy believed until his death that the primary reason *The Dynasts* had been censured was *odium theologicum*; his philosophy – again overstated by his critics as 'pessimistic' – was he thought, the real bone of contention, and not the art, or lack of art, of his creative work. That philosophy had been attacked before, most notably in the outcry that greeted the sardonic notation about 'Justice' and 'the President of the Immortals' that Hardy devised to conclude the fifty-ninth chapter of *Tess*. Indeed, there is little in the concept or the descriptions of the Will in *The Dynasts* that could not have been anticipated from mutterings about Fate, the gods and the temporal nature of any human happiness in Hardy's earlier works. The images of an illuminated Will – as in that extraordinary scene in Milan Cathedral, when Napoleon places on his own head the crown of Lombardy and, in Hardy's words, 'there is again beheld as it were the interior of a brain which seems to manifest the volutions of a Universal Will, of whose tissues the personages of the action form portion' (I, I, vi) – do not alter the substance of the metaphor. Hardy's deterministic philosophy had settled into familiar tracks by the 1870s, and was, in fact, of a degree and kind familiar to many intellectuals of the age. Much has been made of Hardy's indebtedness to Schopenhauer and Von Hartmann, who had also written about a supreme and universal Will; but Hardy was at least equally under obligation to British philosophy, and in a letter to Helen Garwood he wrote, 'My pages show harmony of view with Darwin, Huxley, Spencer, Comte, Hume, Mill, and others, all of whom I used to read more than Schopenhauer.'[11] In fairness to Hardy – who generously acknowledged both the nature and extent of his borrowings throughout a half-century of authorship – one should note the justice of his repeated attribution of deterministic views to generations of speculators on the nature of 'the Cause of Things', including many of the Church Fathers,

St Paul, St Augustine and Calvin. Determinism was not a doctrine novel to the late Victorian age, nor popularized for the first time by Hardy.

Despite his disinclination to develop a 'systematized philosophy warranted to lift "the burthen of the mystery" of this unintelligible world', Hardy explored at greatest length, and most explicitly, the implications for himself – and for 'a great many ordinary thinkers', as he wrote to Alfred Noyes on 19 December 1920 – of a doctrine in which the Immanent Will governs all human action. This 'fixed foresightless dream' holds together all mankind, and Hardy says as much in the Fore Scene: 'the anatomy of life and movement in all humanity and vitalized matter' is exhibited 'as one organism'. Hardy was not consistent about the possibility of free will in such a universe, and his English heroes certainly behave as if their choices genuinely exist. Perhaps the fullest statement explaining the distinction between the gloomiest deterministic comments of the Spirits and the stubborn refusal of men to believe that all their behaviour is committed in advance may be found in a letter that Hardy wrote on his birthday (2 June 1907) to Edward Wright:

This theory, too, seems to me to settle the question of Free-will v. Necessity. The will of a man is, according to it, neither wholly free nor wholly unfree. When swayed by the Universal Will (which he mostly must be as a subservient part of it) he is not individually free; but whenever it happens that all the rest of the Great Will is in equilibrium the minute portion called one person's will is free, just as a performer's fingers are free to go on playing the pianoforte of themselves when he talks or thinks of something else and the head does not rule them.[12]

In three respects Hardy believed that his concept of the Prime Cause differed significantly from earlier treatments: for the first time the Will was personified in poetical literature; he described the Will as evolving and becoming aware of Itself; and this development, in turn, raised the possibility that the Will might some day become sympathetic towards the nobler ideals and aspirations of the human race. It is sometimes forgotten how resoundingly affirmative the final Chorus of the After Scene was intended to be:

> But – a stirring thrills the air
>   Like to sounds of joyance there
>   That the rages
>   Of the ages
> Shall be cancelled, and deliverance offered from the darts that were,
> Consciousness the Will informing, till It fashion all things fair!

No reader can afford to discuss Hardy's personal convictions about the nature of the 'rapt Determinator' that 'neither good nor evil knows' (II, VI, vii) on the basis of the novels, short stories and *Collected Poems* alone. If we know with reasonable confidence how to assess Hardy's personal views on the dilemma of men and women adrift in a friendless (and, worse, indifferent) universe, we do so by correlating a host of private statements, made in correspondence and conversation, with the more public musings of various *dramatis personae* in *The Dynasts*. Without *The Dynasts*, a great deal of uninformed and unsympathetic criticism of Hardy's achievement might still remain unchallenged.

There is, in brief, an extraordinary largeness of vision about this work, a grasp of the totality of the European community that has few, if any, counterparts in the post-Romantic poetry written by Hardy's contemporaries. The word 'cinematic' has sometimes been used to describe Hardy's descriptions of the Continent, as seen from a great height; the description contained in the Fore Scene is only the most famous of several equally spectacular views:

The nether sky opens, and Europe is disclosed as a prone and emaciated figure, the Alps shaping like a backbone, and the branching mountain-chains like ribs, the peninsular plateau of Spain forming a head. Broad and lengthy lowlands stretch from the north of France across Russia like a grey-green garment hemmed by the Ural mountains and the glistening Arctic Ocean.

The point of view then sinks downwards through space, and draws near to the surface of the perturbed countries, where the peoples, distressed by events which they did not cause, are seen writhing, crawling, heaving, and vibrating in their various cities and nationalities ...

Perhaps John Wain exaggerates by describing the entire work as a shooting-script, and by emphasizing the alternations between 'wide-angle shots' and 'close-ups' that contain dialogue, as if the completeness of Hardy's 'cinematic range' were, in itself, sufficient explanation of a reader's instinctive satisfaction that much has been imagined greatly in *The Dynasts*. But Wain's major argument, that Hardy's 'visual sense was always superb', is unexceptionable, and a reminder that metaphysics is being drama-tized, history is being recreated, a huge cast is going through its paces, *before our eyes*. Nothing less than such a soaring perspective can render justice to the naval struggle off Cape Trafalgar, where 'the broad face of the ocean is fringed on its eastern edge by the Cape and the Spanish shore'; or to Vimiero, where the English 'fight for their lives while sweating under a quarter-hundredweight in knapsack and pouch, and with firelocks heavy as putlogs ... the land abruptly terminating two miles behind their backs in lofty cliffs overhanging the Atlantic'; or to the Old West Highway out of Vienna, travelled by eighty carriages that look 'no more than a file of ants crawling along a strip of garden-matting'; or to the Ford of Santa Marta at Salamanca, crossed by infantry regiments during an electrical storm ('The lightning is continuous; the faint lantern in the ford-house is paled by the sheets of fire without, which flap round the bayonets of the crossing men and reflect upon the foaming torrent'); or to the brief interlude between battles at Mont Saint-Jean, in front of Waterloo, when the French 'lie down like dead men in the dripping green wheat and rye, without supper and without fire'.

For many readers, however, the primary attraction of *The Dynasts* will be related to what Hardy has done to the historical Napoleon. After all, much of the work was laboriously worked up from historical records, ranging from the twenty-volume *Histoire du Consulat et de l'Empire* by A. Thiers to brief and perhaps not wholly reliable newspaper accounts; much of the parliamentary debating and convoluted diplomatic manoeuvring that slow our reading pace are reconstructed from notes taken in the British Museum; details about dispositions of armies and battle tactics may sometimes seem excessive. Indeed, Hardy – in 1907 – spoke of himself as 'an old campaigner'. He works best with the people of Wessex and the speaking-roles of Londoners in the streets, and, as might be expected, convinces us completely of the authenticity of his ordinary soldiers and sailors.[13] Napoleon, however, is the central character; has the most lines; and obsesses the conversation of the Spirits no less than of his human contemporaries. Hardy could not afford either to take Napoleon's utterances at face value, or to present the Emperor as the Boney who, according to the woman at Rainbarrows' Beacon, Egdon Heath (I, II, v), 'lives upon human flesh, and has rashers o' baby every morning for breakfast – for all the world like the Cernel Giant in old ancient times!' Hardy's greatest challenge may well have been the feat of reconciling the Emperor's conviction that he dominated and shaped events with his own conviction that such men (in the words of the Spirit of the Years, as it looks down upon the Wood of Bossu after Waterloo):

> wade across the world
>   To make an epoch, bless, confuse, appal,
> and 'in the elemental ages' chart' are
> Like meanest insects on obscurest leaves
> But incidents and grooves of Earth's unfolding;
> Or as the brazeb rod that stirs the fire
> Because it must. (III, VII, ix)

It is no disservice to Hardy's memory, or even necessarily a commentary on the failings of the epic-drama, to note that he failed to stabilize these warring elements; that the richness of human personality remains almost as mysterious at poem's end as at the beginning; that the poem, in brief, does not *define* Napoleon. Nevertheless, Hardy's intention – that the reader should witness rather than dispute the workings of history – finds its main focus in Napoleon's dealings with his generals, fellow-dynasts and various women (Josephine, Queen Louisa of Prussia and Marie Louise). Those relationships are limned as shrewd, tinged by more than a little cruelty, and appallingly direct. Napoleon – a consummate liar and often a hypocrite – is not to be believed save in those moments when he soliloquizes; yet to an important degree his conviction that his personal ambition involves the destiny and glory of France makes him more than a mere opportunist. Moreover, Napoleon's career is marked by more than one moment of self-awareness that he may not control events: as in the scene at Milan Cathedral, where the Spirit of the Pities whispers in his ear (I, I, vi); or at the Bridge of Lodi; at Tilsit (II, I, viii); or on the banks of the Niemen, near Kowno (III, I, i), when the Emperor muses despondently on the workings of inexorable law.

The 'spectral questionings' which finally overwhelm him after the defeat of Waterloo
leads to his recognition that he

> came too late in time
> To assume the prophet or the demi-god,
> A part past playing now . . .
> Great men are meteors that consume themselves
> To light the earth . . . (III, VII, ix)

Hardy has shown in both the Second and Third Parts the moral deterioration of
Napoleon by means of a long series of images of physical decay. If at the end of his
career Napoleon can no longer be said to retain elements of greatness – in his own
words, Waterloo is his 'burnt-out hour' – he has been portrayed consistently as com-
plexly unpredictable and even, on occasion, open to self-doubts about his right 'to
shoulder Christ from out the topmost niche/In human fame . . .'

And at what a cost! In suffering, in dislocation of entire populations, in blasted
hopes, in mutilation and death: *The Dynasts* provides dozens of eloquent, heart-
rending images of what war, modern war, really means to those caught up within
its coils. Hardy was fully conscious of how glorious an appearance parading soldiers
could make, and even as late as Waterloo the Spirit of the Pities can say, of Ney's
cavalry charge (which the Spirit knows is foredoomed):

> Behold the gorgeous coming of those horse,
> Accoutred in kaleidoscopic hues
> That would persuade us war has beauty in it! (III, VII, iv)

But war is barbarous, and Hardy, in scene after scene of vivid slaughter, gives full
credit to its savagery. As the Emperor watches 'with a vulpine smile', a battery fires
on Russians crossing the ice covering the Satschan Lake: 'A ghastly crash and splash-
ing follows the discharge, the shining surface breaking into pieces like a mirror,
which fly in all directions. Two thousand fugitives are engulfed, and their groans of
despair reach the ears of the watchers like ironical huzzas.' (I, VI, iv). Many such
quotations might be amassed to show how, to the grim historical record, Hardy
added the poet's imaginative touch, as in the phrase 'like ironical huzzas'. Two
additional moments may be cited here to identify the commitment of the poet: II,
VI, iv, when the shattered limbs of the dead steam from their own warmth 'as the
spring rain falls gently upon them', followed by the deeply moving lamentation of
the Pities:

> *What man can grieve? what woman weep?*
> *Better than waking is to sleep! Albuera!*

And III, VI, viii, the second moment, when the Chorus of the Years, viewing the
cornfields around La Belle Alliance, reminds us of the unwilling creatures of the
field that are drawn into the insanity of men: coneys startled by thudding hoofs,

moles whose chambers are crushed by wheels, larks whose eggs are scattered, snails crushed:

> Trodden and bruised to a miry tomb
> Are ears that have greened but will never be gold,
> And flowers in the bud that will never bloom.

They too were present, and Hardy has written their testament.

The last long composition of Hardy's career was cast in a more conventional dramatic form than *The Dynasts*. Hardy began *The Famous Tragedy of the Queen of Cornwall* in 1916, after a visit to Tintagel which stirred up memories – perhaps never really forgotten – of the Lyonnesse where, in 1870, he had met his 'dearest Emmie'. For some reason inspiration faltered, and he set the romance aside; but after seven years he returned to it, completing a rough draft in April 1923. Publication by Macmillan, and production by the Hardy Players, followed a half-year later, and Hardy was to revise the play and enlarge the number of scenes on the basis of rehearsal experiences.

Hardy had called Emma 'an Iseult of my own', and told Sir Sydney Cockerell that she 'of course' had been 'mixed in the vision of the other'.[14] Autobiographical elements underlie the play like a granitic substratum. Hardy was recalling the scenery of Cornwall that he had already written about at length in *A Pair of Blue Eyes* (1873) and in a large number of lyrics. He wrote to Alfred Noyes (17 November 1923) that his play had been '53 years in contemplation'. The problem of a divided love – Tristram caught between the yearning of Iseult of the White Hands and the claims of Queen Iseult – may have been, during a crucial year, the question that tormented a younger Hardy whose engagement to Tryphena Sparks had not ended before he met and fell in love with Emma Lavinia Gifford. And the understandable bitterness of the Queen – one of Hardy's original contributions to the Tristram story – has suggested to more than one critic the strains in Hardy's marriage relationship during the last two decades of Emma's life.

Hardy freely adapted the varying versions of the legend by Malory, Bédier and Wagner to his own purpose, citing as his precedent the Greek dramatists, 'notably Euripides', and the play, no less than *The Dynasts*, is based upon a lifetime of readings in dramatic literature and active play-going. Merlin, who introduces the play – the rôle was created for T. H. Tilley of the Hardy Players, reminds the audience that the play is constructed of familiar materials: 'The tale has travelled far and wide . . .' The Chanters – 'Shades of Dead Old Cornish Men' and 'Shades of Dead Cornish Women' – are dressed 'as in the old mumming shows', and Hardy, referring to their function as that 'of a Greek Chorus to some extent',[15] obviously wanted them to speak monotonically, as he had specified in his Preface to *The Dynasts* for 'such plays of poesy and dream': 'with dreamy conventional gestures, something in the manner traditionally maintained by the old Christmas mummers, the curiously hypnotizing impressiveness of whose automatic style – that of persons who spoke by no will of their own – may be remembered by all who ever experienced it.' The setting of the play is the Great Hall of Tintagel Castle, 'round or at the end of which the audience sits'. Hardy's distaste for accessories on a stage had led him, on more than one earlier occasion, to advocate something very similar to theatre in the round, for only if spectators could sit 'to a great extent round the actors' would they be able to see the *play* (Hardy's emphasis); the appeal would then be to their imagination rather than to their eyesight. Moreover, Hardy took great pride in the fact that in this play dramatic time coincided perfectly with real time: '. . . the rule for staging nowadays should be to have no scene which would not be physically possible in the time of acting.'[16] His observance of the unities was more consistent here than in the only other occasion he remembered attempting it, in *The Return of the Native*. The effect of beginning the play just before the catastrophe was to intensify the inevitability of the final knotted action, in which three of the four major characters die.

Hardy's modernization is perhaps most original in its final moments, when the Queen stabs her husband Mark, leaps over the cliff while 'the wind rises, distant thunder murmuring', and Iseult the Whitehanded discovers the bodies of Mark and Tristram. It may be that Hardy, attempting to avoid historical accuracy ('it would have been impossible to present them as they really were, with their barbaric manners and surroundings') at the same time that he tried to avoid turning them into 'respectable Victorians' in the manner of Tennyson, Swinburne or Arnold, gave to his characters a clotted, uneasily mixed speech that over-complicates the task of dramatic presentation. It is not too surprising that a poet four-score and upwards should have found it necessary to intensify romantic passion by transcribing at least eight passages from his own *A Pair of Blue Eyes*.[17] But overall the elaborateness of the rhymes, the occasional soaring eloquence (as in the Queen's sad lyrics, vii, and Tristram's song, xi) and Hardy's continuing control of theatrical elements are impressive for this hour's traffic on the stage. Minor work it may be, but there are several moments of dark beauty that finally stir in the audience a genuine sense of pity for the plight of Iseult the Whitehanded. It is no mean achievement to close an illustrious career with a recension of one of the greatest love stories of the western world that so originally and masterfully illustrates, on so many fronts, Hardy's familiarity with and love of the theatre.

NOTES

1. The painting is reproduced in *Concerning Thomas Hardy*, edited by D. F. Barber (London: Charles Skilton Ltd, 1968), following p. 136.
2. Carl J. Weber, *Hardy of Wessex: His Life and Literary Career* (Hamden, Conn.: Archon Books, 1962), pp. 246–57.
3. *Thomas Hardy's Personal Writings*, edited by Harold Orel (London: Macmillan, 1967), p. 142.
4. Ibid., p. 145.

5. *One Rare Fair Woman: Thomas Hardy's Letters to Florence Henniker 1893–1922*, edited by Evelyn Hardy and F. B. Pinion (London: Macmillan, 1972), p. 114. Cf. Richard Little Purdy's *Thomas Hardy: A Bibliographical Study* (London: Oxford, 1954), p. 122.

6. The total consists of 1470 lines of prose, 7931 of blank verse, and 1152 of rhymed verse. Thirty rhyme-schemes are used. Elizabeth Cathcart Hickson, *The Versification of Thomas Hardy* (Philadelphia: University of Pennsylvania, 1931), pp. 86–90.

7. Florence Emily Hardy, *The Life of Thomas Hardy 1840–1928* (London: Macmillan, 1962), p. 413.

8. William R. Rutland, *Thomas Hardy: A Study of His Writings and Their Background* (New York: Russell and Russell Inc., 1962), p. 271.

9. Walter F. Wright, *The Shaping of The Dynasts: A Study in Thomas Hardy* (Lincoln: University of Nebraska Press, 1967), p. 150.

10. A full study of the ways in which Hardy differentiated his Spirits is contained in J. O. Bailey's *Thomas Hardy and the Cosmic Mind: A New Reading of The Dynasts* (Chapel Hill: University of North Carolina Press, 1956).

11. *Thomas Hardy's Personal Writings*, p. 23.

12. *Life*, p. 335.

13. Wright, *The Shaping of the Dynasts*, pp. 124–27.

14. *Friends of a Lifetime: Letters to Sydney Carlyle Cockerell*, edited by Viola Meynell (London: Jonathan Cape, 1940), p. 284.

15. *Life*, p. 423.

16. Ibid., p. 234.

17. Reginald Snell, 'A Self-Plagiarism by Thomas Hardy', *Essays in Criticism*, II (January, 1952), 114–17.

PART 3

The genius of Thomas Hardy

🌿 *Hardy's Wessex*

DENYS KAY-ROBINSON

In Chapter L of the original serial version of *Far from the Madding Crowd*, published in the *Cornhill Magazine* for November 1874, occurred the words, 'Greenhill was the Nijnii Novgorod of Wessex'. It is a momentous date in the world created by Thomas Hardy: not because of the surprising comparison (Greenhill is Weatherbury Hill close to Bere Regis), not even because of the spelling of Nijni Novgorod, but because this was the first time Hardy had used the term 'Wessex'.

As evolved by him it signifies neither the Wessex of history nor (as some publicists imply) an alias for the County of Dorset. In fact it covers six counties: Berkshire (North Wessex), Hampshire (Upper Wessex), Wiltshire (Mid-Wessex), Dorset (South Wessex), Somerset (Outer Wessex), and Devon (Lower Wessex); Cornwall, rather unexpectedly in view of Hardy's early associations, is not part of Wessex, but Off-Wessex. He was specific about these boundaries; when Jude goes to Christminster (Oxford), it is carefully stated that he leaves Wessex to enter the city; the poem 'The Abbey Mason', set in Gloucester, invites us to 'take a brief step' beyond Wessex to visit the cathedral. What Hardy would have thought about the recent boundary changes, which take Lumsdon (Cumnor), Alfredston (Wantage), Cresscombe (Letcombe Bassett), the Brown (Red) House, and even worst of all Marygreen (Fawley), out of North Wessex into the outer darkness of Oxfordshire, does not bear contemplation.

As a modern literary expression the name Wessex was not coined by Hardy, although a sentence in his 1895 preface to *Far from the Madding Crowd* implies that he thought it was. William Barnes had used it in its proper historical sense in 1844 and in Hardy's picturesque sense in 1868 (in the preface to *Poems of Rural Life in Common English*).

Hardy's originality was in extending it to the whole of south-west England east of the Tamar, and in popularizing it into an everyday term.

He had already embarked on the nomenclature that was to go with the Wessex conception. Indeed, the general reader today may be excused for thinking he had never used anything else, since even in *Desperate Remedies*, his first published novel, some of the 'regulars' appear: Casterbridge, Knapwater House, Budmouth Regis, Tolchurch. But for several years yet they were to be used alongside earlier codenames that were gradually discarded as the definitive list grew. Thus in *An Indiscretion in the Life of an Heiress* (1878) Weymouth turns up as Melport instead of

Budmouth, Stinsford is not yet Mellstock but Tollamore, and Kingston Maurward (Knapwater) House makes its debut as Tollamore House.

Now and then he devised a name in his definitive code, but later, it seems, switched its application from one village to another. Lower Longpuddle in *Under the Greenwood Tree* and *Far from the Madding Crowd*, both early works, stands unmistakably for Puddletown, otherwise coded as Weatherbury. The latter novel actually contains the phrase, referring to Puddletown, 'Weatherbury, or Lower Longpuddle as it was sometimes called'. But a couple of decades later, when 'A Few Crusted Characters' appeared, a careful examination of the internal evidence results in the firm conclusion that Lower Longpuddle now stands for Piddlehinton. Similarly Trantridge in *Tess of the D'Urbervilles* can only be Pentridge, an interpretation confirmed by its position on Hardy's own Wessex map. But again in 'A Few Crusted Characters', in the anecdote called 'The Adventures of George Crookhill', Trantridge refers to a place on the main Salisbury–Blandford road where there is an inn. Neither of these requirements is filled by Pentridge, and the most probable candidate is Tarrant Hinton, especially since in the first version of the story the fictional name is Tranton.

But in the main once Hardy had decided on his Wessex nomenclature he kept to it, and we are left to play the pleasant game of identifying the reality beneath each disguise. Many pseudonyms are straightforward, either genuine archaic names – Shaston for Shaftesbury, Ivell for Yeovil, Durnover (from the Roman Durnovaria) for Fordington – or sufficiently like the real name to be easily translated – Abbots Cernel for Cerne Abbas, Stagfoot Lane for Hartfoot Lane, Evershead for Evershot. Others are derived from topographical features – Kennetbridge for Newbury, a town with a bridge over the River Kennet; Havenpool for Poole, conspicuous for its large natural harbour; Cresscombe for Letcombe Bassett, a village formerly noted for the growing of watercress. History, personal or otherwise, is sometimes involved – Marygreen for Fawley, where Hardy's paternal grandmother, Mary Head, spent some unhappy childhood years; Alfredston for Wantage, birthplace of King Alfred.

Other code-names that present little difficulty are those of places described so accurately that their identity can hardly be in question, or with which Hardy is known to have been associated at the time when he was preparing the relevant piece of writing. No one, for example, could have any doubt at all that Mellstock is Stinsford, or that almost every building mentioned in *Under the Greenwood Tree* relates to the author's birthplace and the scenes most familiar to him since childhood, or that the locations in *A Pair of Blue Eyes* spring from his acquaintance with north Cornwall during his architectural and courtship missions to St Juliot. The where-abouts of a fictionalized place are often indicated, too, by Hardy's practice of retaining the real names of large cities – Bath, Bristol, Southampton – and most natural features – High Stoy Hill, Blackmoor Vale, the River Froom (or Frome).

One is bound to ask why Hardy should have gone to the trouble of weaving this great tapestry of semi-disguise – for 'semi' most of it is. Not that he is exceptional among novelists in obscuring settings based on real places. Scott, George Eliot, the

Brontës, to name a few, adopted the device when it suited them. But no one pursued it to the same extent. The explanation lies partly in his feeling that he was freer to make fictional changes in a real-life scene if he gave it a fictional name; for it should never be forgotten that Hardy's Wessex, however valuable a picture of nineteenth-century south-western England it provides, is essentially – perhaps paradoxically – a fictional creation, a dream-world in which fact and fancy are as inseparably inter-twined as the twisting patterns in a piece of marble. So precise does Hardy seem, that it is all but impossible not to forget this occasionally. Carl Weber, one of the most notable Hardy scholars and biographers, fell into the trap and elaborated a theory that all the major Wessex novels were carefully dated to give a continuous picture of Wessex life during the greater part of the nineteenth century. But Hardy's dates are as frequently adapted to his fictional needs as his scenes, and the more Weber's theory is examined the less tenable it becomes.

The other reason for Hardy's play with names is that not infrequently it was politic to disguise the setting of a story in order to avoid giving offence. We come across this first in *A Pair of Blue Eyes*, in which, to conceal the relationship of the narrative to his courtship, he transformed St Juliot into West Endelstow, thus affording himself the opportunity of doubly disguising it by transplanting it nearer the coast. Only in extreme cases did he forgo his preference for a basis of reality and create a place entirely from imagination: The Slopes, home of the nefarious Alec d'Urberville in *Tess*, is one such, and another, in the same novel, is The Herons at Sandbourne (Bournemouth), scene of Alec's murder.

Probably disguised rather than invented, but so heavily veiled that they have yet to be uncovered, are the settings of some of the stories collected in *A Group of Noble Dames*. Scholarly opinion about the collection ranges from derision of the very notion that they could have any factual basis (an attitude that involves discrediting the great John Hutchins, in whose pages the substance of several of the tales is to be found), to the assertion that every tale had its origin in the annals of a well-known family. Since the tales are – or were by the standards of the time – mainly derogatory to the families presented in them, any real family recognizing itself would certainly not have been pleased. Indeed, at least one story – 'The First Countess of Wessex', based unequivocally on the early history of the Earls of Ilchester – caused a great deal of offence in the Ilchester household, and Hardy was forgiven only after a number of years. As to whether the remaining tales (other than those culled from Hutchins) had a factual basis, on three distinct occasions Hardy stated that they did, and in an apparently unpublished article now in the Dorset County Museum one Sidney Heath, writing in 1906, declared all the stories to be transcripts of official documents put into a form of fiction. In a follow-up article he went further, and said they were true down to the minutest detail. According to Heath the head of one family con-cerned ordered all books by Hardy found in the house to be burnt in the courtyard, another threatened to dismiss any servant found bringing a Hardy work on to the premises, and a third forbade the local bookseller to sell Hardy.

If we are to take Heath seriously, a complication arises, for he heads his article 'How Thomas Hardy Offended the County Families of Dorset'; yet of the stories not derived from Hutchins 'The Marchioness of Stonehenge' is seemingly set at Wilton, Wiltshire, 'The Lady Icenway' in Hampshire, with allusions to Somerset, 'The Honourable Laura' in north Devon, and 'The Duchess of Hamptonshire' possibly in Wiltshire. Should Heath properly have rendered his title '. . . Dorset and Other Parts of Wessex', or does he imply that for his most dangerous narratives Hardy took the double precaution of not only disguising the names of the real places but lifting them out of Dorset altogether? Only one of the stories contains much descriptive detail, and this one is also interesting because Hardy published it, under different titles and with minor changes, no fewer than three times. In the final (and volume) version it appears as 'The Duchess of Hamptonshire'.

Here the action takes place at Batton Castle, which is closely described. In the first version, 'The Impulsive Lady of Croome Castle', the same building was Croome Castle. In the middle version 'Emmeline, or Passion versus Principle', it was Stroome Castle. On some, but not all, of the endpaper maps in the Wessex and Pocket Editions of Hardy's works, Batton Castle is marked in the approximate position of Tottenham House, the former seat of the Marquises of Ailesbury in Savernake Forest, east Wiltshire; on the other maps it is omitted altogether. But neither the present Tottenham House nor its predecessor bears the smallest resemblance to Batton/Croome, nor have the events in the story any counterpart in the private annals of the Ailesburys. Again, Batton seems suspiciously like a contraction, along typical Hardy lines, of Badminton, particularly since Croome Castle could have been suggested by Castle Coombe, only a few miles away. But just as with Tottenham House, neither the present Badminton House nor its predecessor answers to the description, and the Beauforts of Badminton repudiate any connection with the narrative.

I have gone thus extensively into the topographical puzzle of this minor work because it is an outstanding example of Hardy's capacity for drawing on the world of reality, yet covering his tracks almost impenetrably when he chose. The key to 'The Duchess of Hamptonshire' may well involve a Dorset family, a building in, say, Somerset, amid surroundings drawn from Wiltshire. 'The Withered Arm' is a story of which Hardy himself vouched for the truth, yet the events recounted in it are not to be found in any Dorset records, and it has been suggested that their factual basis may have become known to Hardy while in Scotland. In *The Woodlanders* Hintock House is a portrayal of a real building, but the prototype (now demolished) stood at Turnworth, several miles east of the main area covered by the novel. The Stancy Castle of *A Laodicean* occupies the position of Dunster Castle, Somerset, but the features of the building are derived from Corfe and Sherborne, the church is that of Puddletown, and the pictures are those on exhibition at the time at Kingston Lacy.

The most elusive of landscapes in the greater novels is that of *The Woodlanders*, partly because Hardy changed many of the locations between editions. Originally Little Hintock was laid somewhere between Melbury Osmond and Bubb Down, but later it was shifted several miles east, close to High Stoy, and of course other places had to go east with it to preserve their relative positions. The reason for the shift was lest the dubious Mrs Charmond be identified by readers with any member of the Ilchester family, whose disapproval Hardy was about to risk (and as we have seen, soon won) with the publication of 'The First Countess of Wessex'; for originally Hintock House had occupied the site of Melbury House, the Ilchester family seat. To the end of his life, although long reconciled with the Ilchesters, he preferred not to have *The Woodlanders* scenes too closely analysed. As late as 1926, two years before his death, he could still deny in a letter that he knew where Little Hintock was, and the list of hamlets that he names as having helped to supply its features spans the terrain from the old setting to the new.

The Woodlanders more than any of his other prose writings illustrates Hardy's capacity for observing nature in close detail, and for remembering the interpretations of what he saw given him by those even nearer to the land than he was. The reader constantly comes across fascinating details such as that young firs are always planted with their longest roots towards the prevailing wind in order to withstand gales, or that pheasants roost towards the outer end of the bough when the weather is set fine, but huddle close to the trunk when storms are due. Small wonder so many people have quoted the poem 'Afterwards' with its key line, 'He was a man who used to notice such things'. Yet his knowledge was almost wholly of countryman's lore as distinct from naturalist's scholarship. His descriptions are devoid of technical comment; his flowers rarely have even English names.

His belief in the effect of environment on human behaviour is little surprising in one whom his own environment had influenced so profoundly during his boyhood. If in the celebrated opening pages of *The Return of the Native* he gives one the impression that Egdon Heath – a stretch of moorland hardly larger than a good-sized park – is as vast as Dartmoor and as desolate as Bodmin, that is because this is how it had seemed to the boy brought up on its fringe, and the adult was reliving the boy's impressions. Among the major novels, only in *Jude the Obscure*, written at the close of Hardy's prose career, is one allowed to feel that factors other than the Wessex scene predominate in determining the characters' actions, perhaps because in that novel the settings are too many and too varied. Hardy could even go one better and make us feel the power of a place while scarcely introducing man at all. His most forceful piece of descriptive prose is probably the so-called short story 'A Tryst at an Ancient Earthwork': 'so-called' because it is virtually an essayist's account of Maiden Castle by day, by night and during a thunderstorm, with the human element of no more moment than the traditional figures in a landscape painting. Yet no reader of this short piece can doubt Hardy's belief in the influence of the great earthwork on anyone coming into close or prolonged contact with it.

When Henchard, in *The Mayor of Casterbridge*, uses it as a vantage-point from which to observe the meetings between Elizabeth Jane and Farfrae on the Weymouth road, he is too preoccupied and his contact too brief for the fortress to affect him. Furthermore in this novel of great technical brilliance the author has already enlarged on the significance of using Maumbury Rings as a rendezvous, and wisely avoids making the same points about a second ancient enclosure. *The Mayor of Casterbridge* is interesting on several counts relevant to the subject of Wessex. It demonstrates that in Hardy's view the influence of environment is not confined to that of natural environment, but can be as potently exerted by a town; it illustrates his great interest in the past, whether the remote past of the Romans or the period of his own childhood; and it is an example of his taste for centring his major novels round one or two leading rural activities. Here it is the workings of a corn-marketing town; in *The Woodlanders*, thatching and cider-making; in *Far from the Madding Crowd*, sheep and arable farming; in *Tess of the D'Urbervilles*, dairy farming; in *The Trumpet-Major*, water milling; in *Under the Greenwood Tree*, the work of the village musicians; in *The Return of the Native*, the pursuits of the heath dwellers; and, to a lesser extent, in *Jude the Obscure*, the work of the mason.

Each of these books provides a vivid and as a rule detailed picture of the respective occupations, of much value to the student of Wessex social history; but not until *The Woodlanders* (1887), the eleventh of Hardy's fourteen published novels, is the reader made aware that the 'peasants' experienced any hard times. True, the Mellstock Quire was disbanded, to be replaced by various successive forms of organ, at about the time when the real Stinsford musicians suffered the same fate; but this is not in the same category as the problem of low agricultural wages and atrocious conditions, or of the disappearance of the self-contained community with its group of traders and craftsmen. The *Greenwood Tree* yokels and their successors in *Far from the Madding Crowd* are authentic enough under the veil of good-humoured caricature, but there is no indication that they have any problems of getting enough to eat or maintaining a roof – let alone a sound roof – over their heads, or keeping their children warm in winter. They seem never to have heard of the agricultural riots of 1830, well within the lifetime of the older folk, or of the Friendly Society of Agricultural Labourers formed by the Loveless brothers, or even of the Tolpuddle Martyrs.

In his long article 'The Dorsetshire Labourer' (1883), commissioned for *Longmans Magazine* as one of a series from different authors and the only lengthy non-fictionalized dissertation on the economic condition of the agricultural worker that Hardy ever wrote, he displays curiously little sense of the real position, and can have fired little indignation in those accustomed to regard him as the man who had put the Dorset 'peasant' on the public map. And when, with what at the time must have seemed startling suddenness, he introduced Giles Winterborne in *The Woodlanders* as a figure round which to build a passionate exposition of the plight of the cottage lifeholders, a theme which he developed even more vividly in *Tess*, it was still not the real labourers whose cause he was pleading, but the craftsman/tradesman class just above them.

Certainly the policy of ending the lifeholds had become prevalent enough to need exposure in popular form. The system was one under which a family was granted occupation of a cottage until the last of three specified persons died. The tenure could be prolonged by application to the manor court for leave to insert a new 'life' for one that had expired; but there was no obligation on the court to consent, and the policy in the middle of the nineteenth century was for fewer and fewer to do so; in 1842, for instance, the manor court of Fordington entered on a policy of refusing all renewals outright, although Fordington was part of the royal Duchy of Cornwall. The result (as in *Tess*) was families rendered homeless and forced to migrate, generally to the towns, while their cottages were pulled down, sometimes almost before they had left them. And since these 'livier' households were those of the village blacksmith, shoe-maker, wheelwright, itinerant salesman (precursor of the village shopkeeper) and all the other craftsmen who had made each village an almost independent community, their expulsion was one more factor in bringing about the drastic alteration of the centuries-old rural pattern that took place during Hardy's novel-writing years.

Yet the plight of this class – the class, incidentally, from which Hardy himself had sprung – was certainly no worse than that of the farmworker. Not only was he at the bottom of the social scale, he was at the bottom of the economic scale as well, with no hope – at least before about 1870 – of rising in either. Dorset agricultural wages, at one time only seven shillings a week, were among the lowest in England. Families were crowded into cottages far too small for them even had the buildings been sound – the 'model' cottages of Milton Abbas, built by the First Earl of Dorchester to house the population of the town he was about to erase, were as overcrowded as any. In fact the majority were on the point of collapse and sometimes did collapse, like part of Swithin St Cleeve's grandmother's in *Two on a Tower*; the type of hovel familiar in the paintings of such artists as George Morland is no romantic exaggeration. Rheumatism, typhus and tuberculosis were common, clothing and bedding ragged and verminous. Sanitation was of course non-existent.

All this was true even during the so-called Golden Age of agriculture during the 1850s and 1860s. But already a change was taking place. Because the repeal of the Corn Laws had opened the way for huge imports of grain from overseas, particularly from the United States, more and more livestock farming was being substituted for arable – the prominence of dairy farming in Dorset as depicted in *Tess* is a true picture; and the old-style historian's account of the great depression of the 1870s is now recognized as largely a depression suffered only by the farmers who stuck to grain. Meanwhile labour had become increasingly migratory, and by the early 1870s more and more farmhands were accepting the advice of Joseph Arch, the leading advocate of power through the trade union, and refusing to bind themselves by long-term contracts. At long last the more intelligent agricultural workers were beginning to see the possibility of breaking free from their centuries of serfdom, and they were right. Thirty years later Hardy could write (in a letter) of labourers' cottages with carpeted, brass-rodded stairs, a piano in the parlour and sons learning dancing.

As a humanitarian he approved these changes, but as an author and poet, a senti-
mentalist and lover of the past, he deeply regretted the passing – for it was no less – of
the world in which he had grown up. Not for nothing was *The Mayor of Casterbridge*,
written just after he had established himself at Max Gate, set not in the Dorchester to
which he had returned, but in that which he had left. Never was he more sincere than
when he turned his speech on receiving the freedom of Dorchester (1910) into a catalogue of the buildings whose disappearance he deplored and a plea for the preservation of everything of value that remained, despite the fact that all preservation was in
a sense an illusion, since without its occupants a house was but a shell. 'Where is the
Dorchester of my early recollection – I mean the human Dorchester . . . the faces that
used to be seen at the doors, the inhabitants, where are they?'

The answer we might fairly give is, in the pages of his prose and – let it not be
overlooked – his verse. Hardy once said that there was more autobiography in his
poems than in all his novels; he could also have said – and it may surprise some who
are less conversant with Hardy the poet than with Hardy the novelist – that there are
more vignettes of real Wessex people in his verses as well. I do not mean only the
identifiable people – Emma, Tryphena Sparks, Horace Moule, Hardy's parents and
grandparents, his early loves and many others; but the *unidentifiable* people, who we
may be sure are no less factual. Hardy himself admitted the semi-historical nature of
'A Trampwoman's Tragedy', but who were the protagonists in the incident that
inspired 'The Fight on Durnover Moor', for instance, or 'The Slow Nature' or 'By
the Barrows' or the almost unbearably poignant 'The Mongrel', or a hundred other
anecdotal poems? We shall never know, but we do know enough of Hardy's methods
to feel confident that each of these verse narratives arose out of something he had
seen, heard tell of or read in a newspaper, probably the *Dorset County Chronicle*. In any
case, the identity of the characters does not matter; what does, is that cumulatively
the poems of this type give a picture of everyday Wessex people and events that is
more vivid than any learned treatise on social history.

Weddings, funerals, broken betrothals, the problem of the illegitimate baby,
legends, customs, men and women at work and at play, all have their place in Hardy's
poetic record of the Wessex he knew. And naturally, since this is Hardy, the record
includes observation of most moods, seasons and facts of nature. All the splendid
descriptive passages in *The Woodlanders* do not bring the Dorset countryside more
clearly before our eyes than, say, 'Growth in May' or 'The Darkling Thrush'. Tess's
distress at the wounded pheasants does not illustrate Hardy's humanity towards all
living creatures more tellingly than 'The Blinded Bird' or 'Last Words to a Dumb
Friend'.

Hardy's Wessex does not consist merely of places. It consists of people and all
manner of living things, but so integral to, or at least influenced by, their environment
that one is left convinced they could exist nowhere else. Perhaps we gain an
exaggerated impression from subtly exaggerated truth; it is, as I wrote earlier, a
dream-world we are offered, a landscape not photographed but painted by a master.

There is no escaping this paradox of a panorama so historically true yet so uniquely of its creator's devising.

And what is left of it today, more than 130 years after the events of *Under the Greenwood Tree*, getting on for a century after the misadventures of Tess, half as long since Hardy penned the last of his poems? Already, with nearly two decades of his life to run, Hardy was as we have seen bitterly lamenting the passing of so much that he had known. In truth he had deplored some changes much earlier, as for instance the coming of the railway and with it the latest London popular music to oust the old country songs. By the time of his speech on receiving the freedom of Dorchester the railways had reached their zenith, the motor-car was no longer a novelty, the cinema was rapidly gaining ground. In addition to the changes in the agricultural way of life already noted there had been extensive mechanization (acknowledged by Hardy with the introduction of the threshing machine in *Tess*, and even the seed-drill in *The Mayor of Casterbridge*). Workfolk on the farms, though still among the lowest paid – as they remain today – had discovered the power latent in organization and were no longer serfs.

Today, of course, all these changes fade into insignificance compared with what has happened since. And yet the visual differences between modern Wessex and the factual world underlying Hardy's creation are fewer than one might expect from the drastic revolution in the way of life. The lorries and coaches that choke Dorchester's High East and High West Streets are not a fundamental departure from the waggons and carriers' vans that choked it (at any rate on market days) in Henchard's time. We may still identify the prototype of his house, now a bank, his granary, now a printing works, Lucetta's house, now municipal offices, and many more places from Christminster to Endelstow. Hog Hill is still as lonely as when the Three Strangers had their encounter there, though Fennel's cottage has vanished. Fawley is still recognizable as Marygreen and over by the main road a brief stretch of extra deep hedgerow still marks the garden of the first home assigned by Hardy to Jude and Arabella. The old fairs have gone (save at Priddy) but at Weydon-Priors (Weyhill) some of the livestock sheds survive, and the local pub preserves a drovers' room marked 'DR' on the door, with a room alongside for their dogs. On three days in October a pleasure fair fills Salisbury (Melchester) Market Place as it did when the Harnhams lived there in 'On the Western Circuit'. A few changes would have gladdened Hardy: Poxwell (Oxwell) Manor is now a completely reconditioned wealthy residence, a far cry from the dilapidated farmhouse of the Trumpet-Major's day, and it is only one of many farmhouses, formerly manors, that have been similarly rehabilitated.

But the most rewarding links are the old people. It is not hard to find people who knew Hardy – after all, he died less than fifty years ago – or even Emma Lavinia (died 1912), but there are still a few, if you can trace them, whose memories go back to the period of Jude at least, and who recall clearly what their fathers told them about the decades before that. To listen to one of these is indeed to re-enter Hardy's Wessex as Hardy knew it.

Hardy and Cornwall

A. L. ROWSE

Cornwall was immensely important in Hardy's imagination, and even more in his life; for it was there that he met his wife, Emma Lavinia Gifford. Their story began in romance – there could not be a more romantic background: St Juliot, the Valency Valley going tortuously down to Boscastle; Tintagel Castle; the savage cliffs, the sounding surges of the sea. Their courtship came up against opposition from Emma's father; her obstinate belief in Hardy's genius meant everything to him, she helped him forward – to begin with, he was almost as indebted to her as Elgar was to his wife. Then, with the years, estrangement set in – there were no children; Emma was conventional, religious, bent on being a lady. Hardy was lower-class in manner and never lost his sense of social inferiority; on the other hand, he had the courage of his convictions, to challenge religious and social conventions, a radical in his disbelief. His wife was appalled and, estranged, lapsed into sullenness; Hardy's lack of sexual potency may have been an element in her alienation. In her last years she was almost insane, certainly subject to delusions. That was what Hardy had to live with: the fate became a doom.

Nothing entered so deeply into his soul; their life together lasted nearly forty years. When she died in November 1912 Hardy was thrown into poignant remorse and grief; a backward-looking man, whose creative genius sprang out of nostalgia for the past, he at once went back in mind to what their love had been at the beginning, when all seemed fair. A couple of months later – as he remarks himself, forty-three years almost to a day from his first visit – he went back a *revenant* to those scenes. It was then that he wrote the moving series of poems – some of them among his finest – which appear as 'Poems of 1912–13' in *Satires of Circumstance*, and in the succeeding volume, *Moments of Vision*. There are some fifty of these poems. Another group of a dozen or so appears in *Late Lyrics and Earlier*, some of them inspired by his last visit to the spot in 1916, and even a few in *Human Shows and Far Phantasies*. The flame is hardly extinguished with his octogenarian *Winter Words*, for there was his last verse-drama, inspired by Tintagel and the theme he had most at heart. Altogether there must be some eighty poems, a considerable part of his poetic output. They constitute a poignant story of a relationship that turned from joy to anguish – for inspiration and for suffering alike there is no doubt of the debt Hardy owed to her.

It is sometimes held that Hardy was unduly secretive about his life. In fact the extraordinary thing is how much he has told us, in his own terms, for one who was eminently a Victorian, concerned to keep a gentlemanly code in such matters and was by nature reserved. But he was also a penurious, saving soul; in consequence he made use of everything in his work, not a thing was lost – and in the end, he has told us *everything*. It is more possible to do this in poetry – for say a thing in verse, and most people do not know what it means; one can get away with anything.

He told the beginning of it in his novel *A Pair of Blue Eyes*; this is well known, but less so how many circumstances and details of actual experience he wove into it. The plot was of course concocted; more revealing are the ironies of circumstance, to which Hardy was so much attached, while his sensitiveness to atmosphere is equal to Scott or Dickens. 'He was one who used to notice such things': his memory was extraordinarily retentive of every detail. His famous poem of 1915, 'In Time of "The Breaking of Nations"':

> Only a man harrowing clods
>   In a slow silent walk
> With an old horse that stumbles and nods
>   Half asleep as they stalk.

goes right back to the scene he observed in the Valency Valley from the rectory garden, when he heard the news of the battle of Gravelotte in 1870.

All told then, there is the impact of Cornwall on his life and, through that, on his work in general; then there are the specific pieces, in prose – the novel, and an unimportant short story, 'A Mere Interlude', set in the Scilly Isles and Penzance; in verse – some eighty poems, many of them unrecognized, and his last work, *The Famous Tragedy of the Queen of Cornwall*.

Cornwall was to him not a part of Wessex; it lay beyond the border of his kingdom. 'The place is pre-eminently (for one person at least) the region of dream and mystery. The ghostly birds, the pall-like sea, the frothy wind, the eternal soliloquy of the waters, the bloom of dark purple cast that seems to exhale from the shoreward precipices, in themselves lend to the scene an atmosphere like the twilight of a night vision.' Thus, in the 1895 preface to the romance, which he would have liked to call *Elfride of Lyonnesse*. (Shades of the best-seller, Sir Walter Besant, with his *Armorel of Lyonnesse*!)

He describes his first visit to St Juliot in March 1870. How, 'rising at four in the morning, and starting by starlight', he did not reach Launceston till four in the afternoon, whence he drove the additional sixteen miles along that exposed moorland road towards Boscastle. This becomes:

> When I set out for Lyonnesse,
>   A hundred miles away,
>   The rime was on the spray,
> And starlight lit my lonesomeness
> When I set out for Lyonnesse
>   A hundred miles away . . .

We perceive that watching the transmutation of detail from prose autobiography into poetry throws light on the creative process itself: the process is mysterious, but the fact is obvious. There is nothing more obtuse than to say that the biographical and the personal have no importance for understanding the work of art.

Hardy goes on to tell the beginning of the story that ended so ill:

> When I came back from Lyonnesse
>> With magic in my eyes,
>> All marked with mute surmise
> My radiance rare and fathomless,

What he had found there was love, and in it his fate; the tragic colouring of his life, and out of that the inspiration of much of his work.

I

The occasion of his coming – which he nearly missed, for he had not wanted the job – was the restoration of the church at St Juliot, a couple of miles from Boscastle. The parish is that from which came the famous Quaker family, the Rawles of Philadelphia, so prominent in the public life of the city from the time of William Penn. Near the church is the old barton of Hennett, which was their ancient residence. The patron of the living was still a Rawle in Hardy's time, but an absentee living in Antigua.

For generations the place had been neglected, the church hardly attended at all, with a succession of non-resident curates. At last, in 1863, a proper living had been put together from various sources and the Reverend Caddell Holder was appointed the first rector. According to Polsue's *Parochial History of Cornwall*: 'A substantial and commodious modern residence for the incumbent was built in 1847; it is surrounded with beautiful and luxuriant gardens and well-kept shrubberies, in an interesting situation.' But the church was in an advanced state of decay: 'Excepting the south aisle, extreme age has reduced this once superior church to a state of irremediable dilapidation; it is now, 1868, closed for reconstruction. The tower . . . is in a ruinous and falling state. It contained five good bells, but these have latterly been removed to the north transept for preservation.' All this reappears in Hardy's novel, in which the tower and its felling play a symbolic part.

The reconstruction that was carried through by Hardy's employer, Crickmay of Weymouth, was drastic. Crickmay rebuilt the north aisle and demolished the transept and Norman door, of which we have Hardy's drawing. Hardy regretted what was done, but he was called in only to draw the plans and survey the work. We have his drawings of the carved bench-ends and the chancel-screen with its tracery. Such despised relics of the Middle Ages used to be bought up by Parson Hawker of Mor-wenstow to embellish his church. At St Juliot they were all cleared out, the place swept and garnished – and inhabited by the figures we recognize in the novel. Emma's sister was the rector's second wife. Emma writes in her *Recollections*, 'when we arrived at the Rectory there was a great gathering and welcome from the parishioners, and a tremendous fusillade of salutes, cheering, and bell-ringing – quite a hubbub to welcome the Rector home with his new wife.'

For all their evident friendliness, Emma decides, 'I have never liked the Cornish working-orders as I do Devonshire folk; their so-called admirable independence of character was most disagreeable to live with, and usually amounted to absence of kindly interest in others.' Hardy says nothing of this sort, overwhelmed as he was by the romance of it all, the glamour of the Arthurian setting, the splendour of our north coast. Evidently Emma expected to be admired and deferred to.

The two sisters were years younger than the elderly rector, who was liable to be laid up with gout – as he appears in the novel. (Emma is careful to tell us that at Oxford he had been a gentleman-commoner, the son of a Barbados judge.) Their father was a Plymouth solicitor; all the same the Giffords were an old Norman clan in Devon, ancestrally armigerous. She was born in a middle-class house at Plymouth, near the Hoe, where they attended an establishment for the education of young ladies; there were, however, frequent military drills on that exposed spot, 'and then our dear instructress drew down the blinds. My home was a most intellectual one,' she goes on, 'and not only so but one of exquisite home-training and refinement – alas, the difference the loss of these amenities and gentlenesses has made to me.' Nothing can be more dispiriting than middle-class gentility; but in Emma's family there were mitigating circumstances – her father drank and there was a vein of eccentricity. (In my time, half a mile from my home, another Gifford solicitor and his wife were battered to death by a son, and their bodies thrown over the cliffs. But that was on our south coast.)

When Emma's grandmother died, who had had a private income, the family in straitened circumstances left Plymouth and took Kirland House outside Lanhydrock Park. They had been living cheaply in Cornwall for some ten years before Hardy came. Emma's sister – who, she tells us suspiciously, was jealous of her – went as companion to an old lady, apparently a Robartes of the Lanhydrock family, who had retired to Tintagel. This old girl remembered Plymouth in the gay days of the war with Napoleon – Hardy's war. Such a link would account for his knowing Lanhydrock, 'Endelstow' in the novel. When Emma fell ill she was sent to Tintagel to recover.

In the winter the storms were magnificent and the wind dangerous to contend with on the cliffs. I was nearly blown into the Atlantic ocean and clung to the rocks frightened. Strange old-fashioned people with old-world ways lived in sheltered niches on the high ground . . . All this should be seen in the winter to be truly appreciated. No summer visitors can have a true idea of its power to awaken heart and soul.

It was through the old lady at Tintagel that they met the rector of St Juliot, in want of a wife; on her sister marrying him Emma went along too, to keep her company in the lonely rectory and help in the parish. The rector often complained that there was no squire in the neighbourhood, 'no equals in the parish'. So it was a lonely life for Emma, 'scampering up and down the hills on my beloved mare alone, wanting no protection, the rain going down my back often, and my hair floating on the wind'. This was how Hardy remembered her years after, when her life was over, thus, and making music at the piano in the candle-lit rectory in the evenings. He says in the novel: 'Every woman who makes a permanent impression on a man is usually recalled to his mind's eye as she appeared in one particular scene, which seems to be ordained to be her special form of manifestation throughout the pages of his memory.'

Years afterward, when she was dead, there she is in the poem, 'Beeny Cliff: *March 1870—March* 1913':

> O the opal and the sapphire of that wandering western sea,
> And the woman riding high above with bright hair flapping free—
> The woman whom I loved so, and who loyally loved me.

And in 'The Phantom Horsewoman':

> Queer are the ways of a man I know:
>   He comes and stands
>   In a careworn craze,
>   And he looks at the sands
>   And the seaward haze
>   With moveless hands
>   And face and gaze,
>   Then turns to go ...
> And what does he see when he gazes so?
>
> ...
>
> A ghost-girl-rider. And though, toil-tried,
>   He withers daily,
>   Time touches her not,
>   But she still rides gaily
>   In his rapt thought
>   On that shagged and shaly
>   Atlantic spot,
>   And as when first eyed
> Draws rein and sings to the swing of the tide.

Emma was proud of her accomplishment and her long riding habit, 'which had to be caught up to one side when walking and thrown over the left arm gracefully and carefully, and this to be practised during the riding instruction – all of which my father had taught me with great pleasure and pride in my appearance and aptitude'.

She was curious as to what the visiting architect would be like, they had so few visitors. 'I was immediately arrested by his familiar appearance, as if I had seen him in a dream – his slightly different accent, his soft voice . . . He was quite unlike any other person who came to see us.' On his part, he was attracted by her 'liveness', her vivacity – precisely what he lacked. So, to begin with, they complemented each other. Even to the end she had a certain girlish charm; she had a carefree courage, spontaneity, independence. On Hardy's side it was love. Was it on hers? She certainly built up his confidence in himself – he badly needed it; they were no longer young, both twenty-nine, the direction their lives would take as yet undecided. It was she who insisted that his real vocation was writing, not architecture – on which they might have married more easily. They discussed his writing together, plots, scenes of novels, stories, poetry.

It was some four years before they could marry. Hardy made the cross-country journey to that remote spot some three times a year while the restoration of the church went on. Meanwhile his manuscripts went to and fro for her to copy and criticize.

A Pair of Blue Eyes tells us more than the reticent Hardy does in the biography. In the novel he split himself in two, the two lovers of Elfride. Young Stephen Smith is in Hardy's situation, a young architect of lower-class birth; Henry Knight is the London lawyer with literary interests who adversely reviews Elfride's book – its title was *The Court of King Arthur's Castle: a Romance of Lyonnesse*. In actuality, again, Emma did write a novel of her own, *The Maid on the Shore*, with its resemblances to *A Pair of Blue Eyes* in scene and situation, set at Tintagel. Later on, Hardy used an idea from it in *Tess of the D'Urbervilles*.

On Hardy's visits to St Juliot in course of work on the church, he and she would perambulate the coast and countryside, Emma on her mare, he walking beside her.

'Fancy a man not able to ride!' Elfride says 'rather pertly' in the novel. She goes on to discover that Stephen had had a lower-class education, and that his father was not a professional man, but a mere mason. The biography is at this point suspiciously disingenuous. Hardy wrote: 'His own wooing in the Delectable Duchy ran, in fact, without a hitch from beginning to end, and with encouragement from all parties concerned.' This is so contrary to the facts that we must regard it as ironical.

The novel tells us the truth: the marriage of Elfride and Stephen was adamantly opposed by her father. This difference of social class, of which Hardy was acutely aware, forms a main theme of the book. The father imposes his veto in *A Pair of Blue Eyes*, and there are discussions up and down, between the girl and her lover, she and her father, and a showdown between the two men. Emma would have been left single if she had obeyed her father. But she followed her instinct and loyally backed her man; she believed in his genius, above all things upheld his sensitive, diffident spirit. When she took Hardy over to Kirland House to introduce him to her father – in the third year of their courtship, August 1872 – the retired solicitor made it clear that he did not regard the man of genius as her social equal. Indeed, he is said to have spoken of him in opprobrious terms to offer to marry into his family.

What were they to do? In the novel Elfride makes an abortive elopement to London with Stephen – Hardy and Emma must have thought of that. In an early preface to *A Pair of Blue Eyes* he says: 'The conduct pursued, under a similar emergency, by a young girl, supplied the foundations on which I have built this book.' Nothing about it whatever in the biography, official as it is and largely written by Hardy: the experience must have been too wounding ever to be mentioned.

However the success of the novel encouraged them to marry. Its reception, he said, 'surpassed his expectations': it was most appreciated by poets, Tennyson for example, while Coventry Patmore declared that he wished only it had been written in verse. In September 1874 Hardy and Emma were married in Paddington – his part of London; though her uncle, later an archdeacon, performed the ceremony, it does not appear to have been graced by the family, or the presence of her father. The experience which Hardy declared to be the foundation of his book was more than that – it was the foundation of their lives together. The sense of social inferiority on his part – which he never overcame – and of social superiority on hers certainly increased the disaccord which grew more marked with the years, as he became more and more sought after, while she regarded herself as unappreciated and lapsed into sullen resentment. Arthur McDowell, who knew the couple well and wrote the best early book on Hardy, told me that her psychosis later took an unendurable form: she grew jealous of his work, thought he was stealing her ideas and tried to compete. She managed to publish a couple of volumes of slightly crazy verse, while after her death Hardy found among her manuscripts one entitled, 'What I thought of my Husband', which he destroyed.

All the same, what would one not give to be able to read it! One can imagine a good deal of what she would say. She looked down on his lower-class manners, his stinginess about money (for so many years he had had so little to live on). She resented his peasant qualities, his humility, his hang-dog expression. When Jacques-Emile Blanche was painting his portrait Emma besought him not to make Hardy look miserable: 'a real gentleman never does'.

But, of course, Hardy was miserable, though he never told anyone the cause of it. Edmund Gosse noticed that 'the wells of hope were poisoned for him', no one knew why or how. The simple truth was that Hardy was an intensively sensitive, suffering soul, gentle and innately courteous, chivalrous towards women. His was really the feminine nature – hence his quite exceptional insight into women's minds; Emma's was the more masculine character. It was not a good recipe for happiness.

She was the dominant partner; but she found that she could have no effect in the realm that mattered all in all to Hardy: he would not sacrifice intellectual and artistic integrity, especially in those matters where he most offended Victorian conventional opinion – over the relations of the sexes and religion. Actually his work became more challenging and controversial than it need have been, with *Tess of the*

D'Urbervilles. And when *Jude the Obscure* was written, Emma went to the publishers to try and stop its publication.

There could be nothing more agonizing for a writer of genius than interference in the most sensitive area of his mind, the seed-bed from which he creates. Emma lapsed into sullen resentment, 'a closed and shuttered mind', a kind of living death in the same house with him. No wonder his later work is obsessed with the theme of mismating, marital misery, the malignity of fate. To this had the early promise come.

There was a premonition of this as early as 1872. Hardy was on a visit to her friends, the Serjeants, who lived at ancient St Benet's at Lanivet – formerly a monastic cell or hospital. 'Near Lanivet, 1872' describes the shudder he felt when Emma went up to an old Cornish cross and extended her arms along it. (The cross was that on the road to St Austell; for Hardy the poem had a special significance.)

> "—Something strange came into my head,
>   I wish I had not leant so!"
>
>   . . .
>
> And we dragged on and on, while we seemed to see
>   In the running of Time's far glass
> Her crucified, as she had wondered if she might be
>   Some day.—Alas, alas!

It is difficult for us in our day to realize the extraordinary strength of Victorian class-consciousness, and its rigid exclusiveness. When Elgar married a lady of good class, her family stopped her allowance – just what the couple most needed: they had to go round peddling Elgar's songs. There is no doubt the iron entered into his soul: an abnormally sensitive man, he bore the stigmata to his dying day; nothing consoled him, not all his success and fame. Hardy had more confidence in himself and his Dorset origins – Nelson's Captain Hardy, afterwards Admiral, was after all a distant connection. All the same, Hardy never graduated from his social *gaucherie*; it is a tribute to his latent masculinity – if he had been at all homosexual he would have been more flexible, more socially adaptable.

The evidences are written not only all over *A Pair of Blue Eyes* but throughout his work and in his life. Though the famous novelist dutifully went the round of the London season, religiously attended its parties and met people in Society, he was always a fish out of water. The country boy was mesmerized by the mysterious life of the gentry, yet his imagination never could penetrate into its interior – any more than Henry James's could into that of the lower classes.

There was something else, which Hardy tells us – in verse. The couple were sitting together, their family portraits around them, when they both heard a sigh – it was another of those queer, extra-sensory experiences to which Hardy was so prone. They could not explain it:

'Then its meaning',
Said we, 'must be surely this; that they repine
That we should be the last
Of stocks once unsurpassed,
And unable to keep up their sturdy line.'

In the poem 'The Interloper' Hardy does not hesitate to give the trouble its name – the word 'psychosis' had not yet been invented, but the epigraph reads, 'And I saw the figure and visage of Madness seeking for a home' – another strange idea.

There are three folk driving in a quaint old chaise
And the cliff-side track looks green and fair;
I view them talking in quiet glee
As they drop down towards the puffins' lair
By the roughest of ways;
But another with the three rides on, I see,
Whom I like not to be there!

Thus was their later life rendered miserable, when all had seemed fair at the beginning:

Innocent was she,
Innocent was I,
Too simple we!
Before us we did not see,
Nearing, aught wry –
Aught wry! . . .

Yes, the years matured,
And the blows were three
That time ensured
On her, which she dumbly endured;
And one on me –
One on me!

Anyone who knows the area well will recognize the places, the scenes, the names sometimes under an easily penetrable disguise. Hardy tells us in his later preface to *A Pair of Blue Eyes*: 'One enormous sea-board cliff in particular figures in the narrative . . . this cliff was described in the story as being without a name.' It is in fact Beeny Cliff, of the later poem; here takes place – for all the creaking old-fashioned machinery of the novel – one of the most exciting scenes in fiction: Knight's rescue from slipping down the face of the cliff. In the course of his ordeal – breath-taking to the reader – there is one of those strange 'moments of vision', the phrase Hardy used for title of a volume of poems. Clinging to the face of the stupendous cliff – it is nearly 800 feet high – Knight's eyes are fastened to:

an imbedded fossil, standing forth in low relief from the rock. It was a creature with eyes. The eyes, dead and turned to stone, were even now regarding him. Separated by millions of years in their lives, Knight and this underling seemed to have met in their place of death. It was the single instance within reach of his vision of anything that had ever been alive and had had a body to save, as he himself had now.

Actually this clinging to the cliff adventure had been Emma's years earlier, as a girl at Plymouth.

Hardy informs us: 'The mansion called "Endelstow House" is to a large degree really existent, though it has to be looked for at a spot several miles south of its supposed site.' In fact it is the Jacobean mansion, Lanhydrock, not far from Lanivet. Elfride married the peer who was the owner of 'Endelstow', Lord Luxellian. Hardy got this name from the parish next to Lanivet, Luxulyan (pronounced by us Luxillian – the second u being a Cornish u, like a French u; the name means *locus* Sulyan, the place of St Sulyan or Julian). In *The Hand of Ethelberta* Lady Petherwin gets her name from the parish near Launceston.

Many more of our local names appear in novels or poems: Castle Boterel is Boscastle, St Launce's Launceston, Stratleigh (for Bude) and Camelton come from Stratton and Camelford, Parrett Downs are Tresparett Downs, Barwith Sands for Trebarwith Sands, and so on. A couple of rustics are given the straight names Werrington and Egloskerry. Naturally Hardy's rustics do not speak Cornish dialect, they speak broad Dorset. Everything is made use of in his careful way. At a service in church it had fallen to him to read the Lessons, as Knight does in the novel. Stephen Smith has an assignation with Elfride in the church-porch, just as it is, looking out over the V-shaped Valency Valley.

So too is Plymouth, and the Hoe, where Elfride-Emma was born and grew up. There is the girl making music for him in the evenings, as in his diary, and getting up very early in the morning to set him off on his journeys. Even the episode of the tumbler lost in a crevice of the rocks, at a picnic, appears in a poem, 'Under the Waterfall', as also in a sketch with Emma searching down the slope, long ringlets tumbling forward. Once, one evening, they were locked within Tintagel Castle on the headland. The medieval chapel within the castle – rendered famous by Geoffrey of Monmouth all over the world – had the same dedication as St Juliot, i.e. Julitta, a martyr with her son Cyric in Diocletian's persecution: hence its popular appeal to medieval sentiment. Oddly enough, when Hardy was well enough off to build his own house outside Dorchester, Max Gate at Fordington, he bought the land from the Duchy of Cornwall, which owned the manor.

That was the scene of their last, unhappy years – about which I have heard from several who knew them there, not only Arthur McDowell, but Q. (Quiller-Couch), and Sir Charles Grant Robertson. One day shortly before the end, after long silence, Emma suddenly sat down at the piano and played over and over the old melodies of those first days; then announced she would never play again. This appears in verse, in 'The Last Performance'.

She had expressed her wish to be buried in the family vault at Charles Church, Plymouth – gutted by the Germans in the last war. But the vault had been blocked up and she gave up the idea. Hardy:

There was one nook, indeed, which was pre-eminently the place where she might have lain – the graveyard of St Juliot, Cornwall – whose dilapidated old church had been the cause of their meeting, and in whose precincts the early scenes of their romance had a brief being. But circumstances ordered otherwise. Hardy did not favour the thought of her being carried to that lonely coast unless he could be carried thither likewise in due time. On this point all was uncertain.

'Circumstances' – to their irony Hardy was acutely and constantly alive – ordered that the unbeliever should be buried in Westminster Abbey.

2

Emma died on 27 November 1912.

> Why did you give no hint that night
> That quickly after the morrow's dawn,
> And calmly, as if indifferent quite,
> You would close your term here, up and be gone
>   Where I could not follow . . .
>
>   Never to bid good-bye,
>   Or lip me the softest call,
> Or utter a wish for a word . . .
>
>
>   . . .
>
>
>   You were she who abode
>   By those red-veined rocks far West,
> You were the swan-necked one who rode
> Along the beetling Beeny Crest,
>   And, reining nigh me,
>   Would muse and eye me,
> While Life unrolled us its very best.
>
> Why, then, latterly did we not speak,
> Did we not think of those days long dead,
> And ere your vanishing strive to seek
> That time's renewal?

This is what Hardy now did alone. Early in March, at just the time of year he had first approached St Juliot, he returned. His purpose was to arrange for a memorial to her in the church; but it was much more than that – it was to renew the time, in his own phrase, to retrace his steps into the past. Fidelity, above all, fidelity to the past, was the keynote of Hardy's mind. He was now an old man of seventy-three; but the time's renewal gave him his last burst of inspiration, out of which came some of his finest poems. Besides this, the whole body of verse gives us the most revealing record of the whole relationship, his real autobiography. The first harvest provides the section, 'Poems of 1912–13', in *Satires of Circumstance*, to which he provides the key: *veteris vestigia flammae*. The next volume, his finest, *Moments of Vision*, includes a similar number on the same theme.

> I found her out there
> On a slope few see,
> That falls westwardly
> To the salt-edged air,
> Where the ocean breaks
> On the purple strand,
> And the hurricane shakes
> The solid land.

He had come back to recover the magic of their first meeting, before the long corrosion of the years:

> Woman much missed, how you call to me, call to me,
> Saying that now you are not as you were
> When you had changed from the one who was all to me,
> But as at first, when our day was fair.

He recalled everything, every scene and movement, even the air-blue gown she had worn at St Launce's; by these details the magic was re-woven, even if it seemed only a dream remembered on waking.

> Why go to Saint Juliot? What's Juliot to me?
>   Some strange necromancy
>   But charmed me to fancy
> That much of my life claims the spot as its key.

Had it been a dream that there had been a woman there as in hiding:

> Fair-eyed and white-shouldered, broad-browed and brown-tressed
> And of how, coastward bound on a night long ago,
>   There lonely I found her,
>   The sea-birds around her,
> And other than nigh things uncaring to know.

· · ·

Does there even a place like Saint-Juliot exist?
> Or a Vallency Valley
> With a stream and leafed alley,
Or Beeny, or Bos with its flounce flinging mist?

There follows one of the most moving of the poems, 'After a Journey':

Hereto I come to view a voiceless ghost;
> Whither, O whither will its whim now draw me?

. . .

I see what you are doing; you are leading me on
> To the spots we knew when we haunted here together,
The waterfall, above which the mist-bow shone
> At the then fair hour in the then fair weather . . .

And then the sad harvest of the later years:

Summer gave us sweets, but autumn wrought division?
> Things were not lastly as firstly well
> > With us twain, you tell?

But he is unchanged:

Trust me, I mind not, though Life lours,
> The bringing me here; nay, bring me here again!
> > I am just the same as when
Our days were a joy, and our paths through flowers.

Hardy wrote this at Pentargan Bay: a heart-breaking poem, when one knows all that it encloses.

Here, all round him, unaware of her spirit's passing,

> > She had, in her flower,
> Sought and loved the places—
> > Much and often pined
> For their lonely faces
> > When in towns confined.

There follows the splendid evocation of 'Beeny Cliff' in all its colour, haunted by its ghost. In the next, driving to Boscastle, he sees,

Myself and a girlish form benighted
> In dry March weather. We climb the road
Beside a chaise. We had just alighted
> To ease the sturdy pony's load . . .

. . .

> It filled but a minute. But was there ever
>   A time of such quality, since or before,
> In that hill's story? To one mind never,
>   Though it has been climbed, foot-swift, foot-sore,
>   By thousands more.

Poets are the truest prophets – that hill is not likely to witness such a moment again, with such after-effects in literature.

Here again is 'Where the Picnic Was':

> Where we made the fire
> In the summer time
> Of branch and briar
> On the hill to the sea,
> I slowly climb
> Through winter mire,
> And scan and trace
> The forsaken place
> Quite readily.

A curious ballad-like poem – like so many of Hardy's, in dialogue form – recalls their misunderstandings, the agonies that 'came thereof', and gives us a clue to their source.

> And as he planted never a rose
>   That bears the flower of love,
>   Though other flowers throve
> Some heart-bane moved our souls to sever
> Since he had planted never a rose . . .

At Launceston there is the dream again:

> Slip back, Time!
> Yet again I am nearing
> Castle and keep, uprearing
>   Gray, as in my prime.

. . .

> Here I hired
> Horse and man for bearing
> Me on my wayfaring
>   To the door desired.

. . .

> If again
> Towards the Atlantic sea there
> I should speed, they'd be there
> Surely now as then? . . .

Never a one. And the same on the way back through Plymouth:

> Nobody thinks: There, there she lay
> In a room by the Hoe, like the bud of a flower,
> And listened, just after the bedtime hour,
> To the stammering chimes that used to play
> The quaint Old Hundred-and-Thirteenth tune
>   In Saint Andrew's tower
>   Night, morn, and noon.

During the war, in 1917 – at the age of seventy-seven – Hardy published his fullest and finest collection of poems, *Moments of Vision*. The volume is hardly less dominated by these familiar themes than the preceding one. A dated poem, like 'It never looks like summer here', written during his stay at Boscastle, indicates that some poems go back to the extraordinary harvest of that visit. They give us other facets to her personality, enable us to penetrate further into the mystery of their relations. 'The Riddle' says:

> Stretching eyes west
> Over the sea,
> Wind foul or fair,
> Always stood she
> Prospect-impressed; . . .
>
>
>   . . .
>
>
> Always eyes east
> Ponders she now—
> As in devotion—
> Hills of blank brow
> Where no waves plough.
> Never the least
> Room for emotion
> Drawn from the ocean
> Does she allow.

In other words, psychologically, Emma was an obsessoid.

It is clear that it was Hardy who had been in love – the waves themselves beneath the headland re-echoed:

> In the sway of an all-including joy
>   Without cloy.

But on her side, the next says:

> Why be at pains that I should know
>   You sought not me? . . .
> Come, the lit port is at our back,
>   And the tumbling sea;
> Elsewhere the lampless uphill track
>   To uncertainty!
>
> O should not we two waifs join hands?
>   I am alone,
> You would enrich me more than lands
>   By being my own.

He was the wooer: he *needed* her, and she fulfilled his need. We know now what she accomplished for him – and hers was the sense that it was fated.

The poem, 'The Change', written between her death and his going back, registers their fate:

> O the doom by someone spoken—
>   Who shall unseal the years, the years!—
> O the doom that gave no token,
>   When nothing of bale saw we: . . .

The beautiful poem, 'Quid hic agis?'—

> When I weekly knew
> An ancient pew,
> And murmured there
> The forms of prayer . . .

describes their experiences in St Juliot church, the occasion when it fell to him to read the lessons to the few farmers and women in the congregation.

> But now, at last,
> When our glory has passed
> And there is no smile
> From her in the aisle,
> But where it once shone
> A marble, men say,
> With her name thereon
> Is discerned to-day; . . .

It seems from 'The Young Churchwarden' that Emma had another admirer in church:

When Love's viol was unstrung,
Sore I wished the hand that shook
Had been mine that shared her book
While that evening hymn was sung,
His the victor's, as he lit
Candles where he had bidden us sit
With vanquished look.

Such a young man would have been a local farmer – an even more unsuitable match for Solicitor Gifford's daughter than the visiting architect's assistant. 'She, her father, I', appear together rather ominously in 'At the Wicket-Gate':

Of the churchgoers through the still meadows
No single one knew
What a play was played under their eyes there
As thence we withdrew.

No one knows now who the young churchwarden was; but his admiration for Emma may have given an edge to Hardy's suit, and suggested the remarkable poem 'The Face at the Casement'.

Yes, while he gazed above,
I put my arm about her
That he might see, nor doubt her
My plighted Love.

The pale face vanished quick,
As if blasted, from the casement,
And my shame and self-abasement
Began their prick.

. . .

Long long years has he lain
In thy garth, O sad Saint Cleather:
What tears there, bared to weather,
Will cleanse that stain!

St Clether is a remote moorland parish between Camelford and Launceston: Hardy seems to imply a fragment of experience buried in the churchyard there.

Other poems, sometimes worked up 'from an old note' go back to minute details in his obsessive memory; Q. told me that, whenever he met Hardy in these last years, all he would talk about was Boscastle and those scenes. Locked in memory, he turned and twisted, sometimes reproaching himself, sometimes her – as in 'An Upbraiding':

> When you are dead, and stand to me
>   Not differenced, as now,
> But like again, will you be cold
>   As when we lived, or how?

It would seem that, whatever the complex mesh of reasons – nobody's 'fault', but something irremediable in her nature, Hardy's the tenderer – Emma's heart had turned to stone.

Hardy wrote an antiphon to 'When I set out for Lyonnesse', which sums up the conclusion of it all as that more famous poem had its beginning. In this later poem, 'I Rose and Went to Rou'tor Town' (i.e. Camelford), 'she, alone' is speaking:

> I rose and went to Rou'tor Town
>   With gaiety and good heart,
>   And ardour for the start,
> That morning ere the moon was down
> That lit me off to Rou'tor Town
>   With gaiety and good heart.

. . .

> The evil wrought at Rou'tor Town
>   On him I'd loved so true
>   I cannot tell anew:
> But nought can quench, but nought can drown
> The evil wrought at Rou'tor Town
>   On him I'd loved so true!

That poem should stand at the end of the story.

3

But it is not quite the end.

In 1914 Hardy married his second wife, Florence, who for some years had acted as his amanuensis and kept house for Emma. In September 1916 they went down to Cornwall 'to see if Hardy's design and inscription for the tablet in the church had been properly carried out and erected.' While at Tintagel they had an unfriendly reception in the church. The Hardys took their seat at the corner of the transept, 'when the vicar appalled us by coming to us in his surplice and saying we were in the way of the choir. He banished us to the back of the transept.' When he began his sermon the couple walked out; the vicar was vexed, thinking it was done to be even with him. He could have no idea of the real reason. They had come there in memory of Emma, who as a young woman had made a water-colour drawing of the nave before it was 'restored'. They wanted to look down the length of the nave to compare it with Emma's sketch. 'It was saddening enough that we were inhospitably received in a church so much visited and appreciated by one we both had known so well.'

Once more a visit to that so poignantly remembered spot inspired, besides poems, a poetic drama; the first draft of *The Famous Tragedy of the Queen of Cornwall* was written that year, when Hardy was seventy-six. He did not take it up again till 1923, when he finished it in his eighty-third year, and equipped it with a couple of drawings still delicate and firm in line. The play is a curious little work, easy to underestimate or misconceive, yet unmistakably his. He was quite clear as to his artistic intention – a mummers' play, to be performed rather ritually, the chorus chanting their verse in unison (as in Eliot's verse-plays). Hardy says that he 'tried to avoid turning the rude personages of, say, the fifth century into respectable Victorians, as was done by Tennyson, Swinburne, Arnold, etc.' He wanted to conjure up the brute reality – perhaps an impossible task – and to lend distance to the spectacle, suggesting that it was a dream conjured up from the remote past by Merlin. To this end the archaic idiom, the *gaucheries* of phrase which would ruin the effect in a modern theatre – for which, after all, it was hardly intended. It was one more evocation of all that past. (I do not know how it could be performed, unless by film, with the visual and sound-effects of that coast, the barbaric headland, the castle, the sea-birds and the thundering sea.)

The aged Hardy wrote to a friend, 'I visited the place forty-four years ago with an Iseult of my own, and of course she was mixed in the vision of the other.' The unhappy Iseult of Brittany is given 'corn-brown hair', like Emma's. The theme of the play is mismating:

> Why did Heaven warrant, in its whim,
> A twain mismated should bedim
> The courts of their encompassment
> With bleeding loves and discontent!

Yet he suggested an alternative ending, the chanters singing an earlier poem, 'A Spot':

> In years defaced and lost,
> Two sat here, transport-tossed,
> Lit by a living love
> The wilted world knew nothing of: ...

> ...

> But lonely shepherd souls
> Who bask amid these knolls
> May catch a faery sound
> On sleepy noontides from the ground:

> "O not again
> Till Earth outwears
> Shall love like theirs
> Suffuse this glen!"

There was the split experience, the love and the suffering, that made Hardy's life and work what they were. And all inextricably intertwined with these places; so he dedicated it to the remembrance 'of those with whom I formerly spent many hours at the scene of the tradition – E.L.H., C.H., H.C.H., F.E.H.' There they all are brought together in the dedication of his last work: Emma, her sister and husband, the rector of St Juliot, and Florence Hardy, who knew the whole story and witnessed its end.

4

In those days of horse-drawn traffic, the nearest railway junction sixteen miles away at Launceston, St Juliot was certainly sequestered. Even today I have made the journey across the county from my home very few times, usually in winter as Emma suggested. My first visit was on such a March day as Hardy remembered, dry and cold, but an exquisite day of clear sunlight on crisp rime, lighting up the churchyard path, the valley beyond. I went there last on a day of storm, high wind and rain, the water sheeting across the steep hill up from Boscastle. Then down the long lane that leads to Lesnewth – hugging the shelter of the high Cornish earth-and-stone 'hedges' – past the rectory to the church on the edge of the valley. There was the old south aisle and granite porch, that had escaped Hardy's ministrations, now whiskered with moss.

Within, all was quiet – though the wind raged in the trees and was blowing great guns up the hollow valley – and recognizable enough. There were the pitch-pine pews in place of the carved bench-ends, the thin Victorian screen in place of the traceried medieval one with its relics of gilding, even an ancient harmonium – could it be Emma's? – with copies of Hardy's drawings behind.

On the wall of the north aisle he built there are three memorial tablets to the characters in the story. There is first the rector, incumbent for twenty years, who died in 1882 – erected by his widow. Next: 'To the dear memory [that is how Hardy thought of her, after the years had fallen away] . . . Before her marriage she lived at the rectory 1868–1873, conducted the church music [a Hardy touch for playing the harmonium], and laid the first stone of the rebuilt aisle and tower. She died at Dorchester 1912 and is buried at Stinsford, Dorset. Erected by her husband 1913.' Next again:

Thomas Hardy, O.M., Litt.D., author of many works in verse and prose and in early life architect, made drawings in March 1870 of this church in its ancient state and later for the alterations and repairs executed 1871–2, which he assisted to supervise. He died 1928 and is buried in Westminster Abbey. Erected 1928 as a record of his association with the church and neighbourhood.

Hardy's philosophy

A. O. J. COCKSHUT

I

'It is my misfortune,' Hardy wrote in a letter of December 1920, 'that people *will* treat all my mood-dictated writing as a single scientific theory.' This should never be forgotten, and it should help us to distinguish the senses in which Hardy can and cannot be called a philosopher. I remember once a friend of mine who was a university lecturer in philosophy was invited to a club lunch to meet some Manchester businessmen. When, in answer to their inquiry about his work, he said he was a philosopher, he was greeted with incredulous guffaws. To them a philosopher was typically, a chauffeur or gardener, who said things like: 'Well, sir, as it's been a hard winter, I expect we'll get a cold spring and a wet summer.' The idea that anyone could waste their talents and education in giving lectures on philosophy, and be paid for it, struck them as bizarre. Hardy was much nearer to the chauffeur than he was to the lecturer. He was a reflective, self-educated, sensitive man. Reason was the least developed of his faculties. When we speak of philosophy in Hardy, we mean his general temperamental approach to the universe. This sense is old-fashioned; but that need not worry us, since everything about Hardy was old-fashioned. His house was old-fashioned, and his clothes, and his loyalties, and his fictional technique. And in one of the older senses of the word 'philosophical', its application to him seems very just. Hardy was philosophical in the sense that his was a mind with a strong tendency to generalize. Tess was very like her creator, and like most of his heroes and heroines, when she tried to guess the nature of life on other planets from her own experience on this one. She was also, like her creator, very illogical.

We can best delimit Hardy's philosophical bent, then, by contrasting it with its opposites. On the one hand, he was totally unlike the professional philosophical reasoner; on the other, he was equally unlike the man (Arnold Bennett, say) who is satisfied with describing men and things as they appear, and brushes aside further questions by saying, in effect, 'There you are, that's how the world is – what more do you want?' Hardy always wanted more; he always saw the particular case as some shadowy illustration of a general truth. There is always for Hardy something behind the facts. He was a man who always felt what Plato expressed by his myth of the cave. We are all like men watching shadows of people moving behind us, unable to turn and see them as they are. Hardy's deep impressiveness as a novelist, even at his worst, rests for me on two contrasted temperamental traits. The first is the sense of Plato's cave; the second is the intense sympathy with which he feels and makes the reader feel the particular case, especially in its sufferings.

In Hardy's novels there are two groups of characters, strongly contrasted, who might be labelled philosophical. In the first group come Clym Yeobright in *The Return of the Native*, Jude and his son Father Time, and, at a less consciously reflective level, Michael Henchard. These are people who try to make some general system of life out of their experience. Clym Yeobright is the first and most fully analysed of these. Hardy says:

He already showed that thought is a disease of the flesh, and indirectly bore evidence that ideal physical beauty is incompatible with emotional development and a full recognition of the coil of things. Mental luminousness must be fed with the oil of life, even though there is already a physical need for it; and the pitiful sight of two demands on one supply was just showing itself here.*

Notice how he takes it for granted that thought is an *emotional* function. The idea of a dry, logic–chopping, uncommitted philosopher does not appear, even in order to be repudiated; if Hardy could have imagined any such being, he would have thought him trivial, and perhaps made him a minor figure of comedy. Thinking, for Hardy, involves the whole man; it drains energy and increases pain. The disinterested intellectual pleasure which philosophers, scholars and scientists may obtain from hard thinking scarcely comes within Hardy's purview. And from his own point of view, he is perhaps right to ignore it, since it can only be enjoyed by those who are leading a reasonably contented existence. Few of Hardy's characters attain contentment, and those that do are of another kind.

But why does thought increase pain? It does so because for Hardy the gloomiest speculations seem the most convincing. Schopenhauer is a brooding presence behind the presentation of Clym Yeobright and Little Father Time. At the same time thought reminds us of systems of belief which do give comfort, and which Hardy could never either accept or forget. Most important of all, it distracts us from the instinctive traditional life of the country in which thinking has a humbler and more useful rôle, concerning itself only with the best ways for men to feed and clothe themselves, and to enjoy the few modest pleasures that life affords.

This brings us to the other set of characters who can be called philosophical in a different sense. Henchard's daughter, Giles Winterborne and Marty South are the most impressive; and it is in *The Woodlanders*, to which the last two belong, that Hardy gives the most sustained and memorable account of instinctive, traditional, affectionate, enduring life, and seems most strongly to endorse it. The events of *The Woodlanders* are unhappy, the loves are unfulfilled, but the pessimism is muted by the adjustment of the characters to the environment, and through that to life. If Hardy had finished writing novels with *The Woodlanders* in 1887, instead of with *Tess* (1891) and *Jude* (1895), he would not have his reputation for extreme pessimism. Up

* *The Return of the Native*, Book II, Chap. VI.

to *The Woodlanders* the world of his novels is narrow and at times sad and sombre, but relieved with many touches of contentment and even gaiety. There are many reasons, no doubt, for the grimmer qualities of his last two novels. But one is especially significant. Tess, to a great extent, and Jude, completely, have lost touch with their roots. They are wanderers among people they do not know; their work is variable, and their life has no rhythm. In Hardy's world this is inevitably fatal.

To say that thought is a disease is, obviously, very extreme; and it is certainly not a fair account of Hardy's own thinking. His own meditations, in his poems, in the reflective passages of the novels, and in diaries and letters do not strike the reader as diseased. Why then is he so sweeping in his condemnation of the intellect? Partly, I suggest, because he had a very abstract and rigid conception of what thinking is. Or rather, he knew of no theoretical equivalent for the kind of general, balanced, felt meditation from which issue his own most satisfying writings. When he describes thought as a disease he means something very harsh, repellent, inhuman. He never seems to have heard of Pascal's spirit of finesse, or remembered that Newman said that reason was only the map of the mind's progress. Both these phrases might be applied to his own riper reflections. But he would not have dignified them with the name of thinking. The thought, the reasoning that he respected and hated and feared was hatchet-like, reductive, mechanical. Thus we have the paradox that one of the most thoughtful and thought-provoking of our greater writers often spoke as if thought was a curse.

We can see this paradox more clearly if we consider the place of traditional superstitions and irrational customs in his novels. They are shown as human, significant, vaguely comforting and, often, as containing a core of moral truth. Sometimes, it is true, like the mummer's Christmas play in *The Return of the Native*, a traditional custom is portrayed as feebly preserving a phantom life when public interest in it had been lost. But that, too, is a matter for regret to Hardy. Now Hardy assumes, without apparently contemplating any alternative, that all these things depend on ignorance. What is absent from his thinking, and what at times it seems to require, is a philosophical outlook like that of Burke. This would have helped him to bridge the gap between unthinking, illogical, comparatively contented countryman, and tortured, cerebral, bodiless, potentially suicidal educated man.

Burke, or some thinker of the same school, could have helped him to see that men are not really divided in this way. Educated and intellectual men are just as much creatures of the senses as other men. Furthermore it is possible to have a highly sophisticated and philosophical defence of the respect paid to tradition by the uneducated countryman. At times Hardy comes near to saying, 'Hodge or Schopenhauer, that is choice.' And he goes on to imply that with the spread of education Schopenhauer will come into the ascendant and Hodge gradually fade away. Yet how far he himself was from being either Hodge or Schopenhauer. Whatever is the place of primitive instinctive life in philosophy, there can be no doubt of its importance in art. If it was impossible for him to achieve the detachment to see this in his own art, he could have observed it in his great predecessors and contemporaries. The greatest literary artist of Hardy's early years, Charles Dickens, was in many ways an eternal boy.

But Hardy was oblivious of all this, and it may have been part of the price he paid for being an autodidact. He did not think of the philosopher as a wise man, like Pascal or La Rochefoucauld, or as a master of an academic discipline. He thought of him as a man with a neat, destructive system that would probably tend to show that life was not worth living. He showed his respect for this kind of philosopher and his dislike and fear of him by embodying him in the person of Little Father Time in *Jude*.

For our purpose it does not matter that Time is an unsatisfactory character in a novel that is written, for all its strangeness, in the tradition of realistic fiction. The reader of *Jude* may well complain that he cannot consent to give literal credence to an allegorical figure. But what does the boy mean? First, he is clearly a personification of the feelings of Jude and Sue, his father and stepmother. After watching a wedding, both are disturbed and disgusted, and Sue says:

> Everybody is getting to feel as we do. We are a little beforehand, that's all. In fifty, a hundred years the descendants of these two [the bridal couple they have been watching] will act and feel worse than we. They will see weltering humanity still more vividly than we do now, as shapes like our own selves hideously multiplied, and will be afraid to reproduce them.★

Schopenhauer no doubt lies somewhere behind this passage, but its compelling source is a strong personal distress, partly caused by his own marital troubles. So it does not occur to Hardy, who has tricked himself into thinking his own agonizing reflections the QED line of a cool piece of geometrical reasoning, that nothing is more irrational and unphilosophical than to make confident predictions about the distant future of this surprising and inconstant world.

Time himself, the embodiment of these fears, is equally a combination of an impulsive emotional nature with an appearance of cool reasoning. He is a natural philosopher in that he 'seemed to have begun with the generals of life, and never to have concerned himself with the particulars'.† But he is also, of course, a child with all, or more than all, a child's ignorance of life. He would like the flowers very much, if he didn't keep on thinking that they'd all be withered in a few days. Surely the most hasty and illogical ground for cosmic despair, because a longer view would remind him of the coming spring and the cycle of nature. His naïvety makes him unintentionally comic, as when he says, 'If I was you, mother, I wouldn't marry father.' Not knowing how babies are born he accuses Sue of having 'sent for another', just as if it was done by application to a government department. In fact he knows nothing of life.

Of course we may say that is natural enough in a child. But that is not quite the

---

★ *Jude the Obscure*, Part v, sect. iii.
† Ibid.

point. As every reader has felt, and as Hardy probably knew, he is quite unbelievable as a child. It is better, perhaps, to think of him as a savage portrait of the philosopher as Hardy saw him, a man whose emotional growth is stunted by thought, who reasons about things, but does not understand anything. This kind of thought is indeed a disease, or would be, if it could really be attributed to anybody. It is ironical that Hardy should have shown his essential healthiness by presenting this unreal, bloodless kind of thinking as diseased, but at the same time, because of his limited idea of what thinking could be, accorded it an unwilling and unjustified respect. Little Time, without in the least deserving the honour, becomes a universal authority in the novel. It may sound like a contradiction to say this and to say at the same time that Hardy feared what Time represents. But the point is that at the time he wrote *Jude* Hardy was in the state of mind when anything seems certainly true if only it denies all our hopes and aspirations. This was hardly a settled conviction with him, more a recurrent mood which may have been stronger in the mid-nineties than at any other time in his long life. I doubt, though, whether Hardy perceived the full irony of the famous death message, 'Done because we are too menny', left by Time when he killed himself and his siblings. The boy-philosopher is not only violent, impulsive, irrational, but also ignorant and illiterate. To view philosophy like that was the inevitable price Hardy paid for his limited idea of it, for his failure to recognize the complexity possible to the thinking mind.

I have referred, rather vaguely, to some of Hardy's philosophical sources. How important to him are they? We may approach this question by considering a celebrated passage from the end of *Tess of the D'Urbervilles*: ' "Justice" was done, and the President of the Immortals, in Aeschylean phrase, had ended his sport with Tess.'

This is memorable rhetoric. But if it is more than an antiquarian note, it means something which is plainly untrue – that Aeschylus's and Hardy's conception of the working of divine justice in the world are similar. There is nothing in the book corresponding to Aeschylean hubris and excess; and the Greek idea of crimes being visited on the descendants of the offender is present only in the most shadowy way. Vague remarks about the possible crimes of Tess's aristocratic ancestors cannot provide any equivalent for the terrible background of the Thyestean feast. Moreover the 'justice' in Hardy's passage is a false human justice, represented by the death penalty awarded to the much-suffering victim of two men's selfishness.

But it would be a mistake to argue from this that Hardy was trying to endow his tale with a spurious classical authority. He was not cheating; indeed he strikes us always as a man of singular intellectual honesty. He was recalling, unguardedly and emotionally, an intense literary experience. Any sensitive reader, especially one to whom thoughts of destiny and doom are familiar, will be deepy moved by the *Agamemnon*. It will tend to recur to his mind when he is contemplating a tragic scene. He makes Jude refer to it again in his moment of supreme agony. In both cases it was the literary quality of Aeschylus that brought him into Hardy's text; though in saying that we must be careful to add that for a meditative, wide-ranging reader, general reflections about life (which might loosely be called philosophical) are natural fruits of literary experience of this kind. The obverse is equally true; the influence exercized by a professional philosopher, like Schopenhauer, is a literary one. Hardy is not concerned with his reasoning but with the *tone* of his thinking.

2

Hardy saw all the world and all time and space as one vast system, all in a sense alive. Perhaps the simplest way to summarize his thinking in a phrase would be to call him a pessimistic pantheist. So it is that his descriptive passages often read like a piece of Wordsworth turned upside down. Take this for instance from *The Woodlanders*:

On older trees huge lobes of fungi grew like lungs. Here, as everywhere, the Unfulfilled Intention, which makes life what it is, was as obvious as it could be among the depraved crowds of a city slum. The leaf was deformed, the curve was crippled, the taper was interrupted; the lichen ate the vigour of the stalk, and the ivy slowly strangled to death the promising sapling.*

The sense of an informing spiritual life is just as strong as in a Wordsworth landscape. Without articulating for himself a theory to explain it, Hardy feels impelled to judge nature morally, to attribute to it a purpose, and to say that it had failed. Other passages in his work, notably the ending of *The Dynasts*, give a somewhat more optimistic tinge to this idea of imperfectly realized purpose.

Pantheism, of course, is a very ancient view of life, and also a very natural and obvious one. But it raises difficult questions about the status of man. Here Hardy was in a dilemma, and like all his dilemmas it was emotional rather than intellectual. On the one hand, he instinctively regarded man as a part of the universal system, differing in no fundamental respect from stars, animals and earth. At the beginning of *The Return of the Native* there is a characteristic descriptive passage, in which a hill, an ancient burial mound, and a woman standing on the mound are seen as a single homogeneous grouping which 'amounted only to unity. Looking at this or that member of the group was not observing a complete thing, but a fraction of a thing.' And here a recent thinker came apparently to reinforce this ancient pantheistic intuition. Darwin seemed to justify the view that men and animals were not fundamentally different.

We should not take Darwin's influence too seriously. His work can be interpreted in accordance with the tenets of almost any philosophy. Cardinal Newman welcomed it much less dubiously than Hardy did. Darwin's importance for Hardy is this: he gave a modern slant to an ancient intuition, and allowed a man who was really governed by ideas of immense antiquity to suppose that he was also being fashionable and up-to-date. Even so, Darwin cut both ways. This is well shown by two letters written in his sixties. In the first, after a bitter attack on blood sports, he goes on:

* *The Woodlanders*, Chap. VII.

A Dorset hurdle-maker; these movable hurdles were used both for the penning of sheep, and for sheltering ewes in lamb. 'Detached hurdles thatched with straw were struck into the ground at various scattered points, around and under which the whitish forms of his [Gabriel Oak's] meek ewes moved and rustled.' *Far from the Madding Crowd.*

ABOVE The hurdle-maker at work.

RIGHT Haymaking. 'They [the haymakers] consisted in about equal proportions of gnarled and flexuous forms, the former being the men, the latter the women . . . In the first mead they were already loading hay, the women raking it into cocks and winnows, and the men tossing it upon the waggon.' *Far from the Madding Crowd.*

ABOVE A scene on Egdon Heath, 'the vast tract of unenclosed wild . . . It was at present a place perfectly accordant with man's nature – neither ghastly, hateful, nor ugly; neither commonplace, unmeaning, nor tame; but, like man, slighted and enduring; and withal singularly colossal and mysterious in its swarthy monotony.' *The Return of the Native.*

LEFT A timber merchant, probably in a lesser way of business than Mr George Melbury, '. . . the timber, bark, and copse-ware merchant . . . the middle of the area was now made use of for stacking timber, faggots, hurdles, and other products of the wood'. *The Woodlanders.*

ABOVE Sheep-washing. 'The meek sheep were pushed into the pool by Coggan and Matthew Moon, who stood by the lower hatch, immersed to their waists; then Gabriel, who stood on the brink, thrust them under as they swam along . . .' *Far from the Madding Crowd.*

RIGHT Sheep-fair and pleasure-fair on Greenhill (Woodbury Hill). '. . . the busiest, merriest, noisiest day of the whole statute number was the day of the sheep-fair.' *Far from the Madding Crowd.* 'All these bleating, panting, and weary thousands had entered and were penned before the morning had yet advanced . . . Alleys for pedestrians intersected the pens, which soon became crowded with buyers and sellers from far and near.' *Far from the Madding Crowd.*

ABOVE The tranter, or carrier. 'His [Dick Dewy's] errand was to fetch Fancy, and some additional household goods, from her father's house in the neighbouring parish to her dwelling at Mellstock.' *Under the Greenwood Tree.*

RIGHT The cobbler. 'He [Mr Penny] sat facing the road with a boot on his knees and an awl in his hand, only looking up for a moment as he stretched out his arms and bent forward at the pull . . . Rows of lasts, small and large, stout and slender, covered the wall . . .' *Under the Greenwood Tree.*

ABOVE An itinerant cider-press. 'He [Giles Winterborne] was likely to return to Hintock when the cider-making season came round, his apparatus being stored there, and travel with his mill and press from village to village.' *The Woodlanders*.

RIGHT Cottage interior. 'In the room from which this cheerful blaze proceeded he [Mr Percomb] beheld a girl [Marty South] seated on a willow chair . . .' *The Woodlanders*.

A group of elderly country characters, among whom might be found Tranter Dewy, or Grandfather William, or Malster Smallbury, or old Durbeyfield, and many others.

'"Don't cry! Don't cry!" said Henchard.' An illustration of the scene in *The Mayor of Casterbridge* when Elizabeth-Jane has just heard that it is Henchard, not Newsom, who is her real father.

RIGHT A postcard from 1922 illustrating the national affection for a literary monument.

BELOW One of several sets, by several hands, of scenes from 'Hardy's Country' which shows how early the West Country legend sprang up and how Hardy encouraged the legend.

82 – AND NOT OUT!
MAY HIS INNINGS BE INDEFINITELY PROLONGED!

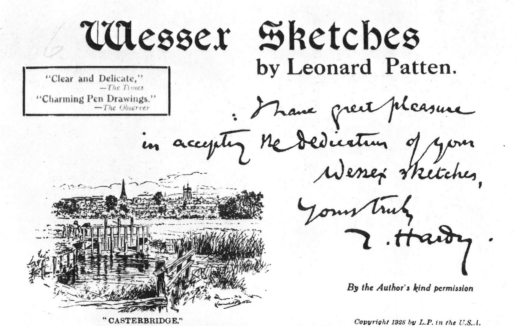

Wessex Sketches
by Leonard Patten.

"Clear and Delicate,"
—The Times
"Charming Pen Drawings."
—The Observer

: I have great pleasure in accepting the dedication of your Wessex sketches, yours truly T. Hardy.

By the Author's kind permission

"CASTERBRIDGE."

Copyright 1928 by L.P. in the U.S.A.

A performance by the Hardy Players in 1922 of *A Desperate Remedy*, Hardy's first published novel.

A modern-day poster from the Hardy Country illustrating the ever-increasing attraction of the legend.

In the present state of affairs there would appear to be no logical reason why the smaller children, say, of overcrowded families, should not be used for sporting purposes. Darwin has revealed that there would be no difference in principle.*

In the second he said:

The discovery of the law of evolution, which revealed that all organic creatures are of one family, shifted the centre of altruism from humanity to the whole conscious world collectively.†

In fact you could take your choice. You could use Darwin to support treating men like animals, or you could use him to support using animals like men. As we would expect, Hardy, with his usual obliviousness to logic, blandly confuses origins with values in both passages. But if Darwin only provided a rather specious justification for a deep pantheistic intuition, he could not mitigate Hardy's dilemma. He believed that men were part of the stuff of nature, as like all the rest as a spike to a helmet, as he expresses it in another part of the descriptive passage from *The Return of the Native* previously quoted. But he *felt* that men were unique, above all in their capacity for sympathy and their capacity for pain. In a deeply feeling and only intermittently rational man like Hardy the feeling will generally take precedence of the thought. If we respond to his stories and feel with his characters, we find, despite all the theorizing, that man has his old dignity and passion. However much he may be at a loss to explain it, Hardy endows man with a soul.

But there is another respect in which Darwin (and the geological writers like Lyell who preceded him) chimed in neatly with Hardy's natural way of thinking. The scientists gave the earth and organic life and the human race a time scale immensely longer than their predecessors in earlier centuries had done. Many people found this frightening. Hardy found it grand and inspiring. It was natural to him to speculate about prehistory; and he was fortunate to live in the age he did, when geologists had licensed his imagination to wander back thousands or even millions of years. Perhaps the best general description of the impression made on a sensitive reader by Hardy's work as a whole is still that of Lionel Johnson:

A rolling down country, crossed by a Roman road: here, a gray standing stone, of what sacrificial, ritual origin, I can but guess; there, a grassy barrow, with its great bones, its red-brown jars, its rude gold ornaments, still safe in earth: a broad sky burning with stars: and a solitary man.‡

The neat cosmology of the eighteenth century, with its ignorance about primitive human civilization, could have provided nothing for such an imagination to work upon. Here was a natural and artistically fruitful affinity between Hardy's personal bent and the scientific speculations of his age. No one but Hardy, perhaps, would

---

* Florence Emily Hardy, *Life*, Chap. XXVII.
† Ibid., Chap. XXIX.
‡ Lionel Johnson, *Thomas Hardy* (1894). It is worth noting that this was written before the appearance of *Jude the Obscure*.

have shown a man desperately clinging to a cliff-face, facing certain death if he relaxed the grasp of his fingers, and then continued as follows:

> ... opposite Knight's eyes was an imbedded fossil, standing forth in low relief from the rock. It was a creature with eyes. The eyes, dead and turned to stone, were even now regarding him. It was one of the early crustaceans called Trilobites. Separated by millions of years in their lives, Knight and this underling seemed to have met in their death.*

But once again it is a question of mood and feeling not of reason to determine whether these new-found aeons of time increase or reduce human dignity. Is he dwarfed by the past, or aggrandized by the unimaginable number of the centuries that prepared for his coming? Hardy himself was in doubt and inclined to give different answers at different times. But his readers are unlikely to be in doubt. For them Hardy's past is enriching, not impoverishing. And, if he was lucky in his scientists, he was also lucky in his native Dorset, which is so full of visible signs of the antiquity of man.

This brings us to Hardy's nostalgia. It has become fashionable to use this word disapprovingly; and a close reading of Hardy may well make us wonder whether the fashion is a sensible one. No doubt there are trivial versions of nostalgia which those who are most eager to condemn it have in mind. There is nothing in Hardy corresponding to the talk of 'high noon of Empire, when it never rained during the cricket season'. Nor does he favour the older and more serious idea of a Golden Age of innocence and simplicity as in pastoral poetry or the landscapes of Poussin. A painless, carefree life was something Hardy was incapable of conceiving.

Hardy's nostalgia is one common to many sensitive spirits, though few have expressed it so poignantly; it is nostalgia for a predictable rhythm of life. The old rustic world he shows is hard, but its comforting feature is that even its disasters are known beforehand, because they are the same as those suffered by previous generations. Unable to attain religious or metaphysical certainty, Hardy clutches all the more avidly at the certainties of everyday.

To illustrate this we may turn to two painful scenes in *Tess*. In the first Tess and her companions are working on the vast swede-field of Flintcomb Ash in a bitter winter; in the second she is loading a grain-elevator. Both scenes are bleak and hard. But it is characteristic of Hardy to make the first scene more endurable. The miseries of the swede-field are grand and simple. The girls are felt to be, and perhaps feel themselves to be, the last in an endless series of toiling generations scratching at an unresponsive earth. In the second scene a new technical development which is supposed to save labour and time, is unwelcome because the stress and anxiety of change outweighs the relief to the muscles. There is a new, nervous, almost claustrophobic tone in Tess's suffering. This aspect of Hardy's nostalgia is simply a longing for a limit to experience. Coarse-grained people find this easy to despise; they seldom reflect that it is only the intensely sensitive, the minds on which nothing is lost, who

* *A Pair of Blue Eyes*, Chap. XXII.

experience enough to have such a feeling at all. If the grain-elevator had been a hundred years old, it would have alarmed Hardy and Tess no more than a farm-cart.

But there is another, deeper note in the nostalgia, a longing for faith. Hardy described himself as 'churchy' and said that as a child to be a parson had been his dream.* The poem about going to see the oxen kneel at midnight on Christmas Eve is an extreme statement of a life-long feeling. Here Hardy was unfortunate. It was natural to a man of his long, fond memories to associate religion with country churches and uneducated countrymen. On the other hand, the autodidact in him took the half-truths of the fashionable agnostic writers of his day far too seriously, and his untrained mind was oblivious of the begged questions and false reasonings that abounded in their works. They represented for him, as they were to do for Yeats some twenty-five years later, an authority which could be resented, but which allowed no possibility of appeal or rebellion. Over and over again, in diary, letters, novels and poems, he repeats the cliché that simple people have religion and educated people don't. This was untrue at the time, and has become more blatantly untrue since. But it takes on the character of a fixed idea; and as in paranoiac delusions any threat to it, any piece of evidence that does not conform to it, only causes irritation. Hence the contempt with which he speaks of men like Browning, 'the last of the optimists'. Did it never occur to him that Browning's mental powers were quite as good as Huxley's and his erudition much wider? Probably it did, and hence the irritation and contempt.

Of course there were several different kinds of longing combined here. He does not always distinguish clearly between a deep spiritual desire for a loving God and an antiquarian delight in village superstitions. But that need not prevent us from distinguishing them. We may say that for all the quaintness of kneeling oxen and the like, Hardy did possess this deep spiritual longing. It was his great misfortune that he located it in the past, forgetting that the only point where eternity touches time is the present moment.

But in other ways his nostalgia may have helped to save him from the ravages of some of the dominant delusions of his time. He was unaffected by the progress myth. Of all the great Victorians one may guess that Newman and Hardy would be least astonished by the world we know today. Both would find it uncomfortable, and Hardy would be particularly distressed by the rapidity of technical change. But neither would find anything to upset the principles by which he had lived or the expectations of the future he had formed. One cannot say the same for Carlyle or Macaulay or Mill or Arnold.

There is a paradox here. In an age of rapid change Hardy was, as we have seen, intensely sensitive to change. But at the same time he recognized its superficial quality. From one point of view his Wessex is a doomed stronghold of an ancient way of life. But from another it may be seen as poetic equivalent for the necessary conditions of all human life. More than all his contemporaries among novelists he

* *Life*, Chap. XXXIII.

deals with the fundamental things that local variations cannot really alter. This means that while his ideas, which are mostly second-hand, may appear dated, his feelings never do.

And yet there may be doubt about the healthiness of those feelings. He has often been censured for morbidity, and just as often praised for the sublimity of his compassion. How are we to explain this? A recollection of his fourth or fifth year may help to resolve the contradiction:

Also he remembered . . . being in the garden at Brockhampton with his father on a bitterly cold winter day. They noticed a fieldfare, half-frozen, and the father took up a stone idly and threw it at the bird, possibly not meaning to hit it. The fieldfare fell dead, and the child Thomas picked it up and it was as light as a feather, all skin and bone, practically starved. He said he had never forgotten how the fieldfare felt in his hand: the memory had always haunted him.*

He was recalling this scene after more than eighty years. The feeling described is not very unusual in its nature; what is unusual is its intensity. Hardy had less of a mental skin than most people, even sensitive people; and along with this he had at times a perverse desire to worry at the sensitive nerve, to test his own courage, as it were, by imagining horrors. And, though he did not literally believe in a supernal mocking power of the kind suggested by the Spirit Sinister in *The Dynasts*, yet his instinctive pantheism made it natural for him at times to invent or imagine such a power. The scenes in his writings which have with some justice been called morbid are those where this imaginary sinister force seems for the moment to be real.

It is a difficult problem of detailed critical judgement to decide just when Hardy is fairly to be held culpable in this way. There is never likely to be general agreement about each case. But the essential point is that Hardy's occasional morbidity is at the opposite pole from callousness. He was tempted at times by his sympathy for all suffering creatures to shape his account into a seductive aesthetic artefact. He played at the problem of pain sometimes, not because he took it lightly but because, never being able to forget it, he needed relief from the burden of always taking it gravely.

In any case it is wrong to put morbidity in the centre of our impressions of his work. If we detach our minds from detail and think of our experience of all his books over many years, I think two features of his many-sided personality appear dominant: the sense of dignity and the sense of awe. The dignity is shared by all his leading characters, and is something curiously separate from their deeds. Summarize the story of Michael Henchard or of Tess, and they will appear reckless, crazy, even intermittently wicked. Read the whole book, and this impression is overborne by their power of endurance. They have dignity even in their folly and crime.

The sense of awe is directed not towards God, but towards the whole structure of things. Preoccupied as they were with moral questions, his contemporaries, even

* *Life*, Chap. XXXVIII.

when most in earnest, do not generally convey this sense. I spoke earlier of 'Wordsworth turned upside down'. Certainly Hardy's doctrine is different and much less comforting. But perhaps in the end this contrast is less important than a deeper likeness. Both do what few English writers do; they excite in their reader a sense of timelessness, as if the concerns of everyday were tiny and faint against the grandeur and strangeness of a universe comprehended only by momentary glimpses.

Hardy and architecture

SIR JOHN BETJEMAN

Anyone whose first introduction to Hardy was *Wessex Poems and Other Verses* (1898) might have supposed that the poet was an architect or architectural draughtsman by profession. The illustrations are distinctly architectural – a brick-built turret with a sundial on it and a conical tiled cap; a late fifteenth-century country church with square western tower; the cross-section of a church showing a Transitional Gothic arcade of two and a half bays furnished with box pews and at one end poppy-head bench-ends, underneath in section are shown coffins, a catacomb and various skulls and bones; fortification at Valenciennes; the High Street of Dorchester with Georgian buildings in sharp perspective; the market-place at Leipzig in evening light; the Georgian bay-window of an inn; some Jacobean panelling; the top stages of the twin Romanesque towers of Exeter Cathedral; an Empire-style couch with a dead body laid out on it; a Gothic church key such as might have been designed by Pugin; a Grecian urn containing dying wild flowers; an accurately and tenderly drawn perspective of the interior of the nave of Salisbury Cathedral looking eastward and with Sir Gilbert Scott's iron screen still there to add mystery and depth to the choir and sanctuary. There are certain quaint touches about these illustrations which even if the monogram T. H. was not on them would lead one to suppose that this was no ordinary architectural draughtsman. As for the meticulously drawn landscape, the rising swell of down; the outline of earth-works; prehistoric or Napoleonic ramparts; a winding foot-path; an hour glass with butterflies poised on it – they give the country an air of passivity as though it was waiting for some crime to be committed on it.

In 1856 before he had written any novels Hardy was apprenticed to a local Dorchester architect John Hicks. To be an architect in the nineteenth century was socially better than being a builder or a carpenter. Building and joinery were 'trade'; architecture was a 'profession' and enabled the architect to stay in the country houses of his clients – those who employ architects are 'clients' not 'customers'. Thus was Hardy able to stay in Cornwall with the rector of St Juliot and meet his first wife, the rector's sister-in-law. Parsons in those days were men of standing and second to the squire. Sometimes the rector was squire and parson in one.

The Architectural Notebook of Thomas Hardy (Dorset Natural History and Archaeological Society, 1966) is thought by its copious and painstaking editor, Dr C. J. B. Beatty, to contain work done mostly between 1866 and 1871, though there are earlier and later sketches. The drawings are very much those of any Victorian architect.

That is to say there are sections of timber construction, profiles of mouldings, minute calculations and notes in ink about colour and materials. There are also plans roughly sketched out for a house and even quite a large house. Apart from Hicks and another local architect, Crickmay, Hardy also worked for a very distinguished church architect, Sir Arthur William Blomfield (1829–99), who had an office in London. Blomfield was himself the son of a bishop of London and possibly this church connection accounted for the immense amount of church work which went through Blomfield's office. Hardy was sent as clerk of the works on behalf of the London diocese to superintend the digging up of old St Pancras churchyard, a very full cemetery through which the Midland Railway had to pass on its way to a terminus in the parish of St Pancras. The experience deeply affected Hardy who was then twenty-six years old. Professor Jack Simmons quotes from Mrs Hardy's *Life of Thomas Hardy*:

There after nightfall, within a high hoarding that could not be overlooked, and by the light of flare lamps, the exhumation went on continuously of the coffins that had been uncovered during the day, new coffins being provided for those that came apart in lifting, and for loose skeletons; and those that held together being carried to the new ground on a board merely.

The scene is described in one of Hardy's *Satires of Circumstance* called 'In the Cemetery'. It describes mothers squabbling over the graves:

"One says in tears, "*Tis mine lies here!*'
Another, '*Nay, mine, you Pharisee!*'
Another, '*How dare you move my flowers
And put your own on this grave of ours!*'
But all their children were laid therein
At different times, like sprats in a tin.

"And then the main drain had to cross,
And we moved the lot some nights ago,
And packed them away in the general foss
With hundreds more. But their folks don't know,
And as well cry over a new-laid drain
As anything else, to ease your pain!"

Another poem on the same theme is 'The Levelled Churchyard'.

Let it not be thought that Sir Arthur Blomfield was a hard and gloomy man who put his young assistant onto this task. The times were hard. And Hardy had a country-man's matter-of-fact point of view about death. He and Blomfield got on very well together. Mrs Hardy remarked in her biography fifteen years after he had left the office on how Hardy discussed with Blomfield the puzzle of a coffin that contained a skeleton with two skulls, Blomfield opening with the remark, 'Do you remember how we found the man with two heads in St Pancras?' One of his earlier poems, 'Heiress and Architect', was written while he was in Blomfield's office and describes a capricious lady who wants all sorts of dainty oddities in her new mansion and each time the architect puts her down with robust commonsense. The poem is dedicated to Blomfield.

The *Notebook* shows that Hardy had a wide training in architecture and was not a wholly Gothic revival man. Nor was Blomfield, one of whose earliest churches was the Byzantine building St Barnabas, Oxford (1869). It was bringing the gospel to the poor in a part of West Oxford called Jericho where Hardy pictures Jude the Obscure having a room. St Barnabas, because it was of brick was condemned as a cheap church. Blomfield, as Canon Clarke quotes in his *Church Builders of the Nineteenth Century*, replies thus:

The idea usually conveyed by this term (cheap church) is that of a showy exterior, flimsy construction, and a mean and disappointing interior. Now, as the exact opposites of these are found in St Barnabas', I object to its being classed with cheap churches; it is true that no money was wasted on it, and it was in that sense economically designed and economically carried out; but, as I have before said, no expense was spared to secure strength and solidity of construction; the work was put without any competition into the hands of a thoroughly good contractor, and not one single item of the design from first to last was altered or cut down in the slightest to reduce the cost; everything was carried out as originally designed, and this is more than can be said for many churches that have cost three times as much.

Blomfield's best-known London buildings are the 'Lombardized' interiors of St Mark's, North Audley Street and St Peter's, Eaton Square. He also designed the fine Gothic nave of Southwark Cathedral and Lower Chapel at Eton and many suburban churches, some in brick and some in stone.

Hardy's house of Max Gate is of red brick and has a tower with a conical cap, not unlike that shown in the illustration to *Wessex Poems*. It is quite unlike any other house built in Dorchester before it. Most of the larger houses were Italianate and stone or stucco. I wonder if he was thinking of it in the second stanza of 'Architectural Masks':

> In blazing brick and plated show
> Not far away a "villa" gleams,
> And here a family few may know,
> With book and pencil, viol and bow,
>   Lead inner lives of dreams.

Max Gate was designed on the 'L' plan which Hardy shows or rather hints at in his notebooks. He used plate-glass and sash windows and wooden glazing bars in sunny rooms to reduce glare. The house was clearly designed to look out across the bleak pastoral landscape west and south of Dorchester. It was comfortably contained in a long brick garden wall within which was also a walled garden.

Hardy, like his master Blomfield, was not a rigid Gothicist. *The Architectural Notebook* shows in the sketches and details Hardy's knowledge of, and delight in, Gothic moulding and details of joinery and ironwork as well as practical house plans for St Juliot rectory in Cornwall. They also show his pleasure in what might be called 'late' by rigid Gothic revivalists.

In north Cornwall Hardy had sole supervision of the restoration of remote St Juliot church near Tintagel. Here he was working in the early seventies and went to much trouble to preserve seventeenth-century carved bench-ends which are still there and a medieval screen at a time when screens were not approved of by purists. The screen is rather a botched job, for the carpenter took it out of Hardy's hands and produced his own version – to Hardy's dismay.

St Juliot is an interesting contrast with its adjoining parish Lesnewth which was restored by J.P. St Aubyn, far more violently, in 1866, only five years earlier. There the walls were scraped of plaster, the pews destroyed and replaced by pitch pine as roofs and floors were altered and new windows inserted in a style considered correct by the architect. I do not think Hardy would have had much sympathy with St Aubyn as a church restorer.

Hardy would have been in sympathy with the advanced architects of his time, that is to say, Norman Shaw and Philip Webb. He would have approved of the Arts and Crafts as practised by William Morris. He admired craftsmen. In the touching story of the old workman who breaks his back carrying too heavy a load, the last stanza might be Hardy – and his works:

> "Yes; that I fixed it firm up there I am proud,
> Facing the hail and snow and sun and cloud,
> And to stand storms for ages, beating round
>   When I lie underground."

Hardy the historian

LORD DAVID CECIL

I

Thomas Hardy's modest, old-fashioned, little study reconstructed in the Dorchester Museum, has a great many history books on its shelves; many more than will be found on the bookshelves of most great writers. For history meant more to Hardy than it did to them. Circumstances and temperament alike disposed him to such an interest. He was by birth and upbringing a countryman; and he remained one. His long life was spent almost entirely within a few miles of his birthplace. This fact conditioned his imaginative development and coloured his creative process, which was to operate at full power only in the context of the region which he called Wessex. His knowledge of this, his homeland, was intimate and his curiosity about it insatiable.

This curiosity was as much about its past as about its present. Hardy was born with an intense personal sense of the past. He could only love things or places if they evoked memories for him. What he says of Fitzpiers the doctor in *The Woodlanders* was true of himself.

But whether he meditated the Muses or the philosophers, the loneliness of Hintock life was beginning to tell upon his impressionable nature. Winter in a solitary house in the country, without society, is tolerable, nay, even enjoyable and delightful, given certain conditions; but these are not the conditions which attach to the life of a professional man who drops down into such a place by mere accident. They were present to the lives of Winterborne, Melbury and Grace; but not to the doctor's. They are old association – an almost exhaustive biographical or historical acquaintance with every object, animate and inanimate, within the observer's horizon. He must know all about those invisible ones of the days gone by, whose feet have traversed the fields which look so grey from his windows; recall whose creaking plough has turned those sods from time to time; whose hands planted the trees that form a crest to the opposite hill; whose horses and hounds have torn through that underwood; what birds affect that particular brake; what bygone domestic dramas of love, jealousy, revenge, or disappointment have been enacted in the cottages, the mansions, the street or on the green. The spot may have beauty, grandeur, salubrity, convenience; but if it lack memories it will ultimately pall upon him who settles there without opportunity of intercourse with his kind.

For Hardy this feeling for the past extended to the historic past. His interest in Wessex was an interest in Wessex throughout the ages. Throughout his life he kept notebooks in which, in his neat legible handwriting, he carefully noted down facts that had struck his interest. A large proportion of these are about local history; bits of information about the history of Wessex towns and villages and roads and buildings, anecdotes of human beings connected with them. He was particularly interested to learn anything about his own ancestors: for the name of Hardy figures in Wessex history. One Hardy had founded the Dorchester Grammar School in the sixteenth century; another, Captain Hardy, had knelt to listen to Nelson's last words as he lay dying in the hull of the *Victory*. Interest in his own family went along with an interest in other peoples'. Thomas Hardy saw people in terms of their heredity and believed them to be deeply influenced by it.

Hardy's sense of the past was primarily personal and local. But it broadened naturally into a more general historical curiosity. Wessex was soaked in English history. So much had happened there and had left its mark, and, since it was a rural area, these marks had not been obliterated by much later development. Its downs are dimpled by prehistoric barrows and scarred by the remains of Roman camps and Roman fortifications. Medieval Christianity has built churches in its villages, and these churches in their turn are peopled by the tombs of the English gentry who were the local overlords; crusaders with crossed legs, beruffed Elizabethans kneeling at prayer with their children behind them, periwigged Georgians with florid flattering inscriptions cut in classical lettering on their monuments. These same gentry have ornamented the countryside with mansions and manor houses and their names are also commemorated in traditional tales about their public and private doings; personal dramas of love or hate, the parts they played in the Civil War or the Rebellion of Monmouth. Finally the sea coast is marked by the remains of outposts and fortified places erected in the Napoleonic era to defend the country against invasion. Each of these phases of history left a freight of traditional stories to be learned and listened to by Hardy and written down in his notebooks.

They appealed to the poet in him as well as to the historian. His interest in history was intensified by the fact that it fed and fired his romantic imagination. Hardy was very much a child of the Romantic Movement, acutely sensitive to the picturesque appeal of the past, to the sentiment associated with old customs, old songs, old tales, to all that was expressive of the spirit of bygone days, keeping it alive to enthral the men and women of later ages and to set them dreaming.

Certainly it set Hardy dreaming. It also started him reflecting and questioning. He studied the various phases of man's long history in order to note what was permanent in it and what transitory, to discover what laws, if any, operated and determined the course of human destiny. History for him threw light on what was always the subject of his profound and unsleeping preoccupations; the nature of the basic human situation. Thus his concern with the past stimulated the philosopher in him as well as the historian and the poet.

No wonder his writings are saturated with it. His novels, even when they are set in his own time, are resonant with historical overtones. We arc never allowed to forget that Casterbridge of which Henchard was mayor was an ancient township, with its medieval churches and Georgian inns and the great prehistoric earthwork of Maiden Castle brooding over it from the south-west. Jude, roaming the streets on his first night at Christminster, is haunted by the ghosts of the thinkers and scholars who have meditated there in bygone ages; Knight marooned on the Cliff without a Name, Clym wandering desperately over wild Egdon are both visited by visions of the painted and primitive men who, millions of years before, had looked on these same places; Tess's labourer father broods on his descent from the ancient family of d'Urberville, whose sculptured tombs could still be seen in the church of Kingsbere; Swithin St Cleeve surveys the stars from the top of a tower erected to commemorate an Englishman killed in the American War of Independence. Hardy also takes every opportunity to describe ancient customs like the mummers' play in *The Return of the Native* or the Skimmity Ride in *The Mayor of Casterbridge* or the midnight carol-singing in *Under the Greenwood Tree*. Among our novelists only Scott has put the same stress on the historical past of his imagined world.

Hardy also sought to recreate the past: in one novel *The Trumpet-Major* and a handful of shorter pieces, 'The Duke's Reappearance', 'A Tradition of 1804', 'A Committee Man of the Terror', 'The Melancholy Hussar'. As might be expected, the inspiration of these is regional. They all take place in Wessex and most of them are founded on local tradition. 'The Duke's Reappearance' relates a legendary incident handed down in the family of Hardy's mother, while all the tales of the Napoleonic period are inspired by anecdotes told to Hardy in his boyhood by old people surviving from those days.

The Trumpet-Major, set in the same period, contained more material drawn from hearsay and traditions than any other of Hardy's novels. He made good use of it. It is one of the best historical novels in the language; for me the only rival to the best of Scott's, that is to say those about eighteenth-century Scotland. This is because, like them and unlike most of its rivals, it successfully solves the special problem facing all historical novelists, namely how to reconcile the claims of history with the claims of life. A fictional world is only living and real for the reader if he feels that its inhabitants are like real living people. Now the only real people whom the novelist knows are his contemporaries. But he also knows that people of past periods were different from his contemporaries in some important respects and that he must make this clear in his picture of them. How then is he to create characters who are true to their period and yet convince us as living individuals? Most novelists fail on one count or the other. The average historical novel, inspired as it is by the wish to give its readers something pleasantly and romantically exotic, is peopled by figures dressed with careful accuracy in the costumes of their period, but who are in themselves conventional puppets. On the other hand most of the distinguished novelists who have tried writing historical novels succeed in presenting us with living characters; but although incongruously apparelled in fancy dress, these are characters of the novelist's own time with the thoughts and assumptions of that time. In contrast to them the characters in *The Trumpet-Major*, like those in *Redgauntlet* and *The Heart of Midlothian*, are living flesh and blood human beings who are also unmistakably natives of the ages in which their stories are set. So much so that these books pass the highest test to which an historical novel can be subjected; we can turn from them to an actual record of the time they describe without being jarred by the slightest change of key.

This is partly because both Scott and Hardy did see their fellow beings – contemporary as well as in the past – 'historically', that is to say as products of their historical environment. Among the first things each noticed about a man were those characteristics that revealed his ancestry and the culture from which he sprang. Scott and Hardy therefore did not need when writing about a past age to shift their angle of vision as much as most novelists would: to them, the past was always part of the present. The second reason for their success is that in these particular books the age they write about is not far from their own. They have chosen to recreate a past world which is as close to them as a past world can be; set in their native country and near enough in time for the people in it to be very like people they have known. All the more because they are members of those humbler ranks of society whose mode of life changes least with the passage of time: 'I have sought my principal personages,' says Scott in the preface to *The Antiquary*, 'in the class of society who are last to feel the influence of that general polish which assimilate to each other the manners of different nations.' He might have added 'the last to lose the tradition of customs and manners inherited from former ages'. Hardy could have said the same thing about the characters in *The Trumpet-Major*. All his cast is drawn from the inhabitants of the little village of Overcombe on the Dorset coast.

This does not mean he was oblivious of a larger context. Hardy viewed Overcombe in its wider historical setting and in relation to the Napoleonic Wars taking place at the time. The great historical events take place off the stage; but we hear them talked about and some of the main characters in the story play a part in them. Of the two heroes, John Loveday is a soldier who goes off in the end to lose his life in the Peninsular Campaign and Bob, his brother, a sailor on board the *Victory* at the Battle of Trafalgar. We may note that he gets permission to serve on the *Victory* from Hardy's relative, Captain Hardy: Captain Hardy is one of the two actual historical characters to make a brief appearance in the story. The other is George III, who stops to speak to Anne, the heroine, on her way back to watch the *Victory* on its voyage to Trafalgar. We are also given a distant glimpse of George III and his family on the way to stay at Weymouth, called Budmouth by Hardy, and, later, reviewing the troops on the neighbouring downs. Another true incident is recalled when a rumour that Napoleon has landed in England leads the villagers to make a panic flight from their homes in the middle of the night. In these occasional glimpses Hardy opens our eyes to perceive a vaster and more momentous background behind the rural drama which fills the foreground of the book and shows us that this is influenced by the great historic drama which is being played out all over Europe.

Once or twice Hardy steps out of the period to survey his scene, as it looks when revealed against the background of past or future time. John Loveday's fellow soldiers visiting his family in the Old Mill of Overcombe walk over a paved floor worn by 'the ebb-flow of feet that had been going on there ever since Tudor times': after King George's review of the troops outside Weymouth:

The King and his family left the hill. The troops then cleared off the field, the spectators followed, and by one o'clock the downs were bare. They still spread their grassy surface to the sun as on that beautiful morning not, historically speaking, so very long ago; but the King and his fifteen thousand armed men, the horses, the bands of music, the princesses, the cream-coloured teams–the gorgeous centre-piece, in short, to which the downs were but the mere mount or margin – how entirely have they all passed and gone! lying scattered about the world as military and other dust, some at Talavera, Albuera, Salamanca, Vittoria, Toulouse, and Waterloo; some in home church yards; and a few small handfuls in royal vaults.

Hardy extends his view to include these wider vistas very rarely; but the effect of his doing so is such as to modify our vision of his whole drama and to invest it with a mysterious sublimity. Deliberately he moves outside it the age he was writing about to make a comment from his own personal and timeless viewpoint. So whether his story is set in the past as in *The Trumpet-Major* or later as in his other novels, he always keeps us aware of his story as an episode in the great process of human history. Yet that episode remains a lively, accurate re-creation of its period.

2

History inspired Hardy the poet as well as Hardy the novelist. Sometimes it is the history of a place; as for instance 'A Spellbound Palace', that haunted and haunting poem where the spectacle of Hampton Court on an autumnal afternoon evokes for Hardy the spectres of Wolsey who had built it and Henry VIII his master, 'the Shade of a straddling King, plumed, sworded, with sensual face'. Hampton Court is an exception among Hardy's historic poems in that it is about a place not in Wessex. Wessex scenes, Wessex traditions are as always his main inspiration; medieval in 'A Lost Pyx', seventeenth-century in 'At Shag's Heath', eighteenth-century at 'In Sherborne Abbey', early nineteenth-century in a whole Napoleonic group. Hardy's interest in this past period grew so strong as to take him out of Wessex to compose ballads about Leipzig and San Sebastian and to reflect lyrically on his feelings when visiting the bridge of Lodi, when he was travelling on the continent. This same continental journey stirred his sense of the past to write the series called 'Poems of Pilgrimage'. In these, Gibbon's garden at Lausanne, Keats's grave in Rome, Caligula's palace on the Palatine all suggested to him melancholy, ironical, typical musings about the contrast or the likeness between past and present which led him on to further melancholy, ironical, typical general conclusions on the riddle of human destiny. The past could do this for Hardy in a way the present could not, let alone the future. He was once invited to the United States of America but refused the invitation. He wrote a poem explaining why.

I

My ardours for emprize nigh lost
Since Life has bared its bones to me,
I shrink to seek a modern coast
Whose riper times have yet to be;
Where the new regions claim them free
From that long drip of human tears
Which peoples old in tragedy
Have left upon the centuried years.

II

For, wonning in these ancient lands,
Enchased and lettered as a tomb,
And scored with prints of perished hands,
And chronicled with dates of doom,
Though my own Being bear no bloom
I trace the lives such scenes enshrine,
Give past exemplars present room,
And their experience count as mine.

3

Hardy's most ambitious excursion into past time is that queer mammoth-size mixture of history and philosophical allegory which he entitled *The Dynasts*. In this he presents ten years of European history – the ten years between Trafalgar and Waterloo – as an example of the permanent human situation and of the forces controlling it. Hardy had meditated writing *The Dynasts* many years before he started it, and had done a great deal of research with it in mind. The result is an accurate and detailed word picture, covering nearly five hundred pages. It is presented in a curious three-tiered form: an allegorical framework encapsulating dumb-show panoramas of historical scenes in narrative prose, which in their turn introduce dramatic scenes composed in a convention derived from Shakespeare's historical plays; that is to say they are divided between blank verse scenes about the leading historical personages in the story – Napoleon, Nelson and so on – and prose scenes of humble life about imaginary characters. These last in spirit and manner recall *The Trumpet-Major*. They are just as good and more poignant; for, in *The Dynasts*, we see these characters not only at home in quiet Wessex but actually taking part in great historic events – agonizing in the retreat from Corunna, lying on the field of Waterloo wounded and in their death throes. These prose scenes give Hardy a chance to display both his comic and his tragic genius and he takes it. At the same time he never fails to make them convincing evocations of past history.

Like the prose scenes the dumb-show panoramas combine historic accuracy with imaginative power. But this time the power manifests itself in a different strain of

Hardy's genius, his extraordinary gift of visualization. The pictures he paints are as correct as he can make them: they are made up entirely of facts he has discovered in the records he had studied. But he has brooded on these so long and so intensely that they seem to have become part of his own experience. He describes Trafalgar and Corunna and Waterloo as if he had been present at them; with an immediate reality made individual by the characteristic imaginative light with which he has flooded them, the odd vivid Hardyish images with which he brings them before our mental eye.

The Field at Waterloo

An aerial view of the battlefield at the time of sunrise is disclosed.

The sky is still overcast, and rain still falls. A green expanse, almost unbroken, of rye, wheat, and clover, in oblong irregular patches undivided by fences, covers the undulating ground, which sinks into a shallow valley between the French and English positions. The road from Brussels to Charleroi runs like a spit through both positions, passing at the back of the English into the leafy forest of Soignes.

The latter are turning out from their bivouacs. They move stiffly from their wet rest, and hurry to and fro like ants in an ant-hill. The tens of thousands of moving specks are largely of a brick-red colour, but the foreign contingent is darker.

Breakfasts are cooked over smoky fires of green wood. Innumerable groups, many in their shirt-sleeves, clean their rusty firelocks, drawing or exploding the charges, scrape the mud from themselves, and pipeclay from their cross-belts the red dye washed off their jackets by the rain.

At six o'clock they parade, spread out, and take up their positions in the line of battle, the front of which extends in a wavy riband three miles long, with three projecting bunches at Hougomont, La Haye Sainte, and La Haye.

Looking across at the French positions we observe that after advancing in dark streams from where they have passed the night they, too, deploy and wheel into their fighting-places – figures with red epaulettes and hairy knapsacks, their arms glittering like a display of cutlery at a hill-side fair.

If the historical sections of *The Dynasts* had been confined to its dumb shows and prose scenes, it would have been Hardy's most successful attempt to re-create a vanished age. Alas, it was not so confined! There are also the scenes in blank verse and these take up even more space. Now and again and at moments of tragic climax – when Villeneuve decides to commit suicide or Napoleon recognizes at long last that his career has ended in failure – they achieve a stern majesty. But for the rest the reader is faced with many hundreds of lines where parliamentary debates and diplomatic discussions, in their original form prosaic and pedantic, are conscientiously translated into a prosaic and pedantic blank verse which, while keeping them dull, makes them stagey. This fatally weakens the illusion of historical reality produced by the prose scenes and panoramas.

Nor, for all its length, does *The Dynasts* reveal so embracing a historical perspective as do the novels. For in it Hardy confines himself to one period; his scheme did not allow him to refer to other ages, so that he never gets a chance, as in the novels, to give us his sense of the whole huge historic process, to show us glimpses of the human story stretching forward and back through time in dim and endless vista. The presence it is of these glimpses that makes Hardy's historical vision sublime. It also makes it unique in our literature; and, so far as I know, in any other.

Hardy and the natural world

MARGARET DRABBLE

There are surprisingly few novelists who have written much about nature and the natural world. Poets, yes, but not novelists. Most of the early novelists in the English language were Londoners, and if their characters made excursions into the country, it was into a countryside of coaching inns and highwaymen rather than of trees and moors, birds and animals. Nature, as Hardy was to say in *The Trumpet-Major*, was at their stage 'hardly invented'. Jane Austen, who wrote after the romantic revolution, and who was certainly no Londoner, nevertheless addresses nature but briefly: it is never more than a background for her human performers. A respect for accuracy led her to inquire of a friend about the state of hedges in Northamptonshire, and her heroines enjoy a turn in the shrubbery, or even a ramble along a muddy country lane, but her poetic descriptions of nature, in the mouths of Fanny Price and Marianne Dashwood, are banal, and intended to be so. Later in the century, Dickens and Thackeray wrote largely of city life: George Eliot and Trollope of towns, villages, cloisters, country houses. This is not surprising. The novel was a middle-class form. read by middle-class readers, and its material was social and human relationships. Descriptions of nature were left, on the whole, to the poets: so were descriptions of natural beauty.

There are, of course, exceptions to this generalization. Scott, the romantic, wrote of landscape, and George Eliot, though more celebrated for other achievements, wrote with first-hand knowledge of rustic life. Her scenes in the Rainbow Inn in *Silas Marner* were hailed as fine examples of a certain kind of portrait, and Hardy's scenes of choric peasant life bear a marked family resemblance to them. There are dairy scenes in *Adam Bede*, foreshadowing those in *Tess*. And in *Middlemarch* there is a fine episode in which farm labourers in smock frocks threaten intrusive railway agents with their hay forks, in defence of their land. But the smock frock, in George Eliot's work, already wears a quaint air of survival in the bustle of the commercial nineteenth century. Hardy's peasants were still wearing it some decades later, but Hardy knew that it would not be seen for much longer, even in his remoter, more agricultural district. He was aware that he was, in certain of his scenes, writing in a *genre*: *Under the Greenwood Tree* is subtitled 'A Rural Painting of the Dutch School', a description that would certainly have fitted George Eliot's rural scenes.

As far as the use of landscape is concerned, however, the only novelist who re-sembles Hardy is Emily Brontë: her sense of the unity of man and nature, her evocation of a particular location in particular detail, are very close to his. In both their works, landscape is seen to determine character, and descriptions of it are as significant a part of the novel as the people who live in it. For this same sense in other writers, one must look to the poets – to Wordsworth, to Coleridge, to Crabbe. And it is interesting and paradoxical to note that Hardy, himself a fine poet, who regarded poetry as his most serious form, wrote less of nature in his verse than one might expect. In many of his poems there is a natural background, but most of them deal with speculations or emotion or relationships: very few are straight natural descriptions. It is for this reason that this essay will be concerned with the novels: in them, Hardy's feelings about the natural world find their fullest expression.

Hardy wrote about nature because he was a countryman. Unlike most of his predecessors, he was born in a rural, though not isolated district, in an exceptionally attractive part of the country, where nature lay around him in his infancy, as the moors lay beyond Emily Brontë's back windows. He could hardly have avoided it. He was also one of the very few novelists whose origins could have been described, however roughly, as 'working-class', a fact about which, in later life, he was to prove sensitive. Emily Brontë was a parson's daughter, a cultural exile, who communed with nature partly because she had no choice, but Hardy's family were deeply rooted in the land where they lived, and Hardy grew up in close touch with a whole community. He knew at first hand of the wealth of farmers and the poverty of agricultural labourers, he knew the ways of the peasants and the ways of the local gentry, and he observed, not as a historian but as a fellow countryman, the changes that were taking place in traditional village life. He was brought up in a world of folklore rather than of science, where each object had its familiar name, and each complaint a home-made remedy; he was familiar with the cycle of the seasons and the duties attached to each time of the year in each rural occupation. Although he sometimes laughs at the simplicity of his peasant characters, he does it with the licence of an intimate rather than the patronage of an outsider. Although he was, as he grew older, much perplexed by questions of progress and tradition, and less and less convinced that simplicity was necessarily a virtue, he remained an accurate recorder of country speech and customs. Some of his scenes are set in social regions untouched by the novelist, because unknown to him: one thinks of the scene in *Far from the Madding Crowd*, set in Warren's Malthouse, where Shepherd Oak is greeted in a friendly fashion with a not-very-clean two-handled communal mug of cider from the ashes, and a piece of bread and bacon, with the advice 'Don't ye chaw quite close, Shepherd, for I let the bacon fall in the road outside as I was bringing it along, and may be 'tis rather gritty.' (Gabriel Oak agrees, politely, like the gentleman that he is, that he has no objection to 'clane dirt'.)

Not all the rustic scenes are equally affectionate: Hardy rarely falls into the easy rôle of sentimentalizing his peasants. They are at times ignorant and superstitious: one of them sticks a pin into Eustacia Vye, to see if she is a witch, and Lucetta Farfrae is destroyed by the barbaric old custom of the skimmity ride. Giles Winterborne is shamed by his low neighbours, in the scene where Grace finds a slug in her lettuce. (The slug is hotly defended by its cook, Robert Creedle, who declares it was 'well boiled, I warrant him well boiled . . . they were born on cabbage, and they've lived on cabbage, so they must be made of cabbage.') Even the farmhands in *Far from the Madding Crowd*, who through most of the novel are seen in a nostalgic pastoral light, are, like a Shakespearian crowd, too easily swayed: they get drunk at Troy and Bathsheba's wedding, and are nearly responsible for the loss of her ricks. But even when Hardy is using his chorus in an unfavourable rôle, his observation of behaviour is still acute: they are real people, not stock peasants, in museum clothes.

Both the drink offered to Gabriel Oak, and the slug salad offered to Grace, illustrate a side of Hardy's awareness of nature which is more significant that his knowledge of rural manners. Like old Jacob, Hardy does not differentiate too sharply between dirt and drink, man and beast. Let the bird eat too, is the boy Jude's thought, when the farmer tells him to stone the bird from the field. To Hardy, the whole of the natural world has a strong organic unity, which he apprehends at times with a mystic clarity: borderlines are blurred, and man becomes part of nature. Clym Yeobright, furze-cutting on the heath, is surrounded by creeping and winged things 'which seemed to enrol him in their band . . . huge flies, ignorant of larders and quite in a savage state, buzzed about him without knowing that he was a man.' Hardy constantly uses anthropomorphic imagery about natural objects, with startling effect: a pool glitters like a dead man's eye, a path across a moor is like a parting in a head of hair, bonfires in the night are like wounds in a black hide, the surfaces of plants are glossy like lidless eyes. Conversely, some of the works of man, like the barrow on Egdon, are so ancient that they resemble the works of nature, and in Casterbridge the country is so close to the town that the distinction between the two is constantly confused: Hardy writes in Chapter IX:

Casterbridge was the complement of the rural life around; not its urban opposite. Bees and butterflies in the corn-fields, who desired to get into the meads at the bottom, took no circuitous course, but flew straight down the High Street without any apparent consciousness that they were traversing strange latitudes. And in autumn, airy spheres of thistledown floated into the same street, lodged upon shop fronts, blew into drains; and innumerable tawny and yellow leaves skimmed along the pavement, and stole through people's doorways into their passage, with a hesitating scratch on the floor, like the skirts of timid visitors. . .

Throughout the description of Casterbridge, the prosperous market-town with its fine new buildings, there is an insistence on its ancient history: Roman remains and prehistoric remains form a part of each landscape, so that the works of man are seen as part of a slow continuous process, not an aggression against or defiance of nature, but a part of a natural process of evolution. Modern man may cut himself off by thought and aspiration from the world he grew from, but essentially man's history hitherto has been one of infinitely slow change, where the animate and the inanimate were part of the same large slow pattern. Hardy's characters have an instinctive feeling for plants and animals, and are often compared to them: Tess yawns like a sunned cat, her mouth opens pink like a snake's; Thomasin Yeobright is a heron, a kingfisher, a swallow; Gabriel Oak can read the behaviour of sheep and cows; Giles Winterborne plants trees as though they were (which they are) living beings. In these descriptions, Hardy is not writing simply of an inherited skill, of country lore: what he gives us is a sense of ancient unbroken sympathy between man and the creation. It would be easy to view this as pathetic fallacy on a large scale, were it not for the fact that Hardy also gives us the other side of the picture: in *Jude the Obscure*, a novel which deals more with thought than with instinct, and more with the town than the country, there are few rural scenes, and the most striking of those is the one where the instinctive Arabella proves much more adept at the age-old task of pig sticking than the over-sensitive Jude. Man is not always kind to animals: sometimes he tortures and destroys them. In the same novel, the image of a rabbit screaming in a gin trap is used to symbolize marriage. (Man also tortures his own kind, however, another example of lack of differentiation between species: Grace Melbury walks not into a rabbit trap, but a man trap.)

Nature has its darker side, and much has been written about Hardy's sense of the hostility of nature, and his use of it as a dramatic ingredient in his novels. It is true that he rejects the idea of nature as the Great Comforter, an idea much more common in the nineteenth century than the Darwinian concepts that were beginning to filter through into the popular imagination, and which became obligatory subjects for nature poets to tackle. Hardy holds little sympathy with Matthew Arnold's notion of nature as 'the cool flowery lap of earth', and prefers to confront Darwin. But his attitudes are by no means consistent, and in searching for consistency, one finds only confusion: nature is sometimes benevolent to his characters, sometimes hostile, sometimes indifferent. Like, one might say, the weather: as soon search for consistency in the weather.

In *Jude*, the darkest of Hardy's novels, nature is almost uniformly hostile, represented by stuck pigs, worms, stoned birds, nettles, and dying rabbits. In *Tess*, landscape and season follow the heroine's fortunes, from village green to lush valley, from stony upland to Stonehenge. In *The Woodlanders*, Hardy presents us with a world that is both fruitful and diseased, both friendly and harsh: it is harsh but familiar to Marty South, it entangles the town-bred Felice and the town-educated Grace, and it finally kills its old friend Giles Winterborne. Egdon Heath, in *The Return of the Native*, is nothing but a heath to Thomasin – in fact, she quite likes its 'grim old face' – but to the outsider Eustacia it is an enemy, and at the end she sees its twisted roots and fleshy fungi as 'the rotten liver and lungs of some colossal animal'. In *Far from the Madding Crowd*, in a similar though less powerful and tragic scene, Bathsheba runs from home to find herself in a poisonous swamp where 'fungi grew in all manner of positions from rotting leaves and tree stumps, some exhibiting to her listless gaze their clammy tops, others their oozing gills. . . .'

Nature, in fact, is as likely to be a snare as a comfort. Although Hardy reinforced his picture of the harshness of nature with the alarming ideas of Darwin, his response to that harshness was personal: as a child, he had seen a frozen bird, a starved man, and the images remained with him. He seems at times to have had an almost perverse delight in destroying the convention of a happy, pretty, gentle rural world, where the only vile thing is man: aggressively realistic, he writes of cuckoo spit and thistles, offensive-smelling flowers, slug-slime, fungi, and the bleeding wounds and amputations of trees. Other writers, notably Wordsworth, had dealt with nature's menace and terror: it was left to Hardy to describe her blemishes. Oddly enough, the vegetable blemishes seem to have upset him and preyed on his mind more than the more obvious and bloody signs of nature's cruelty: we hear surprisingly little of beast destroying beast, though Hardy must have witnessed many slaughters, and seen many predators at work. Beasts in his novels are usually harmless, and there is less of nature red in tooth and claw than one would expect, in view of Hardy's plots: few foxes, few hawks, few stoats. In *The Woodlanders*, a novel which dwells on the Unfulfilled Intention in the vegetable world, owls catch mice as unremarkably as rabbits eat winter-greens, and even the snake that kills Mrs Yeobright is beautiful. The dog that destroys Gabriel Oak's sheep is over-enthusiastic, not malicious.

Hardy also deals with the menace of nature on a grander scale than the scale of caterpillar and slug: Egdon Heath is menacing in a grand, Wordsworthian sense. But unlike Wordsworth, Hardy finds some curious explanations for the romantic vogue for blasted heaths and craggy moors. In the first book of *The Return of the Native* (the novel which has the grandest landscapes), Hardy claims that man is now more attracted by the desolate than he used to be, because:

the time seems near, if it has not actually arrived, when the chastened sublimity of a moor, a sea or a mountain will be all of nature that is absolutely in keeping with the moods of the more thinking among mankind. And ultimately, to the commonest tourist, spots like Iceland may become what the vineyards and myrtle gardens of South Europe are to him now; and Heidelberg and Baden be passed unheeded as he hastens from the Alps to the sand-dunes of Scheveningen.

Of course, this passage is in part a prelude to the introduction of the thoughtful and self-punishing Clym Yeobright, diamond merchant turned furze-cutter, as the next sentence demonstrates: 'The most thorough-going ascetic could feel,' Hardy writes, 'that he had a natural right to wander on Egdon ...' Again, we see nature used as a background to character: or is it the other way round? Which came first in the conception of the novel, Clym or Egdon? The two are inextricably connected.

There is something slightly quaint about Hardy's speculations on the taste for the sublime: as so often in his work, the first-hand and the second-hand ideas are oddly mingled. And on a simpler level, his response to the smaller manifestations of nature is an odd mixture of instinct and acquired knowledge. From boyhood he had known the country names of birds and flowers, but as he grew older he studied and read widely, and his novels are a curious jumble of natural knowing and intellectual titbits of information, some of them (like his views of the Roman roads) inaccurate. He refers to the gorse by its Latin name, *Ulex Europaeus*: he makes erudite references to 'Turbaria Bruaria' – the right of heath-cutting. A peasant woman is compared to a sketch by Poussin. At times one suspects that Hardy is trying too hard to prove that he is no mere rustic novelist, but an educated man, who questions tradition and superstition. Yet at the same time he does not hesitate to use superstition as a vital ingredient in his plots. In one short story, a cast-off mistress dreams a dream which withers the new bride's arm; together bride and mistress consult a wise man, who tells them that the only cure is to lay the arm on the neck of a newly-hanged man. One could view this simply as a pot-boiling sensational use of an old wives' tale, but there are other instances that cannot be taken so lightly: in *The Mayor of Casterbridge*, Henchard consults a weather-caster, and receives accurate predictions, which he unfortunately fails to heed. Hardy himself clearly believed in the weather-caster's powers.

This does not necessarily suggest that Hardy, the educated man, believed in local superstitions: half of him at least is a rationalist, who knows perfectly well that there are no witches, and that the fat of fried adders does not cure a snake-bite. On the other hand, he certainly did believe in the possibility of reading nature's signs so closely that one could pick up hints obscure or meaningless to the ordinary peasant or sensitive townsman. In a beautiful scene in *Far from the Madding Crowd*, a scene which has not a hint of the supernatural, Gabriel Oak reads correctly all the portents of the storm – the hot breeze, the 'lurid, metallic' look of the moon, the behaviour of sheep and cows and rooks and horses, the travelling toad, two black spiders, a huge brown garden slug that has come indoors. His intimacy with nature is shown particularly in the brilliant minutely observed description of the toad: 'Gabriel proceeded towards his home. In approaching the door, his toe kicked something which felt soft, leathery and dis-tended, like a boxing glove. It was a large toad, humbly travelling across the path. Oak took it up, thinking it might be better to kill the creature to save it from pain; but finding it uninjured, he placed it again among the grass. He knew what this direct message from the Great Mother meant.' Significantly, Oak sees nature not as a hostile force or an Unfulfilled Intention, but as the Great Mother, even though she has ruined him and robbed him of his flock by the careless agency of a sheepdog. He bears no resentment. Indeed, his first feeling when he loses his sheep is 'one of pity for the untimely fate of these gentle ewes and their unborn lambs'. His respect for the humble toad is characteristic of the man. Only those who listen carefully, Hardy tells us, will hear nature's admonitions, and their knowledge may well appear supernatural to others.

Hardy himself was a careful listener. A solitary person, he listened and watched. One of his most distinctive gifts as a writer was his ability to describe and reproduce almost unnoticeable variations of sound and melody. His feeling for music (a family passion) is perhaps most evident in his own poetry, where Hardy's own characteristic wilting, delicate, hesitating cadences, once so misunderstood and now so admired, show the extraordinary keenness of his ear. But his novels too bear witness to an almost painfully acute awareness of sound in the natural world: his description of the sound of the wind on Egdon is one of the finest passages in his work. He distinguishes each tone of the music – the treble, tenor and bass of the wind, as it flows over pits and prominences, the baritone buzz of the holly tree, and 'the worn whisper, dry and papery' of the 'mummified heathbells of the last summer, originally tender and purple, now washed colourless by Michaelmas rains, and dried to dead skins by October suns'. Only an ear tuned to 'infinitesimal vegetable causes', as he calls them elsewhere, could have picked up so faint a whisper, and traced so beautifully its origins. Neither books nor folklore will teach such knowledge. Hardy hears the creaking of old houses, the rustles of insects, the sound of a leaf turning in its socket: he can distinguish trees by the sound of the wind or the rain in their leaves.

Hardy, then, was perfectly equipped to write of the natural world. By nature, by birth, by training, he was endowed with every gift, and in his best work he writes with a sensitivity and power that none can imitate. Whole landscapes or minuscule details of leaf and root and insect are in his range: he can achieve large effects and small, and can write with equal ease of nature without man, and of man in his country tasks – cider-making, sheep-dipping, reaping, milking, furze-cutting, tree-barking. The appeal of his subject matter, particularly for town readers, has always been strong, and there is no doubt that he could have succeeded simply as a regional nature novelist, a *genre* in which lasting success is extremely rare: Eden Phillpotts, another West Country writer, wrote dozens of West Country novels which were extremely popular in their day, and which are now largely forgotten. Hardy himself was certainly not above writing popular novels – indeed, much of his fiction he did not take very seriously, and some if it succeeds on a popular level. *The Trumpet Major* was written to an infallible recipe of nostalgia and patriotism, and, good though it is, it is easy to see how Hardy could have contented himself with a much lesser rôle than the rôle he achieved – he could have remained 'good little Thomas Hardy', as Henry James patronizingly described him, writing of milkmaids and shepherds, and occasionally, in more daring morbid vein, of hangmen and witches. There is a strong strain of nostalgia in some of his work, a strain characteristic of the regional novel: it has a right to be there, for Hardy was well aware that on one level he was recording a dying England, dying customs, vanishing landscapes. Nostalgia, a harking back towards a perfect Golden Age, has always been evident even in the most powerful of nature poets: a century earlier, Wordsworth was complaining that the May-pole dance had disappeared like a dream before his day, and that the 'times had scattered all these lighter graces . . .' Faithfully, a rural chronicler, Hardy describes the last of the reddlemen, the dying traditions of the mummers, the advance of mechanization. Like Wordsworth, he foresees harsher times. But, also like Wordsworth, he rarely, at his best, appeals to a sense of passive regret.

Successful though he was as a regional novelist, he was far too ambitious to be content with a rustic label; he makes much larger claims for himself. His themes, as he was fond of pointing out, are Homeric or Sophoclean in their scale, and his corner of Dorset was quite large enough for the grandest of tragedies. (His corner is a tiny corner, in these days of the motor car: illimitable Egdon has shrunk to a plantation.) Hardy was by no means content to record the temporal and the quaint: his tragedies are for all time, his nature is eternal, and the changes that we can see in a lifetime are infinitesimal in the scale of evolution. His characters at times move outsize in their woods and fields, like mythic figures of the folk imagination: he makes good his own large claims. It is easy enough to compare Eustacia Vye to a goddess, for heroines are always goddesses: how much more difficult to make us see Giles Winterborne through Grace's eyes as 'the fruit-god and the wood-god in alternation: sometimes leafy and smeared with green lichen, as she had seen him among the sappy boughs of the plantations: sometimes cider-stained and starred with apple pips, as she had met him on his return from cider-making in Blackmoor Vale, with his vats and presses beside him.' This is the character whom we met at the beginning of the novel, standing stiffly, foolishly, yokel-like, embarrassed, holding a sample (rather than a symbolic) apple tree in his hand. The transformation is the greatest tribute to the seriousness of Hardy's art. Man and nature, the real and the symbolic, blend, as they do in that equally fine and famous passage in which Tess (who is after all only a milk maid) is seen as Eve in the first garden, in the 'spectral, half-compounded aqueous light' of early morning. The description of her meetings with Angel Clare, when they seem alone in a non-human world, with the summer fog lying on the meadows 'like a white sea, out of which the scattered trees rose like dangerous rocks', is one of the supreme passages of English literature. There is nothing prettily pastoral or intellectually inflated here, although the scene is a meadow, and Tess is compared to Eve, to Artemis, to Demeter. Man inhabits nature here in a way that no other writer I know has ever achieved, though some may have sensed it. John Clare sensed the union of man and nature, when he was a boy, but as a man he wrote of an Eden lost. Thomas Hardy re-creates Eden, and of all his many achievements as poet and novelist, this seems to me his greatest.

❧ The Hardy industry

GREGORY STEVENS COX

Thomas Hardy won literary fame in 1874 on the publication of his novel *Far from the Madding Crowd*. This fame was enhanced during the following eighteen years until, with the appearance of *Tess of the D'Urbervilles*, Hardy became a national celebrity. *Jude the Obscure* angered many Victorians but copies of the novel sold briskly. Hardy was wicked – but he was read and lionized by the aristocratic hostesses of London. The publication of *Wessex Poems* (1898) and of *The Dynasts* (1903–8) suggested that the naughty novelist of the nineties was proving to be a respectable Edwardian poet and in 1908 the Prime Minister (Asquith) offered Hardy a knighthood. Hardy declined the honour but in 1910 the Order of Merit was conferred upon him. He also received honorary degrees from the universities of Oxford, Bristol and Aberdeen and his name was canvassed as a possible winner of the Nobel Prize. Old age had brought respectability – the radical and permissive Victorian ('Hardy the Obscene') was metamorphosed into a Grand Old Man, the *cher maître* of Siegfried Sassoon, Edmund Blunden, Robert Graves, W. H. Auden, Edward Thomas, Ezra Pound and the rest of the younger generation. When Hardy's ashes were laid to rest in Poet's Corner in 1928 Barrie, Galsworthy, Gosse, Housman, Kipling and Shaw served as pall bearers. Since then Hardy's reputation has fluctuated in the critical annals of English literature but his popularity amongst layfolk has remained constant. It is the purpose of this essay briefly to explore the Hardy cult – the academic, public and commercial response to the life and works of the Wessex novelist during his lifetime and afterwards.

The adjective 'Wessex' is of primary significance. It is commonly stated that Hardy was the first to resurrect this geographical concept from Anglo-Saxon history and to apply it to the contemporary scene. This is in fact erroneous – it was the Dorset poet William Barnes who first revived the term. But while Barnes' poems were little read outside Dorset (except amongst the *cognoscenti*), Hardy's novels enjoyed national popularity. Hardy, then, should receive the credit for establishing the term. Wessex was first mentioned by Hardy in *Far from the Madding Crowd* (1874) and in the succeeding novels he developed the literary possibilities of the concept. There is of course an ontological difference between the fictional world of Wessex and the geographical reality of the area – the author of *The Woodlanders* enjoys the complete right to foreshorten or lengthen distances between two localities for the purposes of his plot whereas the author of a geography book must observe the proprieties of mensuration. Nevertheless, it was Hardy's practice to employ the actual geography of the West Country with such fidelity to nature that 'real' counterparts can be found for almost all the 'fictional' scenes. A study of Hardy's manuscripts suggests to the present writer that the novelist consciously composed his plots in terms of real geography and subsequently translated the actual into the fictional, Stinsford into Mellstock, Dorchester into Casterbridge. Consequently Hardy's Wessex was not a blurred, impressionistic canvas but a realistic 'rural painting of the Dutch school'; not so much a metaphysical Atlantis as a region easily accessible to the steam engines of the Great Western Railway.

The Victorians discovered this and by the 1890s book-lovers were making pilgrimages to Wessex. In October 1891 the newly founded magazine *The Bookman* made tentative steps towards equating the fictional place-names with the real, and commended a tour through the area to its readers. The article counselled the prospective pilgrim to 'trudge the highways and byeways with [the] rustics, fellows of infinite humour and quaint homeliness'. In the years to follow the rustics were to experience much company. In 1901 C. J. Hankinson ('Clive Holland') wrote *A Pilgrimage to Wessex* which, he claimed, was the 'first authorized statement ever published concerning the topographical features of the most famous of the Wessex novels'. A flood of essays and books quickly followed – Windle's *The Wessex of Thomas Hardy* (1902), Sherren's *The Wessex of Romance* (1902), Harper's *The Hardy Country* (1904), Lea's *A Handbook to the Wessex Country of Thomas Hardy's Novels and Poems* (1904) and Clive Holland's *Wessex* (1906) are the more important of the books. The last-named work was finely illustrated with seventy-five colour paintings by Walter Tyndale. The doyen of these topographical writers was Hermann Lea. He had explored Wessex for some sixteen years before he published his first guidebook and in the interim he had become an intimate friend of Hardy. Together they walked, cycled and motored many thousands of miles throughout Wessex. The fruit of this travel was Lea's book *Thomas Hardy's Wessex* published by Macmillan in 1913 in a format and binding which matches the definitive Wessex edition of the novels. This work has rightly become the indispensable *vade mecum* for all serious literary pilgrims. (Of recent years some scholars have detected 'mistakes' in the work. On more than one occasion Hardy remarked that there were only two or three errors in the whole volume and his evidence should be accepted as authoritative; Lea's work represents the geographical identifications as Hardy wished the world to know them. Those identifications that are sometimes represented as mistakes are probably distortions calculated to conceal the true identity of a locality which, for a variety of reasons, Hardy wished to protect from the public ken.) Lea's work was later issued in the *Highways and Byways* series and went through many editions.

The advent of the char-à-banc and the motor car opened up the West Country to thousands eager to view the scenes of their favourite novels. Hermann Lea realized the commercial possibilities of Wessex and at as early a date as 1898 he was involved with the Revd Thomas Perkins in producing postcards of 'scenes from Thomas

Hardy's famous novels' (with Hardy acting as adviser to the series). The cards were marketed in sets of six at 6d ($2\frac{1}{2}$p) per set, and proved very popular. Rival series were soon offered for sale by other firms and somewhat later there appeared six drawings (by Leonard Patten) issued as a set dedicated to the author (who hoped that they would be popular).

The Hardy industry became centred on Dorchester. For not only was this Casterbridge, the heart of fictional Wessex, and an excellent base from which to make one-day excursions to 'Mellstock, Weatherbury, The Hintocks, Sherton-Abbas, Kingsbere, Overcombe, and many other towns and villages round', it was also the town close to Hardy's birthplace (at Higher Bockhampton), the town to which Hardy had returned in 1883 to establish a permanent home. So a visit to Dorchester held the promise not only of a gaze at Henchard's house but also of a glimpse at Max Gate – and perhaps a sighting of the author himself.

The birthplace was inhabited from February 1913 by Hermann Lea and he was warned by Hardy that he would be subjected to a stream of uninvited visitors. Lea formulated an adamantine rule: 'Any visitor who was merely of a curious turn of mind met with a courteous refusal to his or her request to view "the place where Hardy was born"; whereas those who were genuinely interested were to be welcomed and shown such features, or told such facts as I knew Mr Hardy did not regard as sacred.' The birthplace later passed into the keeping of the National Trust and today some 10,000 visitors journey to it annually.

Lea's problems were small compared with those experienced by Hardy. Devoted readers regularly laid siege to Max Gate. One Scotsman waited two whole mornings in the hope of 'just seeing' his hero. He was successful – Hardy emerged to post a letter in the pillar box outside the front gate. But many pilgrims were not so fortunate. Miss Titterington, for many years the parlour maid at Max Gate, has vivid memories of a turbanned Indian sitting outside the front door. When Miss Titterington asked what he wanted, the stranger explained that he had travelled 10,000 miles to see 'the Master'. It was an unrewarded journey. As the disciple sat patiently meditating outside the front door, the Wessex guru slipped out of the little green door at the back.

Some visitors were more persistent. In October 1927 a Chinaman effected an entry into Max Gate despite written refusals to see him. This visitor had a strange story to tell about his own sister, a tale of dishonour, revenge and murder culminating in the 'suicide' of the sister by opium poisoning. The Chinaman's reading of *Tess* had brought him to the realization that he should have reverenced, rather than condemned, his sister. He suggested that Hardy should collaborate in writing the story of the tragedy; and as he left he drew from his pocket a book of poems by Hardy and requested the Master's autograph. As ever, Hardy refused and the Chinaman departed sadly.

For over seventy years the Japanese have been amongst the most ardent of Hardy's enthusiasts and since the visit of Professor Hidaka to Dorchester in 1923 scores of Japanese scholars and students have made their way to Wessex. The reasons for this enthusiasm are numerous and interesting. The first of Hardy's books to be introduced to Japanese students was *Far from the Madding Crowd*. The novel attracted attention in 1890 in the magazine *Kokumin no Tomo* (*Companion of the Nation*). The date is significant. Only twenty-two years earlier the feudal order of society in Japan had been overturned by the Meiji government. In feudal Japan society had been divided into four classes – the warrior class, the agricultural, the artisan and the commercial. The social system was rigid; it was very difficult to pass from one class to another and consequently any love affair between members of different classes was destined to be ill-fated. Nor was this all. In the feudal code of behaviour the parents enjoyed almost absolute power over the destinies of their children. It was not unusual for a father to arrange a marriage for his child to a partner other than the loved one. Consequently the father ranked fourth in the order of dread: earth, thunder, fires and father were the elemental forces feared by the feudal Japanese. These sentiments were based upon, and infused by, the spirit of Confucianism which enjoins obedience to those in authority. This cultural heritage enabled the Japanese to appreciate the nuances of the Wessex class system and its austere demands on some characters. The sad history of the d'Urbervilles and Tess's heroic self-sacrifice for her family's sake are themes readily intelligible to the Japanese.

The advent of the Meiji era brought 'technological progress' and rural Japan was confronted by the unsettling problems of an industrial revolution. Among these problems were those of psychological disorientation, the 'loss of identity' that pervades much modern European literature. *Jude the Obscure* captured the anguish of this revolution and the novel has proved to be very popular in Japan. Translations by Professors Uchida, Ito and Osawa appeared in 1925, 1927 and 1955 respectively; and it is interesting to note that an annotated edition by Ohashi was published in 1943 – at a date when much Western literature was tabu in Japan.

Japan has suffered for centuries from harrowing natural disasters – earthquakes, typhoons, fires – and in the face of these remorseless aspects of an unbenevolent Nature the Japanese have developed a stoical attitude towards Fate and the remorseless law of cause and effect. These attitudes and their Confucian and Buddhist expressions are very close to Hardy's concept of an unfeeling Mover.

These then are the cultural, philosophical and historical factors which explain the enthusiasm for Hardy in Japan – the country which has the oldest Hardy Society in the world. The quality of scholarship promoted by this society is inspiring; for many years a team of ten members has been producing an exhaustive *Hardy Glossary*, and individual members have published fine translations and commentaries.

Hardy's universal appeal is primarily attributable to the fact that he is a poet with philosophical insights rather than the expositor of a rigid and internally consistent 'system'. His empathy, especially for those who suffer, renders Hardy acceptable to the Hegelian German no less than the Confucian Japanese. The popularity of *Der Burgermeister von Casterbridge* in Germany is probably not unconnected with interest in the Nietzschean superman; Sue Bridehead (in *Jude the Obscure*) is more than ready for the couch of a Viennese psychologist or an American psychiatrist; and Elfride Swancourt has some Flaubertian qualities which the French find interesting. Enthusiasm for Hardy is a temperamental and emotional commitment rather than a rational choice. Hence Hardy lovers (and Hardy haters) may be Christian, agnostic or atheist – there is something, somewhere in the novels or poems, to fit nearly every creed. And discovery of the appropriate quotation not infrequently becomes the rationalization for the earlier, emotional, acceptance (or rejection). Hardy's novels have been translated into at least twenty-one foreign languages (including Bengali, Tamil, Lettish and Chinese).

In common with other great writers Hardy received a large and varied correspondence from all manner of public and private persons. Some 4187 of these letters are preserved at the Dorset County Museum and they are of invaluable assistance to any biographer (although, sad to relate, not all scholars have made use of this source). Many of the letters are of a serious nature – from editors soliciting new serials and poems, from philanthropists seeking support for worthy causes, from antiquaries and folklorists discussing incidents in the novels, and so on. A few of the letters are decidedly out of the ordinary. In September 1923 Fanny Butcher wrote asking for Hardy's 'Confessions' for the Chicago *Tribune* and a few weeks later Marjorie G. Lachmund from Yonkers, New York, asked Hardy to close his eyes, draw a pig, and send the resulting sketch to her. The London correspondent of *Izvestia* wrote for Hardy's opinion of Lenin in January 1924 and in November was soliciting Hardy's reactions to the political situation created by the abandonment of the Anglo-Russian Treaties (who more appropriate than the author of *The Dynasts* to tackle such a problem!). There is a request from J. W. Kirby asking the author to send a letter wishing success to the large steam trawler *Thomas Hardy* which had been built for deep-sea fishing off the Icelandic coast; Hardy obliged. There is even a letter from a certain Rose Lucas who offered to sell Hardy the plot for a story. The novelist received his first fan letter in 1874, and when *Tess* and *Jude* were published he was inundated with correspondence from women who sought his advice about sexual problems. In general the writers had pasts like that of Tess and wondered whether they should confess their guilty secrets to their husbands.

Tess of the D'Urbervilles has undoubtedly been the prime mover in the creation of the 'Hardy of Wessex' legend. It is to Talbothays and Wellbridge House, to the Abbot's coffin at Bindon and the d'Urberville tomb at 'Kingsbere' that most of the pilgrims have wished to wend their way. It is no accident that the postcard publishers usually produced the Tess set first! It is hardly surprising therefore that the novel has been dramatized, filmed, burlesqued, turned into grand opera, pirated and plagiarized.

The first dramatization was made by Hardy himself. As a young man he had been interested in the theatre and had even worked as a stage-hand to gain an insight into production techniques. In 1879-80 he collaborated with J. Comyns Carr in making an adaptation of *Far from the Madding Crowd*. This dramatization might well have enjoyed a better run but for a tiresome 'coincidence' – the successful appearance of Arthur Wing Pinero's play *The Squire*. The plot of this latter work bore a striking resemblance to the plot of *Far from the Madding Crowd* and Hardy and Carr levelled charges of plagiarism against Pinero. He vigorously denied the imputations and an acrimonious correspondence was conducted in the press for several months. The episode left a bitter taste and Hardy shunned the stage until the 1890s. By then England was experiencing a theatrical boom. The plays of leading foreign dramatists such as Ibsen were frequently staged and there was a good crop of native genius – Wilde, Shaw, George Moore. It was natural that the outstandingly successful novel *Tess* should have been thought suitable for stage presentation. In response to this demand Hardy made his own adaptation (1894–5), Lorimer Stoddard wrote an authorized dramatization (1896) and Hugh Arthur Kennedy an unauthorized version (1899).

Superficially the novel can be considered as a scenario ripe for theatrical presentation – seduction, deception, confession, partings and reunions, love and remorse, murder and a hanging – this is the very stuff of the stage. Or rather, it is the very stuff of melodrama and this is the great obstacle that adaptors have constantly discovered, sometimes too late. That peerless stylist Max Beerbohm stated the problem with his customary acumen: 'Such characters as Angel Clare demand of a dramatist an extraordinary amount of skill. What the novelist may explain at his leisure, the dramatist must make clear in a few lines.' It has been calculated that Hardy employs some 60,000 words to create the character of a Tess who confesses on her wedding night. These 60,000 words gave him the opportunity to explore nuances and subtleties of character in such a way that the heroine's actions unfold quite naturally and convincingly. The dramatist who has to compress the whole book into 15,000 words labours under great difficulties. Is he to try to cram as much detail as possible into the play (Hardy's method in his own adaptation)? Or should he select a few essential episodes for thorough exploration and subordinate the rest (Lorimer Stoddard's approach)?

Although Ellen Terry, Sarah Bernhardt and Mrs Patrick Campbell (amongst others) were all eager to play the part of Tess, Hardy's dramatization was not performed until the 1920s. Some hitch – of taste, terms or copyright – frustrated all the negotiations between Hardy and the prospective producers of the 1890s.

Lorimer Stoddard's adaptation was performed in America and most accounts indicate that it was very successful. Tess was played by Mrs Fiske who 'had every heart string in her grip' by the murder scene. The rôle won national celebrity for this actress. A bust of her, executed by Max Bachmann, was exhibited; she was held in as high repute as the leading foreign actresses; and the tragic scene in which she wielded the murderous knife became so well known that a farce was centred around it. This burlesque, *Tess of the Vaudevilles*, was performed at the Pleasure Palace, New York, in 1897. The following short extract from a contemporary report gives a good idea of the general level of the humour:

Leading up to the murder scene, Angel Food shouts to Tess, 'We must split, I am going to Brazil, Indiana,' and departs in a frenzy. As Alec [Stoutenbottle] sends out from the wings a mocking laugh of many horse power, Tess sharpens a bread knife with a corrugated edge of her shoe and disappears in the direction of the laughter.

Tess was turned into an opera by Baron Frederic d'Erlanger (music) and Luigi Illica (libretto). The plot was modified considerably and the opera ends with the confession on the wedding night. When Tess realizes that her vision of a happy life with Angel is not to be fulfilled, she drowns herself. Mrs Hardy was not impressed by the London performance of the opera (in 1909). She told Professor Roberts that Angel looked like an Italian organ-grinder and she did not like seeing Prince, the horse, being fed on stage. Mr Hardy, on the other hand, does seem to have enjoyed the production. The performances of the opera in Italy were dogged by ill luck. At the première in Naples (April 1906) the first night coincided with a violent eruption of Vesuvius and the *Manchester Guardian* recorded that 'both performers and the audience were half choked with lava dust, and the noise of falling masonry all round the theatre was an unrehearsed accompaniment to the music'. Hardy wrote to d'Erlanger that the 'volcano was all one of a piece with Tess's catastrophic career'. At a Milan production the musicians went on strike.

In 1908 the historian A. M. Broadley delivered a lecture on 'Napoleon and the Invasion of England' in Dorchester. As a finale to the talk a scene from *The Trumpet-Major* was enacted. This amateur dramatization was a success and within a few months the Dorchester Debating and Dramatic Society was staging a full-length adaptation of the novel. The outside world became fascinated by the spectacle of Dorset folk playing Hardy's characters and the *Dorset County Chronicle* recorded that 'a *posse* of leading dramatic critics [came] down from London especially for the occasion'. Spurred on by their enthusiastic reception the amateurs under the direction of A. H. Evans (and later T. H. Tilley) enacted dramatizations of several of the novels in subsequent years. In 1916 they became styled 'The Hardy Players' and tackled Hardy's own play *Wessex Scenes from The Dynasts*. Eventually confident of the ability of the Players in general and of Miss Gertrude Bugler in particular, Hardy opened a drawer and drew forth the adaptation of *Tess* that he had made in 1894–5. The production of this play was the culminating glory of the local group; no further adaptations of Hardy's novels were staged, as it was felt that any production after *Tess* would necessarily be an anti-climax. However, Hardy's dramatization of *Tess* survived the demise of the Hardy Players and was produced at Barnes (London) in 1925 by a professional cast with Miss Gwen Ffrangçon-Davies starring as Tess. (There have been other dramatizations of *Tess*, and the interested reader could do no better than to read *Tess in the Theatre* by Professor Roberts (Toronto, 1950) – an excellent study which contains the text of Hardy's adaptation, *inter alia*.)

Between 1908 and 1924 the Hardy Players staged fourteen plays and appeared on seventy-six occasions. The London press usually took a kindly interest and although some critics were patronizing and rude the majority were enthusiastic. When

Wessex Scenes from The Dynasts was performed in 1916 Sir James Barrie visited Dorchester and in the course of congratulating the producer told him that he had been utterly unprepared for the delight that he had experienced in 'the Nazareth of Dorchester'.

The rich visual elements in Hardy's pastoral descriptions suggest that the novels are suitable for filming. Movie-makers did, in fact, turn enthusiastically to the Wessex novels at an early date. *Tess* was filmed in 1913 and in 1919 but apparently at least one producer relied on filling his shots with lots of cows to create a bucolic impression and Mrs Hardy was not impressed with the production. In 1924 Goldwyn Pictures Corporation also made a version of *Tess*. At first all boded well for a convincing interpretation. Hardy was able to obtain permission for the American producers to work on location at Bindon Abbey and the director intended to treat the novel 'worthily and reverently'. The result was a fiasco. Tess was presented rushing around in taxis and visiting nightclubs, and she ended up at Stonehenge surrounded by a posse of seven young men who were dressed in American fashion. In the US an illustrated 'Photoplay Edition' book of the film was issued, so the morbidly curious can still see fragments of this production.

In March 1921 Sidney Morgan submitted a cinema scenario of *The Mayor of Casterbridge* for Hardy's comments. Hardy undertook to 'see to the dialect' and appears to have approved of the general arrangements. The corrected scenario was promptly returned to Morgan and the film was produced at Shoreham, Sussex. At the suggestion of Hardy one scene was filmed on location. The cast motored over to Dorchester and Hardy took considerable interest in the filming techniques. According to a contemporary newspaper report he told Miss Pauline Peters (who played Susan Henchard) that she was Susan 'just as I wrote her and just as I wanted to see her'. It would be interesting to see this film version; so far I have been unable to discover whether a copy still exists.

When, in 1923, Hardy was approached by the International Story Company of New York about the motion picture rights in *Tess* and *The Mayor of Casterbridge*, he explained that the rights of these novels had already been sold but he did indicate that the rights for *The Distracted Preacher* and *The Romantic Adventures of a Milkmaid* were available. It is not clear whether these stories were filmed. (There is plenty of scope for research into the whole subject of Hardyan films – postgraduates hunting for an original topic might care to note!) In 1966 a colour film of *Far from the Madding Crowd* was made, starring Julie Christie as Bathsheba Everdene.

In recent years several of Hardy's works have been filmed for television. One of the most successful of these productions was the serialization of *Jude the Obscure* by the BBC. This adaptation has been sold to many foreign broadcasting corporations and the first nude scenes ever to appear on American television came, according to a press release, in two episodes of *Jude*. The film was also sold in the east, to Iran for example. As Hardy's novels first appeared in serialized format (in magazines such as *The Cornhill, Good Words* and *Belgravia*), and as he structured his plots to obtain a dramatic climax at the end of each instalment (this is particularly true of *The Mayor of Caster-bridge*), it is *a priori* probable that television should be an excellent medium for presenting and interpreting the novels.

While film and television can display Hardy's visual artistry, the radio is the best medium for capturing and reflecting the verbal richness of his prose style and the haunting melodies of the poems. A series of imaginative and skilful dramatizations of *Far from the Madding Crowd, The Woodlanders, The Mayor of Casterbridge* and *The Return of the Native* were made by Desmond Hawkins (in the 1950s and 1960s) and broadcast by the BBC West Region. Vaughan Williams was commissioned to compose a theme for *The Mayor of Casterbridge* and this was the genesis of what was later published as *The Casterbridge Suite*.

Throughout his life Hardy was deeply interested in music – especially traditional folk-tunes. As a young boy he had learnt to play the fiddle and often accompanied his father to social gatherings to entertain the guests with music for reels and jigs. Music constituted an important strand in the web of his soul and it pervades both his poetry and his novels. Many musicians have responded to this element in Hardy's work and as a result dozens of his poems have been set to tunes grave and gay. Vaughan Williams, John Ireland and Gustav Holst are perhaps the most famous composers who have written scores for the poems. Holst was also inspired by *The Return of the Native* to write the orchestral symphony entitled *Egdon Heath*. The opening chapter of *The Return of the Native* has been suggested by an eminent music critic as 'required reading' preparatory to listening to Vaughan William's *Fifth Symphony*.

The study of Hardy's life and work has experienced a variety of fashions in the years since 1928. In the twenties some critics wondered whether Hardy should be called a novelist or a poet. ('What matter which?' mused the layman as he browsed among both the novels and the poems in the peaceful groves outside Academe.) In the thirties the fashionable pundits wrote Hardy off – T. S. Eliot inveighed against his morbid pathology, Ford Madox Ford spoke dismissively of 'novels of commerce', F. R. Leavis allowed Hardy a few great poems amidst a pile of rubbish. However, this decade did see the publication of Rutland's fine study (*Thomas Hardy: A Study of his Writings and their Background*, 1938), and the thesis industry was under full sail both at home and abroad. In Germany Ilse Griesbach wrote *The Tragic Universal Sentiment as Structural Principle in Thomas Hardy's Wessex Novels in Relation to Shakespeare in His Lear and Macbeth Period* as a dissertation for the University of Marburg (1934). The war years stifled literary work in Britain, although Edmund Blunden's quiet and judicious work (*Thomas Hardy*) and Lord David Cecil's elegant Clark Lectures appeared in 1942 and 1943. The fifties were notable for Professor Purdy's masterful bibliography (*Thomas Hardy: A Bibliographical Study*, 1954) and the biographies by Professor Weber and Evelyn Hardy. By the 1960s Hardy was in fashion in universities and it was generally recognized that he was an idiosyncratic writer who could not be slotted into any neat literary compartment. C. J. P. Beatty's edition of *Hardy's Architectural Notebook* (1966) and Professor Weber's checklist of *Thomas Hardy's*

Correspondence at Max Gate (1968) broadened horizons for scholars and F. B. Pinion's *A Hardy Companion* (1968) was to be observed in the hands of many Wessex pilgrims. The bombshell of the decade was *Providence and Mr Hardy* by Lois Deacon and Terry Coleman. This work not only raised the perennial 'Life and Art' debate but effected a revolution in Hardy studies by ending the 'armchair biography' style; those who wished to join fully in the discussion prompted by this book had to inspect church registers, school records and local archives in at least six counties. Many interesting and important facts about Hardy's life have come to light as a result of these checkings and cross-checkings. The seventies have already seen the publication of two invaluable reference books – Professor Bailey's *The Poetry of Thomas Hardy: A Handbook and Commentary* (1970) and *Thomas Hardy: An Annotated Bibliography of Writings about him* edited by Helmut E. Gerber and W. Eugene Davis (1973). The latter work summarizes the essence of 3153 essays, pamphlets and books that have appeared in the hundred years since the first publication of *Desperate Remedies*.

The first account of the love affair between Tryphena Sparks and Thomas Hardy appeared as number three in a series of monographs published by James Stevens Cox (the father of the present writer). In 1959 he realized that there were still many people alive who had met Hardy and had interesting recollections about Hardy the man. Stevens Cox (who served as a detective in the Bristol CID during the war) decided to record as many of these recollections as possible in order to preserve the oral testimony for evaluation by future biographers. The death of H. O. Lock (Hardy's solicitor) in December 1962 and of D. A. J. Jackman, J.P., in January 1963 emphasized the urgency of the task. Altogether my father travelled well over ten thousand miles interviewing 203 people who knew Hardy and many other people who had information about him. One journey took him to the west coast of Canada to see a vital witness. The memories that he collected were printed in seventy-two monographs covering 1,276 pages. Copies of the monographs were sold to over forty-two foreign countries, including several Iron Curtain states. During the course of his investigations the editor met some people who, not realizing their importance, had destroyed Hardy letters; he also met some instances of letters being destroyed to suppress certain information. In 1970 the work inaugurated by the monograph series was taken over by *The Thomas Hardy Year Book*, which is now distributed to subscribers in some sixty different countries.

An interesting graph of Hardy's fluctuating popularity among bibliophiles can be produced by a careful study of *Book Auction Records* and booksellers' catalogues. Prices for first editions soared in the year following Hardy's death. In 1929 a copy of the first edition of *The Trumpet-Major* was sold for £100. An almost mint set of this work was recently offered for sale by a leading London bookseller at £70. If inflation be taken into account, it will soon be appreciated just how high the 1929 price was. These records also enable one to gauge the relative popularity of Hardy vis-à-vis other leading Victorian novelists. The first edition of Meredith's *Ordeal of Richard*

Feverel realized £6 10s in 1911, £15 in 1930, £22 in 1944, £12 in 1970. The first edition of Hardy's *The Mayor of Casterbridge* realized £1 18s in 1912, £16 in 1930 (this was the author's own copy with corrections!), $55 (= £13 15s) in 1944, £20 in 1972 (relatively poor copy). The Meredith sold in 1970 was in original cloth, uncut and contained the catalogue called for. The Hardy sold in 1972 was rebound and lacked a half-title (among other defects). Despite the limitations of this comparative method it is nevertheless easy to see the general pattern of the waxing and waning in fashions.

A large proportion of Hardy's novels and poems have appeared in limited and private editions. Between 1914 and 1916 Clement Shorter issued six Hardyan pamphlets, but they were not of the highest aesthetic quality and Hardy did not approve of the way in which Shorter was manufacturing bibliographical curiosities. Accordingly Mrs Hardy took charge of the publishing of pamphlets and the majority were handsomely printed at the Chiswick Press. Messrs Macmillans issued an *edition de luxe* (limited to 500 copies) of the collected works in 1919–1920 (the *Mellstock Edition*) and a limited edition of *The Dynasts* appeared in 1927. More recently the Limited Editions Club has issued several of the novels illustrated with wood-engravings by Agnes Miller Parker, and the Folio Society has produced *The Return of the Native* and *The Mayor of Casterbridge* with a series of outstanding wood-engravings by Peter Reddick.

Other noteworthy editions include the Riccardi Press selection of poems (1921), the limited issue of *The Return of the Native* illustrated by Clare Leighton (1929) and the American edition of *The Three Wayfarers* with four illustrations in colour by William H. Cotton (1930).

There have been numerous festivals centred around Hardy's life and works. The centenary of his birth – 1940 – fell at a time when Britain was struggling against a Dynast far more terrible than Napoleon, and there was little scope for festivities. But the centenary did not pass unnoticed and a very fine selection of critical essays were published in America in *The Southern Review*.

Some exhibitions were held at the time of the Festival of Britain (1951) but the festival *par excellence* was that staged in Dorchester in 1968. The festival was the outcome of spontaneous enthusiasm among Dorset natives and foreign scholars working in Dorchester. The date was not primarily intended to celebrate an anniversary, although it did fall in the fortieth year after the author's death – and a hundred years after Macmillans had rejected the manuscript of Hardy's first novel, *The Poor Man and the Lady*. The programme was inaugurated by a ceremony at Westminster Abbey and during the following three weeks it was possible to attend lectures, musical recitals, play productions, a ball, films, dancing displays, a Victorian cricket match and much else. Casterbridge was *en fête* and local industries responded gallantly. Messrs. Eldridge, Pope & Co. Ltd. brewed a special 'Hardy Ale' of impressive alcoholic strength. Their advertisement proudly proclaimed that 'this beer is about as strong as it is possible to brew beer, and uses best Kent and Worcester hops, and malt from Dorset barley.' It was marketed in pint, half-pint and nip bottles. The same firm also opened an inn – The Trumpet-Major – a few yards from Max Gate. Poole Pottery Ltd produced a Hardy medallion in a limited edition; Messrs. Tate & Lyle's sugar cubes nestled in wrappers which proclaimed Dorset as 'The Hardy Country'; a special 'commemorative cover' envelope was available; Hardy's head was to be seen on napkins, towels and trays. The exhibitions varied from instructive bibliographical displays of first editions to 'an inflatable illuminated polythene heart measuring forty feet long and powered by two vacuum cleaners. From this visual exhibit one got the meaning that Hardy's heart lay deep in the centre of Wessex for all to see. It was not limp and lifeless and forgotten, but full-blown and vibrating through the countryside.' The festival was a success and it has been followed by a series of seminars, lectures and birthday celebrations organized by The Thomas Hardy Society (as the Festival Society is now styled).

At Fort Wayne, Indiana, at the corner of highways 1–69 and US–27 stands a 13,500-square-foot restaurant run by Win Schuler. It is dedicated to Thomas Hardy and decorated accordingly. 'Waitresses and bartenders wear outfits similar to those worn by serving people of Hardy's era. Hardy's thoughts adorn the ceiling beams . . . and there's the Desperate Remedies (bar) and the Devil's Kitchen (coffee shop).' At the other side of the world, in Japan, there are locks of Hardy's hair. Recently a London bookseller offered for sale two chips from the Monkey Puzzle Tree planted by Hardy in Sturminster Newton. In various parts of the world people sleep with Hardy's photograph tucked beneath the pillow. Ogden's Guinea Gold Cigarettes issued a Thomas Hardy cigarette card *circa* 1899 and the birthplace at Higher Bockhampton was no. 10 in a Typhoo Tea series of 'Homes of Famous Men'.

There is a Hardy cult. The visitors to Wessex are the pilgrims. The birthplace has been made the shrine. Unhistorical myths about a self-educated peasant born in a tiny cottage have arisen. The Monkey Puzzle Tree chips are the relics. And the vast literature about Hardy contains the work of hagiographers and of those who have been branded as heretics. The President of the Immortals may have ended his sport with Mr Hardy, but the world has not.

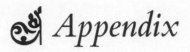 *Appendix*

SOME EARLY FILM VERSIONS OF HARDY NOVELS

A note by G. Stevens Cox

The following brief bibliographical notes have been collected by the writer in the past few years. The list is not complete but it does indicate a number of important sources that are worthy of further exploration. I should like to acknowledge the patient assistance that K. Alain Esq. gave me when I visited the British Film Institute.

MANUSCRIPT MATERIAL

The collection of Hardy correspondence at the Dorset County Museum contains several relevant letters. See: *Thomas Hardy's Correspondence at Max Gate, A Descriptive Checklist* compiled by Carl Weber and Clara Carter Weber, Colby College Press, 1968, in particular the references to letters: 1765, 1885, 1886, 2017, 2018, 2060, 2273, 2292, 2293, 2295, 2296, 2298, 2527, 2570, 2571, 2771, 2772, 2777, 2847, 2985, 2996, 3001, 3008, 3009, 3014, 3124, 3128, 3264, 3269, 3272, 3276, 3278, 3335, 3339, 3493, 3631, 3674, 4268, 4279, 4335, 4400, 4410, 4551, 4553, 4777.

PRINTED MATERIAL

Tess of the D'Urbervilles
(a) Version of 1913.
   Production Co. – Famous Players Film Co.; Distribution by Monopol Film Co.; Producer – Mr E. S. Porter; Cast – Mrs Fiske as Tess. References: *Bioscope* xxi (368) 30.10.1913 p. 391.
(b) Version of 1919.
   Referred to by Marguerite Roberts in *Tess in the Theatre* (University of Toronto Press, 1950), p. 207.
(c) Version of 1924.
   Production Co. – Metro-Goldwyn Pictures Corporation, USA Length – 7,000 ft. Certificate 'A'. The cast included Blanche Sweet (Tess), Conrad Nagel (Angel Clare), Stuart Holmes (Alec), George Fawcett (John Durbeyfield), Victory

Bateman (Joan Durbeyfield), Courtenay Foote (Dick), Joseph J. Dowling (The Priest).

References: *Bioscope*, 9 October 1924 p. 59. (A damning criticism – 'It is difficult to find any justification for the production of this ludicrous travesty' etc. etc.) *Kinematograph Weekly*, 25 September 1924, p. 46.

Tess in the Theatre (op. cit.) p. 207 (a number of contemporary reviews are quoted).

A 'Photoplay Edition' of the film was published in America.

Far from the Madding Crowd

(a) A film by this name (780 ft. long) was issued in 1909 by the Edison Co. A brief resumé of the plot suggests that possibly the only Hardyan feature of the film is the title.

Reference: *Bioscope*, 7 October 1909, p. 96.

There appears to be a copy of *Far from the Madding Crowd* (produced by the Edison Co., USA, 1911) in the Hollywood Film Museum. Is this the same as the 1909 version? The length ('12 minutes') would seem to suggest so.

(b) Version of 1915

Production Co. – Turner Film Co.; Great Britain, 1915. Length – 4,600 ft. Producer – Larry Trimble. The cast included Florence Turner (Bathsheba), Campbell Gullan (Sergeant Troy), Malcolm Cherry (Boldwood), Marion Grey (Fanny Robin), Henry Edwards (Gabriel Oak), Dorothy Rowan (Lyddie).

References: *Bioscope*, xxix (476) 25 November 1915 p. 954.

The Mayor of Casterbridge

(a) On 2 July 1921 scenes were shot at Dorchester for a production of *The Mayor of Casterbridge*. The production was based at Shoreham.

References: *Thomas Hardy Year Book 1972–1973* (Toucan Press, Guernsey, 1973), p. 25 (a reprint of a contemporary press review of the completed film). *One Rare Fair Woman* by E. Hardy and F. B. Pinion (Macmillan, 1972), p. 196–197 text of a letter from Hardy to Mrs Henniker mentioning the filming at Dorchester).

(b) In 1949 The Associated British Picture Corporation commissioned a screenplay; however economic considerations ruled out the production.

Reference: *The Mayor of Casterbridge* – Some Notes by Thorold Dickinson, *Sight & Sound*, vol. 19 (new series), no. 9, January, 1951.

Under the Greenwood Tree

(a) Version of 1929.

Director – Harry Lachman. Production Co. – British International. British production; 8,386 ft.; 'U' certificate. Cast included Marguerite Allan, John Batten and Nigel Barrie.

References: *Bioscope*, 11 September 1929 p. 33 (review).

Kinematograph Weekly, 19 September 1929 (review).

World Film Encyclopaedia (details of cast).

❧ Biographical Notes

MARGARET DRABBLE is a famous novelist, critic and biographer of Arnold Bennett.

TERRY COLEMAN is a distinguished journalist and co-author with Lois Deacon of *Providence and Mr Hardy*.

LOIS DEACON is the leading authority on the strange circumstances surrounding Hardy's secret love for Tryphena Sparks.

SHEILA SULLIVAN, writer and critic, has been a lifelong admirer of Thomas Hardy.

GILLIAN AVERY, author of *Victorian People* and *The Echoing Green*, is an expert on the Victorian era.

J. I. M. STEWART is the author of a major work on Hardy, *Thomas Hardy: a Critical Biography*.

ELIZABETH HARDWICK is an advisory editor for the *New York Review of Books* and is the author of *Seduction and Betrayal*, a study of women and literature.

THOMAS HINDE is a novelist and British Council lecturer on nineteenth-century literature.

GEOFFREY GRIGSON is a well known critic and was the editor of *Hardy's Selected Poems*.

HAROLD OREL is a Professor of English at the University of Kansas and is the editor of Hardy's *Personal Writings*.

DENYS KAY-ROBINSON's book, *Hardy's Wessex Reappraised*, is the definitive work on the subject.

A. L. ROWSE lives in Cornwall and writes eloquently in *A Cornish Childhood* of his love for Hardy, the man and the writer.

A. O. J. COCKSHUT is Fellow and Tutor of English at Hertford College, Oxford, and University G. M. Young lecturer in nineteenth-century studies.

SIR JOHN BETJEMAN is the Poet Laureate.

LORD DAVID CECIL is the author of *Hardy the Novelist*, which provides a special insight into the main characters of the novels.

GREGORY STEVENS COX is a leading publisher of Hardyana.

❧ Acknowledgments

The Editor and Publishers are deeply grateful to James and Gregory Stevens Cox of the Toucan Press for their kind assistance in many directions; for their generosity in allowing access to their collection of Hardyana; and for the selection from their album of photographs, some of which date from the middle of the last century, and many of which were taken by Hermann Lea in the 1890s and early years of this century.

The Editor and Publishers wish to thank the following for their kind permission to reproduce the following illustrations which were not supplied by James and Gregory Stevens Cox: The Dorset County Museum 32, 39, 44; George W. F. Ellis 23; National Portrait Gallery 8; Jorge Lewinski 15, 19, 20.

Index